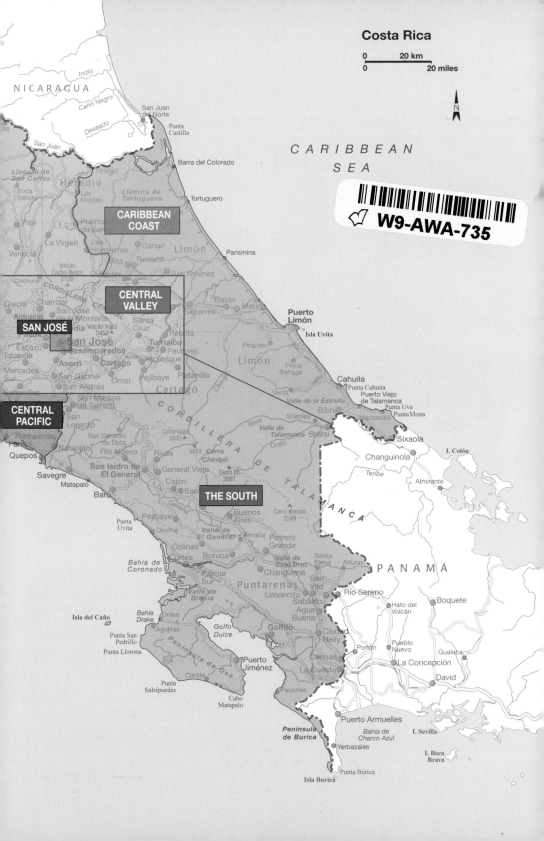

Costa Rica

0 ___ 20 km
0 ___ 20 miles

CARIBBEAN SEA

W9-AWA-735

NICARAGUA

Indio
Caño Negro
Deseado
San Juan
San Juan del Norte
Punta Castilla
Barra del Colorado
Llanura de San Carlos
Boca Sahino
Heredia
Pital
La Virgen
Las Horquetas
Cariari
Roxana
Trinidad
Tortuguero
Llanura de Tortuguero
Parismina
Venecia
Volcán Cacho Negro
CARIBBEAN COAST
Puerto Viejo
Limón
Cinchona
Grecia
Charrizal
CORDILLERA CENTRAL
Santa Cruz
Peralta
Batán
Siquirres
Matina
Puerto Limón
Isla Uvita
Alajuela
San José de la Montaña
CENTRAL VALLEY
Volcán Irazú 3452
SAN JOSÉ
San José
Turrialba
Pavones
Petroleo
Limón
Finca Banaga
Escazú
Tabarcia
Desamparados
Aserri
Cartago
Pacurique
Platanillo
Cahuita
Mercedes Sur
San Gabriel
San Andrés
Orosi
Pejibaye
Cartago
Punta Cahuita
Puerto Viejo de Talamanca
Punta Uva
Punta Mona
Sabonillas
San Marcos de Tarrazú
CORDILLERA
Chirripó
Telire
Shiroles
Valle de la Estrella
Bribri
Manzanillo
CENTRAL PACIFIC
San Lorenzo
San Gerardo de Dota
Cerro Urán 3333
Valle de Talamanca
Bratsi
Sixaola
Puntarenas
Parrita
Naranjito
Río Nuevo
Rivas
3819
Cerro Chirripó
Coén
DE
I. Colón
Quepos
Savegre
San Isidro de El General
General Viejo
Cerro Ell 3097
Changuinola
Almirante
Teribé
Matapalo
Cajón
TALAMANCA
Barú
General
Cerro Kamúk 3549
THE SOUTH
Buenos Aires
Punta Uvita
Pejibaye
Djochal
Colinas
Cortés
Valle de El General
Parraba
Boruca
Potrero Grande
Santa Elena
Alturas
PANAMÁ
Bahía de Coronado
Valle de Coto Brus
Chánguena
San Vito
Río Sereno
Boquete
Isla del Caño
Palmar Sur
Valle de Diquís
Limoncito
Sabalito
Agua Buena
Hato del Volcán
Bahía Drake
Drake
Puntarenas
Aguitas
Golfo Dulce
Golfito
Ciudad Neily
Portón
Pueblo Nuevo
Gualaca
La Concepción
Punta San Pedrillo
Punta Llorona
Península de Osa
Puerto Jiménez
Canoas
La Cuesta
David
Carate
Pavones
Punta Salsipuedes
Cabo Matapalo
Puerto Armuelles
I. Sevilla
Península de Burica
Bahía de Charco Azul
Yerbazales
I. Boca Brava
Isla Burica
Punta Burica

INSIGHT ⊙ GUIDES

COSTA RICA

www.insightguides.com/CostaRica

⊙ Walking Eye App

Your Insight Guide now includes a free app and eBook, dedicated to your chosen destination, all included for the same great price as before. They are available to download from the free Walking Eye container app in the App Store and Google Play. Simply download the Walking Eye container app to access the eBook and app dedicated to your purchased book. The app features an up-to-date A to Z of travel tips, information on events, activities and destination highlights, as well as hotel, restaurant and bar listings. See below for more information and how to download.

MULTIPLE DESTINATIONS AVAILABLE

Now that you've bought this book you can download the accompanying destination app and eBook for free. Inside the Walking Eye container app, you'll also find a whole range of other Insight Guides destination apps and eBooks, all available for purchase.

DEDICATED SEARCH OPTIONS

Use the different sections to browse the places of interest by category or region, or simply use the 'Around me' function to find places of interest nearby. You can then save your selected restaurants, bars and activities to your Favourites or share them with friends using email, Twitter and Facebook.

FREQUENTLY UPDATED LISTINGS

Restaurants, bars and hotels change all the time. To ensure you get the most out of your guide, the app features all of our favourites, as well as the latest openings, and is updated regularly. Simply update your app when you receive a notification to access the most current listings available.

Shopping in Oman still revolves around the traditional souks that can be found in every town in the country – most famously at Mutrah in Muscat, Salalah and Nizwa, which serve as showcases of traditional Omani craftsmanship and produce ranging from antique khanjars and Bedu jewellery to halwa, rose-water and frankincense. Muscat also boasts a number of modern malls, although these are rare elsewhere in the country.

TRAVEL TIPS & DESTINATION OVERVIEWS

The app also includes a complete A to Z of handy travel tips on everything from visa regulations to local etiquette. Plus, you'll find destination overviews on shopping, sport, the arts, local events, health, activities and more.

HOW TO DOWNLOAD THE WALKING EYE

Available on purchase of this guide only.
1. Visit our website: www.insightguides.com/walkingeye
2. Download the Walking Eye container app to your smartphone (this will give you access to both the destination app and the eBook)
3. Select the scanning module in the Walking Eye container app
4. Scan the QR code on this page – you will be asked to enter a verification word from the book as proof of purchase
5. Download your free destination app* and eBook for travel information on the go

* Other destination apps and eBooks are available for purchase separately or are free with the purchase of the Insight Guide book

Contents

Introduction

The Best of Costa Rica 6
The Happy Medium 17
Coast to Coast 19

History

Decisive Dates 26
Before Columbus 31
Conquest 37
Colonialism and
    Independence 44
Modern Times 53

Features

The People of Costa Rica 63
The Rise and Fall of San José ... 74
National Parks 80
The Sports Scene 89
Big Fins and Fresh Fish 94
Tico Cooking 102
Fruits of Costa Rica 106
Coffee 110

Insights

PHOTO FEATURES

A Passion for Plants 84
Going to Extremes 98
Potters, Sculptors, and
    Goldsmiths 158

Costa Rica's Wings
    of Wonder 206
Mountains of Fire 220

MINI FEATURES

The Great Immigration
    Debate 73
A Tropical Forest
    Watcher's Guide 83
City Buses 130
The Vampire Bats
    of Guanacaste 182
The Resplendent
    Quetzal 187
Sea Turtles 236
Ants in Your Plants 244
Island of Wonders 257

Places

Introduction 119
San José 127
The Central Valley 139
The Central Pacific 163
The Northwest Mainland 173
The Northwest:
    Nicoya Peninsula 189
The Northeast 211
The Caribbean Coast 225
The South 241

Travel Tips

TRANSPORTATION

Getting There 260
  By Air 260
  By Bus 260
  By Car.................................261
  By Sea 261
Getting Around.....................261
  To and From the Airport.....261
  By Air 261
  By Bus 261
  By Rail 262
  By Ferry 262
  By Car.................................262
  Taxis 263
  Cycling...............................263

A – Z

Acccommodations.................264
Admission Charges 264
Addresses 264
Budgeting for your Trip 265
Children................................265
Climate.................................265
Conservation 266
Crime and Safety..................266
Customs Regulations 267
Disabled Travelers................267
Eating Out 267

Electricity 268
Embassies and
  Consulates.........................268
Emergencies.........................268
Etiquette 268
Gay and Lesbian Travelers 268
Health and Medical Care 268
Internet 269
Left Luggage 269
Maps 269
Media 270
Money 270
Opening Hours......................270
Photography 270
Postal Services 271
Public Holidays 271
Religious Services 271
Shopping...............................271
What to Buy 271
Student Travelers 272
Telecommunications 272
Time Zone 272
Toilets...................................272
Tour Operators 272
Tourist Information 273
Visas and Passports..............273
Websites 273
Weights and Measures 273
Women Travelers..................273

LANGUAGE

Survival Spanish....................274
  Numbers 274
  Common Expressions 274
  Shopping and Eating.........274
  Getting Around 275
  Driving...............................275
Speaking Tico: Tiquismos 275
Spanish Language Schools ..275

FURTHER READING

Books 276
Other Insight Guides 276

Maps

Costa Rica.............................120
San José................................124
Central Valley........................140
Central Pacific.......................164
Northwest Mainland,
  Monteverde and
  Santa Elena 174
Nicoya Peninsula...................190
Northeast...............................212
Caribbean Coast....................226
The South..............................242
Inside front cover Costa Rica
Inside back cover Costa Rica
  National Parks and Reserves

THE BEST OF COSTA RICA: TOP ATTRACTIONS

From paradise beaches, serene waterways, and magical rainforests to volcanoes and amazing wildlife, this is our guide to the best that Costa Rica has to offer.

◁ **Tarrazú Coffee.** Nothing says Costa Rica like high-altitude coffee from Tarrazú, ranked among the best in the world. Taste a cup in Santa María de Dota in the mountains south of San José. See page 254.

△ **Punta Uva.** Crystal-clear, warm, shallow waters for swimming and an active coral reef close enough to swim to make this beach idyllic. See page 233.

△ **Manuel Antonio National Park.** Small but exquisite, this park packs a wealth of monkeys and birds into a compact jungle edged by three long arcs of white-sand beach. No wonder it's the most popular national park. See page 167.

▽ **Tortuguero Canals.** Drifting silently in a canoe along Tortuguero's narrow waterways overhung with vine-draped trees, you can spot caimans along the shore, iguanas sunning, and monkeys in the trees. See page 229.

△ **Canopy Tour.** Get a bird's-eye view of life at the top, as well as a thrilling ride, as you zip through the forest, suspended from a cable strung along platforms set high in the tree canopy. See page 153.

△ **Osa Peninsula.** Wilderness, wildlife, and adventure: everything the eco-minded traveler comes to Costa Rica to find is here, in the remotest part of the southern Pacific area with its legendary biodiversity. See page 245.

◁ **San José Museums.** The Museo del Oro Precolombino is Central America's largest treasury of ancient gold artifacts; Museo de Jade contains the most extensive collection of New World jade objects. See page 127.

△ **Arenal Volcano.** Picture-perfect, cone-shaped Arenal stands out as the country's quintessential volcano. Although it is temporarily dormant on the outside, it still supplies the geo-thermal power on the inside to heat ever-popular hot springs. See page 213.

▽ **Las Pailas Trail.** Experience some volcanic action up close, along this self-guided loop trail in Rincón de la Vieja National Park. The forest path skirts boiling mud fumaroles and sulfurous hot rocks. See page 177.

◁ **Resplendent Quetzal.** Even for visitors who aren't bird-watchers, catching a glimpse of the shimmering, crimson, and green resplendent quetzal, one of the most magnificent birds in the western hemisphere, is a thrill. See page 187.

THE BEST OF COSTA RICA: EDITOR'S CHOICE

National parks that offer opportunities to see glorious wildlife and hike amid beautiful scenery; beaches for swimmers, surfers, and divers; drives along dramatic mountain roads; plus museums, churches, and markets. Here are our recommendations for a visit to Costa Rica.

Riding on the beach at Montezuma.

BEST WILDLIFE VIEWING

Corcovado National Park. The last frontier for many endangered animals, including Baird's tapir, white-lipped peccary, and jaguar, along with a host of endemic birds. See page 247.

San Gerardo de Dota. One of the most reliable places for spotting the resplendent quetzal, along with other highland bird species, on Cerro de la Muerte. See page 254.

Monteverde Cloud Forest. A misty cloud-forest preserve protects an astonishing range of butterfly, mammal, and bird species. See page 183.

La Selva Biological Station. This wet lowland forest is home to thousands of insect species, plus mammals, snakes, and more than 400 birds, including the endangered great green macaw. See page 218.

Ostional Wildlife Refuge. Nothing beats the nocturnal *arribadas* (mass arrivals) of Olive Ridley sea turtles at this protected beach north of Nosara. See page 204.

Tortuguero National Park. With a sharp-eyed guide, you'll see myriad birds, mammals, and reptiles in this labyrinth of natural jungle canals. See page 227.

Wilson Botanical Garden. Brimming with bromeliads and heliconias, the garden attracts birds and small mammals, while monkeys and snakes inhabit the adjoining primary forest. See page 252.

BEST BEACHES

Nosara. Two beaches side by side: Playas Pelada and Guiones offer surfing, swimming, spectacular Pacific sunsets and yoga-on-the-beach. See page 203.

Punta Uva. The only beach on the Caribbean with a sunset view also has excellent snorkeling, along with warm, shallow water for swimming. See page 233.

Playa Montezuma. Funky, off-the-beaten-path retreat with dramatic crashing surf on rocks, plus wide stretches of sand and horseback beach rides to refreshing waterfalls. See page 194.

Manuel Antonio. Three long arcs of powdery white sand, backed by a jungle park bursting with birds and monkeys. See page 167.

Manzanillo. Swim, surf, dive; watch the local fishermen bring in their catch or follow the beach into the Gandoca-Manzanillo Wildlife Refuge. See page 234.

Playa Tamarindo. A surfer's dream, with eight prime spots to catch a wave, plus a raft of trendy restaurants and a lively night scene. See page 199.

Playa Hermosa. A family-friendly beach on the North Pacific coast, with warm, safe water for swimming, affordable accommodations, and sunset cruises. See page 197.

Manzanillo.

MOST SCENIC DRIVES

Ruta de Los Santos. Charming coffee towns named after saints are strung along a winding paved road in a high mountain valley lined with steeply terraced coffee *fincas*. See page 254.

Braulio Carrillo Highway. The twisting highway to the Caribbean cuts through mountains of pristine primary forest, with dramatic waterfalls and misty green vistas. See page 153.

Orosí Valley. Wend your leisurely way past coffee fields, stopping at colonial-era churches and scenic overlooks for panoramas of this pretty river valley. See page 148.

Costanera Sur. The wide, paved road from Dominical, south to Coronado, combines sparkling Pacific views with dramatic vistas of mountains hugging the coastline. See page 241.

Puerto Jiménez to Carate. Only off-road vehicles should attempt this rough but ruggedly beautiful road, with exciting river crossings and few signs of modern civilization. See page 249.

Paso Real to San Vito. Following a high ridge, the road offers panoramic views of bucolic valleys on both sides and the towering Talamanca mountains to the northeast. See page 253.

BEST HIKES

The Pacific Coastal Path. Heading south out of Drake Bay, this wildly scenic footpath cuts a swath between dense, green jungle and blue Pacific surf. See page 246.

Chirripó National Park. The ultimate hike to Costa Rica's highest peak, climbing through oak forests and alpine moors; for the fittest walkers only. See page 255.

Rincón de la Vieja National Park. A two-hour hike through forests and meadows to La Cangreja Waterfall with thermal springs and a cool swimming hole. See page 177.

Volcán Barva. An uphill hike through magical, mist-enshrouded primary forest above Barva de Heredia leads to a pristine green crater lake. See page 145.

Corcovado National Park. The trail between La Leona and La Sirena stations alternates between beach and forest, with refreshing river dips and scarlet macaws squawking overhead. See page 247.

Carara National Park. Just off the highway, this is one of the most accessible jungle trails, through majestic primary forest to an oxbow lake. See page 163.

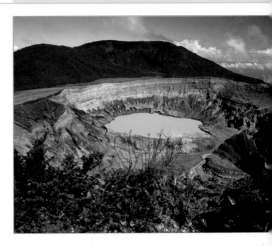

Laguna Botos.

CULTURAL BESTS

Teatro Nacional. Ornate, neoclassical theater modeled after the Paris Opera House, built in 1897, and now the home of the National Symphony and touring performers. See page 129.

Museo del Oro Precolombino. Central America's largest collection of pre-Columbian gold artifacts, arranged to show how gold was woven into indigenous cultures. See page 131.

Basílica de Nuestra Señora de los Angeles. Impressive, multi-domed church in Cartago, dedicated to the country's patron saint whom thousands of pilgrims come to honor in August. See page 147.

Guayabo National Monument. The country's only excavated pre-Columbian settlement has an imposing stone road and ruins of stone aqueducts and buildings. See page 151.

Ujarrás. Romantic ruins of Costa Rica's oldest church; a paradise for picnickers and photographers. See page 147.

Sarchí. You may not need an ox-cart, but watching artisans paint the whirling, kaleidoscopic patterns is worth a visit to this traditional crafts center. See page 156.

Ox-cart wheel.

Birdwatching from an eco-lodge in Carate, Osa Peninsula.

Three-toed sloth in Manuel Antonio National Park.

Tarzan swing in Selvatura Park.

THE HAPPY MEDIUM

Amid the turmoil that often characterizes Central America, Costa Rica is a land more at peace with itself and nature.

Pink torch ginger flower in the Orosi Valley.

Nestled between Nicaragua and Panamá on the Central American isthmus, Costa Rica is a small, democratic country, famous for its natural environment and a peaceful political climate that is unusual in a troubled region.

Since the armed forces were abolished in 1949, the government has been able to devote a large percentage of its resources to education, health, and conservation. About a quarter of the country is protected in national parks, biological reserves, wildlife refuges, and private reserves. With more than 850 species of birds, 250 mammals, and some 6 percent of the world's total identified species, Costa Rica is a paradise for anyone who delights in the unspoiled natural world.

A land of dense jungles, active volcanoes, and pristine beaches, this tiny country is full of geophysical contrasts that make it seem much bigger. More than half the population (total 5 million) live in the temperate Central Valley that houses the modern capital of San José. But as any *Tico* (Costa Rican) will tell you, the 'real' Costa Rica will only be found in the *campo*, or rural areas.

An official at the World Bank first called Costa Rica the Land of the Happy Medium. And while its economy is far from perfect, the high standard of living and social development belie its 'Third World' status.

For over two decades, tourism has been one of the country's leading industries. More than 2 million visitors now arrive every year, the vast

Children in Montezuma.

majority of them coming from North America and Europe. Eco- and adventure tourism are the buzz words that distinguish tourism here, encompassing such diverse activities as birdwatching and whitewater rafting. Costa Rica has come a long way from the sleepy, agricultural land it once was, but it retains a laid-back charm, especially in the more remote areas.

Sarongs in Puerto Viejo,
Caribbean coast.

COAST TO COAST

Costa Rica may be small in area but it is a land of great diversity, with two oceans, rushing rivers, fiery volcanoes, and chilly peaks touching nearly 4,000 meters.

osta Rica lies at the heart of the Central American isthmus and these days few people mistake it for an island in the Caribbean. Traveling around the countryside gives you the sense of being in a large country; geophysically there are so many things going on. In reality, though, it is quite small. From northwest to southwest it measures only 460km (285 miles) and at its narrowest point it is only 120km (74 miles). In total, Costa Rica's land area is just 51,000 sq km (20,000 sq miles), one-third smaller than Scotland.

Stretching between 8 and 11 degrees latitude above the equator, Costa Rica is bounded on the north by Nicaragua, and on the south by Panamá. To the east is the tranquil Caribbean Sea cheek by jowl with the stormier Atlantic. To the west is the tumultuous Pacific Ocean, with many kilometers of surf crashing onto beaches.

Surfer on Playa Tamarindo.

A fertile land

First and foremost, Costa Rica is a rich agricultural land. *Tico* culture is steeped in *campesino* (farmer) traditions, many of which still dominate national life. The soil of the Central Valley is exceptionally fertile, owing primarily to the volcanic ash that has fallen through the centuries. This rich, drainable soil, especially on mountain slopes, is ideal for producing Costa Rica's famous coffee. The tropical climate also guarantees a year-round growing season for plantations of pineapples and bananas.

The fertile central plateau, which lies in the temperate zone at 975 to 1,980 meters (3,200 to 6,500ft), also supports misty cloud forests at high altitudes and, lower down, steaming tropical jungles teeming with tropical flora

and fauna. This wealth of biodiversity has attracted a large international community of conservationists, biologists, birdwatchers, environmentalists, naturalists, and the ecologically attuned.

The coast

Never far away is the coastline. In fact, there are many accessible points from where you can simultaneously view both the Caribbean Sea and the Pacific Ocean. The Caribbean coast measures only 220km (135 miles) in length, while the Pacific coast of Costa Rica, with its deep gulfs and indentations, is several times that length. On the Pacific there are two major peninsulas: the developed Peninsula de

Nicoya to the north, and the more remote Peninsula de Osa to the south. And, remote and mysterious, many kilometers off the Pacific Coast, is the exceptionally beautiful, still pristine Isla del Coco.

Peaks of delight

Although most of Costa Rica's volcanoes are extinct, some are still active. In the Central Valley, Poás Volcano, at 2,700 meters (8,900ft), has one of the world's largest craters, measuring nearly 2km (1.5 miles) in diameter; and Irazú Volcano, at 3,440 meters (11,320ft), is occasion-

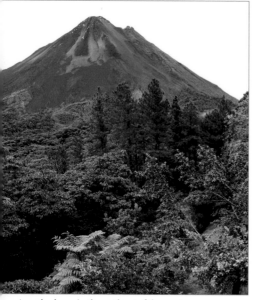

Arenal volcano in the northeast of the country.

ally active. Both these rumbling volcanoes can be viewed at relatively close range.

At 1,633 meters (5,350ft) high, Volcán Arenal to the northwest is the most picturesque of Costa Rica's volcanoes, with a perfect cone shape. It was also the most consistently active, until recently, when it suddenly went dormant. The volcanic action has now shifted west to Rincón de La Vieja, which has just as suddenly become more active. Over on the east coast, Turrialba Volcano also came to life after decades of dormancy and is still fuming away. Its dramatic plumes of vapor and ash can be viewed from as far away as the hills of Heredia, above the capital, San José.

Three spine-like ranges of highland mountains traverse Costa Rica from the northwest to

> Much of Costa Rica's biodiversity is due to mountains, which create a range of 'life zones' at different altitudes. Costa Rica also forms part of a natural 'land bridge' that allows wildlife to migrate between North and South America.

the southeast, rising to more than 3,800 meters (12,500ft). These are the magnificent Guanacaste, Central, and Talamanca ranges. Chirripó Grande, at 3,820 meters (12,500ft), is the highest elevation point in the country. Between the peaks, cool highland valleys with gently rolling, wooded pasture land remind visitors more of Switzerland than of a tropical country.

Climate and ecosystems

Although Costa Rica is geographically situated in the tropics, the great majority of the population live in 'perennial springtime' on the Central Plateau, at elevations between 450 meters (1,500ft) and 1,400 meters (4,500ft), with average temperatures ranging from 20 to 26°C (68 to 78°F), day and night.

Near the coasts, though, temperatures are indeed tropical, with distinct alternating wet and dry seasons, at different times of year for both the Atlantic and Pacific. Tropical downpours arrive with great predictability in the afternoons during the rainy seasons along the coasts and are undeniably awesome. If you are caught out in one, you will never forget the experience.

Away from the humid tropical coasts, the climate is greatly determined by the altitude above sea level. At each level, daytime temperatures remain fairly constant regardless of the time of year. At night, however, the heat of the coastal plains cools only slightly, while high up on the mountains and volcanic slopes, pleasant sun-warmed temperatures plunge dramatically at night, sometimes to just above the freezing mark.

For its size, Costa Rica contains a remarkable variety of natural ecosystems. A journey of just a few kilometers is often enough to take you from one to another, each home to quite different plants and animals.

Dry tropical forest

In the drier parts of Costa Rica where little rain falls for four or five months of the year, the natural vegetation is dry tropical forest, with most trees shedding their leaves soon after the dry season begins. The trees are rarely more than 30 meters (100ft) high, and there is usually a tangled understory of spiny and thorny shrubs. Although the trees are leafless during the dry season, few of them are fully dormant, and many burst into flower soon after their leaves have been shed.

Rainforest

Across most of the Costa Rican lowlands, the climate is wet and warm enough for trees to keep growing for much of the year. The result of this nonstop growth is generally called rainforest. Strictly speaking, though, botanists restrict use of this term to the wettest forests of all. Unlike the trees in tropical dry forests, rainforest trees are evergreen, and their dense crowns form a continuous canopy that casts a deep and almost unbroken shade. These rainforests – both on low ground and also at higher altitudes – harbor an immense variety of life.

Páramo

On Costa Rica's highest peaks, the forest gives way to a treeless landscape known as *páramo*. Cold and frequently swathed in cloud, *páramo* seems a world away from the warmth and lushness of lower altitudes. This ecosystem is dominated by tough, low-growing shrubs that can withstand strong winds. *Páramo* is also found in the Andes, and Costa Rica's scattered patches of it – for example, atop Cerro de la Muerte in the Southern Zone – are the northernmost in the Americas.

Freshwater wetlands

Running as veins of precious ore through the body of the country is an intricate network of waterways, rising and falling through the mountains, then flowing quickly to the sea and providing a steady source of fresh water and hydraulic power.

Smaller forest streams usually flow beneath a continuous overhead canopy, but most rivers are broad enough to allow light to reach the forest floor. The result is a linear 'light gap,' and a profusion of plant growth of the kind rarely seen inside forests themselves.

Aerial view showing the rainforest's density.

VIEWING WILDLIFE

For many visitors, the iconic image that draws them to Costa Rica is a dense rainforest full of wildlife. But actually seeing wild animals is not as easy as it sounds, or as it looks in nature films. With the exception of monkeys, agoutis, and coatis, most forest mammals are nocturnal. And forest creatures are very adept at staying hidden. Even Costa Rica's largest mammal – the 272kg (600lb) Baird's tapir – is capable of tiptoeing through the jungle without being spotted. Some birds do feed on or near the forest floor, making them easier to see, and others travel in noisy, visible mixed flocks, specializing in following columns of army ants and snapping up small insects fleeing the ants' advancing front.

Sudden fluctuations in water level – brought on by tropical downpours – are common events, and freshwater animals are experts at taking cover when flow levels abruptly increase. Along lowland rivers, where water flow is more sluggish, wildlife is more easily spotted, especially on muddy banks, which are home to caimans and alligators.

But the full richness of rainforest wildlife actually takes place in the canopy high overhead, where a complex community of species lives, with only minimal contact with the ground. So if you want to see wildlife, your best bet is to get up into the canopy on one of the raised suspension bridges or on a tree-top platform.

Costa Rica's largest body of fresh water – man-made Lake Arenal – has a distinctly highland feel. In contrast, the shallow lakes and marshes of Palo Verde National Park and Caño Negro in the Northern Zone are seasonal wetlands, attracting numerous wading birds and reptiles.

Coastal waters

Mangroves are the natural vegetation of muddy, low-lying coasts throughout the tropics. In Costa Rica, there are five species of mangrove, and they form extensive forests on both the Caribbean and Pacific shores. Apart from these mangrove swamps, Costa Rica's coastline consists largely of extensive beaches – often of dark volcanic sand – punctuated by low-lying rocks and a small number of offshore islands.

Costa Rica also has some small coral reefs on its Pacific coast, and one significant reef on the Caribbean side, at Cahuita. Reef-building corals need sunlight to grow, and they can only survive in clear water. This limits them to areas well away from the mouths of silt-laden rivers, but it also makes them vulnerable to any

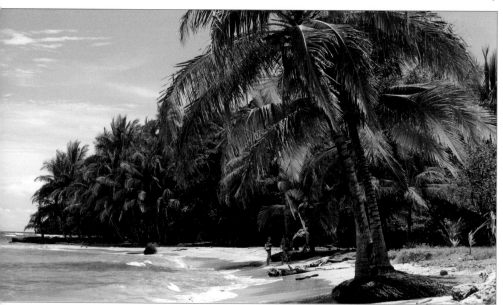

Palm tree-lined beach in Manzanillo.

MANGROVE SWAMPS

Beating a path through rainforests, tourists often miss the equally interesting mangrove swamps. Although inaccessible, smelly, and hot, they abound with life. Mangrove trees have evolved to survive in seawater and saline silt, using mechanisms for getting rid of excess salt, and elaborate roots that anchor them in the shifting mud. Mangrove mud also makes an important contribution to the marine food chain with nutrient-rich algae. Paddling through a mangrove in a kayak, you will spot crabs picking over tree roots and scrabbling in the mud for food, plus huge iguanas draped in branches, and occasional troops of howler monkeys.

increase in silt run-off. Unfortunately, in recent years, almost all of Costa Rica's reefs are threatened by deforestation, which has increased silt levels in the surrounding water.

Despite increasing pressures from development, Costa Rica is fighting hard to retain its reputation as the greenest country in the world, with official moratoriums on building and increased scrutiny or proposed projects along the coasts.

From the edge of the almost tideless Caribbean to the pounding Pacific coast, up and across the slopes of the volcanic cordilleras, and finally to the highest peak of cold, brittle Chirripó, the landscape is endlessly variable and gloriously invigorating.

A basilisk lizard, also known as a Jesus Christ lizard, Tortuguero National Park.

DECISIVE DATES

12,000–4000 BC
First signs of human habitation in Central America.

4000–1000 BC
Earliest settlements, based on crop cultivation.

1000 BC–AD 1500
Expansion of organized farming communities, with trade and communication links.

Pre-Columbian artifact, Museo del Jade.

1502
Christopher Columbus drops anchor for two weeks off the island of Uvita (near Puerto Limón) where he encounters the Cariari tribe.

The Spanish conquest

1572
Colonial period begins. Costa Rica remains poor for 250 years, largely ignored because of lack of mineral resources.

1823
Civil war between conservative imperialists and republicans (*liberalistas*) who finally win.

San José replaces Cartago as the capital.

1824
Juan Mora Fernández becomes first head of state.

1825
The first constitution of the free state of Costa Rica is promulgated.

1832
First coffee exports to Europe, via Chile.

1838–42
Dictatorship of President Braulio Carrillo.

1848
Declaration of the Republic of Costa Rica.

1858
Costa Rica defeats William Walker, who tried to turn Central America into a colony of the southern American states.

1870
Tomás Guardia Gutiérrez takes over power after a military

One of Columbus's ships.

coup and introduces a new liberal constitution.

1871
Railroad construction begins.

Coffee berries.

1880
First banana exports.

1882
Death penalty abolished.

1886
Introduction of compulsory education.

1890
First free and honest democratic elections in Central America bring José Joaquin Rodriguez to presidency. The Atlantic Railroad, from Cartago to Limón, is completed.

1919
A popular uprising ends two-year dictatorship supported by coffee barons.

1934
A strike among banana workers at United Fruit Company leads to establishment of right to strike and minimum wage.

1939–45
Coffee exports stagnate. Costa Rica declares war on Germany, Japan, and Italy.

Ceiling mural in San José's Teatro Nacional.

1940–44

President Rafael Calderón successfully implements social reforms.

1945

The Social Democratic Party (PSD) is founded, later to become Partido Liberación Nacional (PLN), under José Figueres.

1948

Calderón Guardia declares election results to be annulled and reassumes the presidency. Civil war ensues. Junta led by Figueres takes power.

1949

Under the new constitution, the army is disbanded and replaced by a Civil Guard. Figueres hands over power, but governs again from 1953–8 and 1970–4. Blacks and women enfranchised (1949).

1979

The Sandinistas in Nicaragua topple the Somoza dictatorship. During ensuing civil war, Costa Rica becomes a fallback area for guerrilla groups and anti-Sandinistas. Hundreds of thousands of Nicaraguans seek refuge in Costa Rica.

1986

Oscar Arias Sánchez elected president and helps restore peace to the region. For his efforts, he is awarded the Nobel Peace Prize in 1987.

1990

The Social Christian Unity Party (PUSC) wins the elections. Rafael Angel Calderón Fournier becomes president. Costa Rica sends a national team to the soccer World Cup for the first time.

1991

An earthquake strikes Limón province, killing more than 60 and causing extensive damage, destroying the Atlantic railroad.

1994

José M. Figueres becomes Costa Rica's youngest-ever president, but his term is dogged by scandals.

1996

Hurricane César strikes, killing dozens of Costa Ricans and causing massive damage.

1998

New President Miguel Angel Rodríguez (PUSC) encourages foreign investment and privatizes state companies.

2002

Abel Pacheco (PUSC) wins the first-ever presidential run-off vote. Costa Rican astronaut Franklin Chang, aboard US space shuttle, goes for a walk in space.

2006

In close-run election, Oscar Arias Sánchez (PLN) is elected to unprecedented second term as president.

2008

Central American Free Trade Agreement (CAFTA) is ratified following close referendum.

2010

Laura Chinchilla (PLN) is elected the first woman president of Costa Rica.

2011

Costa Rica successfully appeals to World Court in a border dispute with Nicaragua.

2014

Luis Guillermo Solís Rivera of the centre-left Citizens' Action Party (PAC) wins presidential elections. National football team reaches quarterfinals at the World Cup in Brazil.

2015

Turrialba volcano erupts spewing a column of ash 2,500 metres (8,200ft) high and forcing a temporary closure of the main international airport.

Luis Guillermo Solís Rivera.

Monument to Costa Rican workers, San José.

BEFORE COLUMBUS

The early culture of the Amerindians was largely agrarian. Influenced by their Mesoamerican neighbors, they learned to fashion goods from stone, jade, and gold.

On September 8, 1502, Cristóbal Colón (Christopher Columbus) arrived on the Atlantic coast of Costa Rica and took refuge in the calm waters just off the coast, between tiny Uvita Island and what is now the Port of Limón.

The native population greeted the Spaniards with interest and brought out goods to trade with them. They swam out to the ship carrying cotton cloth, shirts, *tumbaga* pendants (an alloy made of copper and gold), and weapons such as clubs, bows, and arrows.

Golden dreams

Dreaming of gold, Columbus had charted the coastal area from Honduras to Panamá and named it Veragua. He was so enamored by the golden mirrors that the Amerindians of Costa Rica wore about their necks, and by their many stories of gold and gold mines along the coast to the south, that he named the area the Rich Coast of Veragua.

Rich though it seemed to Columbus at the time, the newly discovered area was not to be a great, rich jewel in Spain's crown. In fact, the 'Rich Coast' turned out to be one of the poorest of Spain's American colonies. Impassable mountains, impenetrable forests, raging rivers, unbearable heat, floods, disease, swamps, shortages of food and of labor, internal rivalries, lack of natural resources or a way to generate wealth all oppressed the settlers. They were often reduced to living like the 'savages' they had come to conquer: wearing goat-hair garments or clothing made of bark; using cacao (chocolate) beans for currency; eking out a bare subsistence in the fields, using native methods to cultivate native crops.

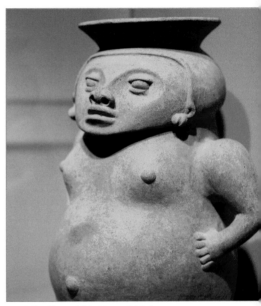

Pre-Columbian exhibit, Museo del Jade.

This bleak reality was yet to come. Columbus naively returned to Spain brimming with dreams of great riches and grandeur, to the point of asking the king to confer on him the title of duke of Veragua.

Natural riches

Unrealistic visions of gold aside, what was life in the newly discovered territory really like? It was a rich land, if not in gold, then in natural resources, with forests, mountains, rivers, grasslands, and abundant animal and plant life. In the Atlantic watershed area, where much of the land is flat, navigable rivers and their tributaries were swelled in some areas by more than 400cm (160ins) of rain a year. In the heavy tropical vegetation grew wild rubber trees, orchids, and ferns. Fish, alligators, and an occasional shark lived in the rivers. Waterfowl, turkeys, iguanas, spider monkeys, howler monkeys, peccaries (wild pigs), and jaguars inhabited the forests.

To the northwest, in the Nicoya region, were tropical dry forests, also abundant in plant and animal life: on the broad, seasonally dry plains grew the beautiful wide, green *guanacaste* tree; the *javillo* with its poisonous sap and thorny trunk; the *cenicero* with its flesh-colored flowers; the *guapinol* with its characteristic seed pods,

Native settlers

Groups of indigenous peoples with diverse languages and cultures lived throughout these areas in small chiefdoms called *cacicazgos*. They were agricultural people, cultivating crops of yucca, corn, *pejibaye* (the bright orange fruit of the peach palm), and numerous other plants. They supplemented their diets with wild fruits and game from the forests, fish and shrimp from the rivers, and crustacea and small oysters from the ocean.

At the time of Columbus's arrival, the people of the Guanacaste/Nicoya region lived in well-

A model display depicts pre-Columbian life in Museo del Jade, San José.

referred to as 'stinky toes;' and many varieties of cacti and spiny shrubs. White-faced monkeys, howler monkeys, red squirrels with gray tails, tapirs, coatis, deer, jaguars, mountain lions, coyotes, and other small animals lived in the forests. In the trees, scarlet macaws and colorful parrots squawked and roosted. Avocados, papayas, guavas, and countless other fruits grew wild.

And the grasslands and swamps of the southern Pacific region, also known as the Diquís region, were lush with life, as were the often misty green hills and valleys of the Central Highlands, where broadleaf evergreen forests, palms, and white oaks grew on the luxuriant hillsides, harboring innumerable species of birds, animals, and plants.

developed settlements, some with populations as large as 20,000. These settlements, supported by the cultivation of corn, were constructed around central plazas, marketplaces, and religious centers.

Guayabo city

In the Atlantic Watershed/Central Highlands area, high up in the mountains near the present-day city of Turrialba, was a city with wide, cobblestoned walkways, freshwater springs bubbling out of stone-lined pools, and a stone aqueduct system carrying fresh water to some of the stone mounds on which houses were built. This ancient ceremonial or administrative center, Guayabo, flourished and disappeared (approximately 1000 BC to AD 1400) before the arrival of the Spaniards. From Guayabo, ancient roads of stone led to towns and may have even reached the ocean.

Other groups within the Atlantic Watershed/Central Highlands region were less settled. They cultivated root crops, and hunted what small game was available, and then moved on to new lands when the soil or supply of game became depleted.

In the Diquis region, people also hunted, cultivated root crops, and lived in well-fortified villages that were strategically laid out to protect villagers from enemy attack.

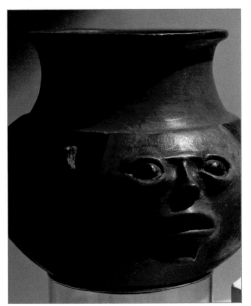

Pre-Columbian vase, Museo del Jade.

Crossroads of the Americas

Influenced by some of the other great indigenous cultures of the Americas, the indigenous peoples of Costa Rica had become skilled in the arts of ceramics, of gold-work and metalwork, fine weaving, and stone carving. Costa Rica, it appears, was a kind of mercantile and cultural crossroads of the Americas. Linguistic and cultural influences, not to mention a wealth of artifacts and materials, were being exchanged both within the country and without, from as far north as Mexico and as far south as Ecuador.

The indigenous peoples of Costa Rican were enthusiastic traders and prized jade pieces and ceramic ware, as well as gold and

stone carvings from Mesoamerica and South America.

The Nicoya area, with its quiet Pacific bays and safe anchorages, provided pre-Columbian commercial ports. Merchant marines from ancient Ecuador, making ports of call all along the Pacific coast of Mexico, Central and South America, frequently stopped at sites in Nicoya, bringing with them the crafts and arts of places they had visited. Perhaps it was they who introduced Olmec influences to the area – or perhaps the Olmecs (and others) came themselves. Regardless, the influence of the Olmecs was evident in the Pacific Northwest in the impressive range of pottery styles; utilitarian articles such as grinding stones; and the practice of certain customs, such as filing human teeth into points.

Over the years, the pottery of Nicoya developed into a vigorous hybrid style that for centuries would be traded around Central America and southern Mexico. A collection of such work is now on view at the National Museum. It is lively, bold, colorful work: large globular jars and vessels; figures of men and women, some with oversized genitals and physical deformities; animals of all kinds; mysterious effigies of man-birds; haunting funerary masks; and some quieter pieces that are almost luminously beautiful.

Mystery of the spheres

The Diquis region is the site of one of the great pre-Columbian riddles. Spheres made of granite, andesite, and sedimentary stone have been found in their thousands along river beds and

WHAT'S IN A NAME?

The Spanish colonists gave the Amerindians the names by which we know them today (which was often the name of the chief at the time of the Spanish Conquest): the Chorotega, Bribri, Cacebar, Coctu, Corobicí, to name a few. We do not know what the people called themselves. Since some groups were completely wiped out before the Spanish arrived, we do not have names for them or know what languages they spoke. Because of this, archeologists usually refer to Amerindian groups by the areas in which they lived: Guanacaste/Nicoya region, the Atlantic Watershed/Central Highlands region, and the Diquis (or Southern Pacific) region.

arranged in cemetery sites. Some are as small as oranges while others weigh up to 14 metric tons, and measure up to 2 meters (7ft) in diameter. They are perfectly spherical to within a centimeter or two and are perhaps the finest example of precision stone carving in the ancient world.

The stone spheres are unique – none have been discovered anywhere else in the world. How were they made? How were they shaped to be so perfectly spherical? How were they transported more than 30km (20 miles) from the source of the stone to the ceremonial sites

techniques, including the 'lost wax' method, to craft all manner of items: gold headbands, arm and leg bands, collars, bracelets, beads, bells; golden ornaments sewn on clothes; gold tweezers for plucking away unwanted facial hair; gold awls, fish-hooks, and needles; gold sheathing for teeth; gold to use on decorative masks.

The Gold Museum in San José (see page 131) – has more than 1,000 of these gold artifacts on display, rearranged to demonstrate how gold was an integral part of early indigenous cultures.

One of the many exquisite gold ornaments displayed in the capital's Museo del Oro.

Gold figurine in Museo del Oro.

where they were arranged? And what do they mean? Today, they stand mute in their new locations, at the National Museum and in the gardens of expensive homes throughout the Central Valley. You can also see them in their original habitat, Isla del Caño, near Corcovado National Park.

Gold and cotton

The Diquis region also abounded with gold, which the Amerindians washed out of rivers, or obtained from shallow digs in the savannahs, under groves of trees on hilltops or on the plains. They became experts in the art of gold-working and employed different

The people of the Diquis region also wove fine, white cotton cloth, which was used to wrap the dead. Although no archeological evidence has been uncovered, since cotton clothing does not survive for millennia, the cloth may also have been made into shirts to be worn by both men and women for ceremonial occasions.

Wars, rituals, and religion

Taken in isolation, archeological evidence on village life, diet, and the arts and commerce of the early Costa Rican people might suggest that life in those times was plentiful, complete, and quite idyllic. In fact it was anything but – war was almost continuous.

In the Guanacaste/Nicoya region, wars were unceasingly fought between rival groups to obtain captives, who were perhaps for human sacrifice (and maybe even consumption). Throughout Costa Rica there were wars to capture women and youths for slaves; to obtain the heads of enemies, which were carried as trophies; and to obtain access to new land. Sometimes, as in the Diquis region, men and women warred together.

Artifacts and skeletons found in unearthed graves suggest that the dead were honored. Funerals and the burials of high-ranking

Pre-Columbian statuettes, Museo del Jade.

people were elaborate affairs: people of rank were buried with riches – and their slaves were sacrificed in order to serve their masters once again in the other world.

Spiritual life

Of their spiritual beliefs little is actually known, although much has been speculated. Phallic images and figures in pottery and stone, emphasizing male and female genitalia, suggest a religion focused on fertility. Fertility rites probably included the music of pottery drums, bone and clay flutes, trumpets, ocarinas, and rattles made of clay or gourds. Large vessels for the fermentation of corn, yucca, or palm fruit suggest ritual inebriation. And there were medicine men – shamans – with vast knowledge of the flora of the forests, who cured illness, forecast the future and dealt with supernatural matters.

The pre-Columbian lineages disintegrated with the arrival of the Europeans, who captured their leaders, disrupted their communities, enslaved their people and destroyed their ceremonial and religious articles. Spirited artistry gave way to a lackluster mediocrity, and dynamic spiritual beliefs were replaced by a half-hearted hybrid religion. Little by little, Costa Rica's rich pre-Columbian traditions were all but extinguished.

Most of Costa Rica's 70,000 or so indigenous people today live on 22 remote reserves. And instead of Columbus Day, which used to be celebrated on October 12, the country now celebrates 'Meeting of the Cultures Day' on the same date.

THE RIDDLE OF JADE

In addition to the enigma of the country's lithic spheres, there is another pre-Columbian riddle in Costa Rica that continues to perplex historians and archeologists: it is the source of jade for the many pieces found throughout the country, as no jade quarries have ever been found in Costa Rica. Guatemala is believed to be the principal source, although some jade may have come from Mexico.

Many of the objects appear to have been treasured for years, passed down as heirlooms; others seem to have arrived in one form, and to have been re-sculpted to the tastes of their new owners.

One interesting theory holds that some of the jade

was brought to Costa Rica by pre-Columbian looters of Mayan burial sites, and this would help to explain the presence of Mayan hieroglyphs inscribed on the stone – which apparently had no value or significance to the Costa Ricans.

The Jade Museum in San José (see page 133) has the largest display of jade in the Americas, with more than 6,000 pieces. Many of the pieces are *col-gantes* (amulets or pendants), generally in the form of birds, animals, or humans, but there is a great variety of other exhibits, including notable oddities such as a tooth with a jade inset, and jade breast supports, thought to have been worn by high-ranking women.

CONQUEST

The conquest of Costa Rica followed the sad pattern of much of Central America, bringing disease, death, and slavery in the largely fruitless quest for gold.

When Christopher Columbus set sail from Spain in 1492 on his first voyage to the New World, he was hoping to find a group of islands near Japan, which he conceived to be about 2,400 nautical miles (4,445km) to the west of Spain. There, he determined, he would build a great city and trade gold, gems, and spices from the Indies with the cities of Europe. He imagined himself as a rich governor, lord of it all.

His ambitions coincided with the interests of the Spanish Crown. The wars to oust the Moors from Spain had depleted the royal treasury and the promise of the wealth of the Indies was very attractive indeed.

The voyages of Columbus

The first of his four voyages took Columbus to the Bahamas, where he established the first Spanish settlement in the New World, at Hispaniola, where present-day Haiti and the Dominican Republic are situated. He built a fort and left 40 men behind to search for gold. He returned to Spain in triumph, with several captive local people.

Columbus set foot in Costa Rica in 1507.

> On returning from his first journey to the New World, Columbus was given a grand reception. He was named Admiral of the Ocean Sea and was ordered to organize a second voyage to further explore Hispaniola.

The second expedition reached Hispaniola only to discover that the 40 settlers had been killed after mistreating the local people. Undeterred, Columbus sailed to the north coast of Hispaniola, where he attempted to establish another settlement.

Leaving his brother Diego in charge, he went off to explore for gold. But the settlers fought among themselves and with the Amerindians. Frustrated gold hunters returned to Spain angry; they grumbled about the disappointingly small amounts of gold and the cruelties of Columbus, who, according to historic accounts, was indeed an arrogant commander.

Nevertheless, a third voyage saw Columbus exploring the Atlantic coast of South America and claiming it for Spain. Meanwhile, Hispaniola was seething with discontent. 'Not enough gold!' was the cry. Columbus tried

'I have seen more signs of gold in the first two days than I saw in Hispaniola during four years,' Columbus wrote to the Spanish king and queen.

to placate the rebels, as would his successors throughout Central America, by permitting them to enslave the indigenous population.

But even that measure failed to satisfy many. Large numbers of men returned to Spain demanding back pay and Columbus's head.

wrote: 'As soon as I got there they sent right out two girls, all dressed up; the elder was hardly eleven, the other seven, both behaving with such lack of modesty as to be no better than whores. As soon as they arrived, I gave orders that they be presented with some of our trading truck and sent them directly ashore.'

While in Cariari, Columbus made repairs to his damaged ships as the near tideless ocean lapped on beautiful beaches and coconut trees swayed in the breeze. The respite was sorely needed: a violent storm off the coast of Honduras had caused considerable damage to his ships,

Vasco Nuñez de Balboa taking possession of the Southern Sea.

Columbus was sent back to Spain in chains. Through the intercession of Isabella and Ferdinand, he managed to secure his release and set out on his fourth voyage.

The 'discovery' of Costa Rica

It was on this voyage, in 1502, sailing up and down the Atlantic Coast looking for a passage to what would later be called the Pacific, that Columbus discovered in Central America the Rich Coast of Veragua.

He spent 18 days in what was later to be called Costa Rica, near the present-day port of Limón, in a place he called Cariari. There, the local people sent out two girls to welcome the party. In a letter to King Ferdinand, Columbus

and his men, one-third of whom were only boys, aged between 13 and 18, were sick and exhausted. Columbus himself, at 51 years of age, was almost crippled with the pains of arthritis.

A difficult passage home

The return voyage was difficult. Columbus's ships had been attacked by worms and were

In 1546, Luis, the grandson of Christopher Columbus, was named Duke of Veragua. He set out with 130 men to claim his legacy, but he was attacked by Amerindians, lost most of his men, and retreated in failure.

battered by foul weather: they were leaking badly. He made it only as far as Santa Gloria, Jamaica, and spent a year there, marooned, unable to get help from the governor of Hispaniola, who was worried that Columbus might usurp his position. There were food shortages and an attempted mutiny, but eventually Columbus and 100 of the original 135 men did return to Spain in 1504, shortly after the death of Queen Isabel.

Columbus spent his final years in increasingly failing health, attempting to secure for himself the governorship, trade and other benefits that had been promised to him by the queen. But the king refused even to see him, and the struggle to attain title, territory, and wealth fell to his sons and in turn their sons (Columbus's grandson was finally named Duke of Veragua in 1546), and to the *conquistadores* who followed him to the Americas. As for his spiritual and material heirs, they too were to encounter hardships.

The conquistadores

It is tempting to characterize the conquest of South America as a brutal cartoon: greedy, ruthless *conquistadores* bungling explorations, slitting each other's throats for gold, territory, or titles; murdering, stealing from, and enslaving the peoples of the land.

It took 60 years from the time of Columbus's arrival at Limón until the first European settlement in Costa Rica was actually established. The rough terrain, the unfriendly oceans, the extreme weather, and a feisty local population all played a large part in the delay. But the continuous, jealous feuding among the *conquistadores* themselves was also a major factor in the failure of the many colonization attempts and should not be overlooked.

Gold was consistently the big theme. When the *conquistadores* asked the Amerindians about the location of gold mines, they simply pointed south to the fabled mines of Veragua. It gave the Spaniards gold fever. But if the indigenous population really knew where the mines were, they never revealed their location, and to this day the great, legendary mines remain undiscovered. The *conquistadores*, spurning the gold to be found in rivers, had to content themselves with taking the locals' gold, which they did – until there was no more. Then they had to determine how to survive, let alone get rich.

The Amerindians of Costa Rica, wearing gold necklaces, guided the Spaniards around the area, and spoke of great mines of gold – pointing south.

More expeditions

In 1506, two years after Columbus returned to Spain, King Ferdinand sent Governor Diego de Nicuesa and a group of settlers to establish a colony at Veragua. It was the first of many ill-fated attempts to establish settlements. Nicue-

Columbus in chains.

sa's ship ran aground in Panamá and he and his group set about walking up the coast to their destination. Food shortages and tropical diseases were acute; the terrain was devastating. Indigenous peoples along the way burned their own crops rather than yield their food. By the time the settlers finally arrived, their numbers had been halved.

Around this time, expeditions from Spain were landing throughout the Atlantic coast of Central America. They were capturing Amerindian slaves and sending them to work in the mines of Hispaniola, stealing their gold and desperately searching for a passage across the continent to the other ocean. Finally, in 1513, Vasco Nuñez de Balboa, a young stowaway escaping debts on Hispaniola, led an expedition across the isthmus and discovered the Pacific Ocean. It wasn't long before rudimentary shipyards appeared on the Pacific coast to accommodate would-be explorers who had sailed into Atlantic ports then walked across the isthmus, ready to set sail on the Pacific and continue their explorations. The unexplored Pacific had better anchorages, and was thought to have more gold.

The adventures of Gil González

The second inland expedition to Costa Rica was led by Captain Gil González in 1522, and

Depiction of the harbour entrance at Punta Arenas, c.1870.

it, too, ended without establishing a settlement. Faulty ships hastily constructed on the Pacific coast of Panamá took on water and forced González and his men to abandon the sea and move forward on foot.

The expeditions of González, which included a walk of 224 leagues (over 1,000km/600 miles) from the south Pacific coast of Costa Rica to the north, and into Nicaragua, have a mythic quality. At the age of 65 – and suffering from arthritis aggravated by the unceasing rain – González sometimes had to be carried on a litter, but he insisted on completing the arduous trip. González rested for 15 days in the home of the Térraba chief near Boruca. According to his accounts, he baptized some 32,000 of the

indigenous people here, and collected golden items of vast value.

He also encountered Chief Diríagen, who appeared out of the blue one day along with 500 Amerindians, each carrying one or two turkeys; 17 women covered from head to foot in gold disks; 10 men carrying standards; five trumpeters and other attendants bringing 200 golden hatchets. The party stopped in front of the house where González was staying, the trumpeters played and then the chiefs, women, and lords entered. When González asked their business, Chief Diríagen replied that they had come to see the men with beards who rode upon strange beasts. Probably Diríagen had come to ascertain the strength of the Spaniards, because three days after his visit, he returned and attacked them. It was an attack that González, with fewer than 20 men, at least according to the legend, easily repelled.

González ran into trouble later on with Pedrarias, governor of Panamá, who was responsible for the deaths of many Spanish *conquistadores*, including Balboa, his own son-in-law, whom he had beheaded. Pedrarias's ire was aroused by the enormous amounts of gold González had collected and by González's refusal to give up his claim on Nicaragua. The affair ended with González fleeing Panamá with his treasure.

Pestilence and slavery

The people of Nicoya and Nicaragua were not so fortunate as González, who got away with his life and his treasure. His expedition had brought smallpox, influenza, and plague to the area, and tens of thousands of Amerindians died. Survivors of the epidemics faced another danger: enslavement. Indigenous peoples from the Nicoya region, who then lived in large population centers, and were vulnerable to such attacks, were captured, branded with hot irons, and shipped off to Panamá and Peru to be sold as slaves.

The second attempted Costa Rican settlement was at Villa Bruselas, near present-day Orotina, not far from the large port city of Puntarenas. It lasted only three years and succumbed to feuding among the settlers and Amerindian attacks.

During this period, the *conquistadores* who arrived in Central America were free to exploit the indigenous population in virtually any way they wished. The Spanish policy of *requerimiento*, which went into effect in 1510, permitted settlers to wage war on those who refused to be baptized, a convenient justification for killing Amerindians and plundering their gold.

Later, *encomienda*, a royal grant from the Crown, gave settlers in Central America the right to force indigenous peoples to labor without compensation – or to demand goods as tribute. It was, in effect, slavery. The Amerindians were relocated to live on the land where they worked, and were considered the prop-

Portrait of Phillip II by Alonso Sánchez Coello.

erty of the grant holder. Without the system of *encomienda*, the *conquistadores* could not realize their aspirations of becoming landed aristocracy. All of the rights and assumed privileges of title had no real value without Amerindians to work the land.

Encomienda was not as widely practiced in Costa Rica as it was in other Central American colonies for a variety of reasons: the Amerindian labor force in Costa Rica was smaller; the Costa Rican Amerindians, outside of the Nicoya area, were not living in as large population centers as were, for example, the Maya of Guatemala. Instead, they lived in smaller, autonomous groups spread throughout the country. Thus the Spaniards

were not able simply to move in and conquer large numbers in a single effort as they had in Mexico.

Moreover, the Costa Rican Amerindians did not adapt well to slavery and fiercely resisted its imposition. Many fought and died avoiding enslavement, and many others fled to the mountains where they could not be followed. Finally, the practice of *encomienda* was abolished well before large numbers of Spanish settlers arrived in Costa Rica.

Church intervention

The Church proved to have an uneasy time with the *encomienda* system. After forceful campaigning by many churchmen, including the Dominican friar Bartolomé de las Casas, who was himself a former *conquistador*, *encomienda* was abolished in 1542.

This set off violent protests among the settlers, who believed they could not survive without slave labor. In Nicaragua, feelings ran so high that an armed uprising of colonists murdered the bishop who had supported the repeal of the *encomienda* system. Settlers petitioned the king, arguing that they had invested their lives and possessions, and the Crown had derived much benefit from their sacrifices. To his credit, the king refused.

Repartimiento

Still, the Crown had to support the colonists' need for labor. *Encomienda* was replaced by a system called *repartimiento* (meaning to divide up) which required all Amerindian men between the ages of 16 and 60 to labor for one week of each month for private individuals, religious institutions, municipalities, and/or government offices.

> Bartolomé de las Casas was to chronicle the methods of Spanish colonization in Latin America in his *History of the Indies*. He later became bishop of Chiapas, in Mexico.

On paper, the system was supposed to provide indigenous peoples with compensation for their labor and leave them free to work their own fields for the remaining three or so weeks of the month. But, in practice, things were very different, and abuses became commonplace.

Columbus thought he had struck it rich. But the riches he dreamed about never materialized. Costa Rica's gold supply was limited to surface and river deposits. The Gold Museum in San José is the country's best, with many of examples of pre-Columbian artifacts housed in a vault-like space.

Local people were required to devote considerably more than a week's labor to the Spaniards, since they had to walk very long distances, sometimes for days on end, from their villages to their places of work. And they were charged for the food and any other goods they consumed – thus using up their miserably small amount of pay.

Years passed and the search continued for the fabled great gold mines of Veragua. But the mines were never found. Spanish *conquistadores* plundered the coastlines, laying claim to whatever booty they could find, capturing local people and enslaving them, and fighting all the while among themselves for claims to the new lands. English pirates appeared on the scene, also competing for gold and slaves.

Spain's Central American colonies were developing, with administrative centers springing up in Panamá, Nicaragua, and Guatemala. In 1539, officials in Panamá used the name Costa Rica for the first time to distinguish the territory between Panamá and Nicaragua. But still there were no permanent settlements.

In 1559, Phillip II of Spain insisted that Costa Rica be populated, this time well inland. In 1561, Juan de Cavallón arrived with a group of 90 Spaniards recruited from Guatemala and Nicaragua, along with a team of black slaves and auxiliary Amerindians from Nicaragua.

Bringing indigenous peoples from one area to another was a common practice among the *conquistadores*, since these displaced people scarcely ever attempted to escape and return to their homes.

Cavallón also brought along livestock, including horses, cows, goats, pigs, chickens, and ducks, to improve the community's chances of success. It was a well-planned and well-financed expedition. Finally, 60 years after Columbus had arrived in Veragua, the first inland settlement in Costa Rica was established. It was christened Garcimuñoz, after Cavallón's place of birth.

Juan Vásquez de Coronado

Hailed by some historians as the true conqueror of Costa Rica, Coronado moved the Garcimuñoz settlement to the Cartago Valley and thence to El Guarco, and it was there, for the first time, that a permanent community took root. Coronado's tactics with the Amerindians of Costa Rica were different from those of his predecessors. While he fully intended to settle their lands and take what gold he could lay his hands on, he was friendly toward them, he treated them with respect, and he requested, rather than demanded, labor and tribute.

Chronicler Bartolomé de las Casas.

Coronado was pressured by his soldiers and the settlers, who weren't particularly interested in peace, to be more aggressive with the indigenous population. The settlers wanted food, gold, and labor, or at least the promise of wealth and an easier life. During this time, they were continually threatening to desert Costa Rica, claiming life was too difficult. Coronado's peaceful strategies were effective, however, and the colony flourished.

Pacification and punishment

Among Coronado's successes was the surrender (pacification, it was called) of a local chief named Quitao. At a meeting of all the chiefs in the area, Quitao announced that he was tired of hiding in the jungles and was ready to submit to the Spaniards. He told the other chiefs they were free to decide for themselves what they would do. The chiefs asked Quitao to decide for them and he replied that they would have to serve the king and his representative. Those who did not go along with this would be severely punished. As a token of his submission, he sent 150 local people to serve the Spanish, an act that was 'cause for great admiration among the Spaniards.'

Coronado's chronicles of his explorations throughout Costa Rica include keen, almost affectionate, observations of the Amerindians. In the Diquis region, visiting the Coctu, he wrote of the well-organized and well-developed villages, unlike any he had previously seen. He noted that the people had a lot of gold, which they acquired from tribes on the Atlantic coast and scooped from the rivers, and wore fine cotton clothing as well. He described them as a very good-looking people, bellicose, skillful in their manners, and very honest, 'a thing rarely seen in indians.'

It was among the Coctu that Coronado met the 'most good-looking indian' he had ever seen, Chief Corrohore, who asked his assistance in recovering his sister, Dulcehe, who had been kidnapped by a neighboring chief. Coronado succeeded and Dulcehe was returned.

The situation was not always peaceful, however. Coronado, known for making peace among some of the warring tribes of Costa Rica, joined them in their wars against one another. There were also Amerindian uprisings in the colony. Returning after an exploration, Coronado found that all the Amerindians of the area, including Quitao, were at war with the Spanish. (The Spanish had been stealing the indigenous people's corn.) Amerindians in Orosi had killed eight Spaniards and their horses. His old friends, the chiefs Aserrí, Currirabá, Yurustí, Quircó, and Purirsí, had been made prisoners. In an attempt to calm the situation, Coronado went to speak to the Amerindians and, in a fit of temper, ordered two of them to be dismembered.

The lack of gold, food shortages, and indigenous revolts imposed continuous hardships on the settlers. Supplies and new settlers were brought in from Nicaragua, but life was almost unendurable for the Spaniards. In 1569, settlers demanded indigenous slaves,

threatening to abandon the colony if their demands weren't met. Perafán de Ribera, Coronado's successor, a frail man of 74 years, defied Spanish law and permitted the settlers to enslave the local people.

A vanquished land

The late 1560s marked the end of the conquest of Costa Rica. By then the majority of the indigenous population of the new colony had been killed, had died of diseases, had submitted to the Spaniards, or had fled to the forested mountains of Talamanca. The land was now

Conquistador statue, San José.

available to the settlers from Spain to come and make a new life.

Some traces of indigenous roots, however, survive to this day, particularly in place names honoring ancient chiefs – Aserrí, for example, is a town south of San José. Columbus's original name for Costa Rica – Veragua – has recently been resurrected and now graces a 1,620-hectare (4,000-acre) nature reserve and rainforest research center on the Caribbean Coast with a view of the spot where the Spanish ships first dropped anchor. Less gloriously, the indigenous word for chief – *cacique* – is now best known as a major brand name for *guaro*, a cheap but potent alcohol made from sugar cane.

COLONIALISM AND INDEPENDENCE

After years as a forgotten penurious colony that received news of its independence by mail, Costa Rica discovered coffee and launched a fledgling democracy.

The Costa Rican colony grew slowly. In 1573, there was a total of 50 families in Cartago, and a fledgling community farther west that would later become San José. Spanish immigrants arrived from Extremadura, in the west of Spain; from Andalucia, in the south, with its strong Moorish influences; and from Castile, the heart of old Spain. The Spanish had also founded colonies on the Pacific coast, at Espiritú Santo de Esparza and Nicoya. Although the population of Costa Rica was slowly growing, life was anything but easy.

During the conquest, *conquistadores* had loaded their ships and lined their pockets with gold, and had sent their obligatory percentages off to the royal treasury, which had swelled with their contributions. But by the end of the 16th century, what little gold there was in Costa Rica was gone. There was little Spanish currency available and it appeared as though there was no way to generate wealth. Cacao beans were used as money and barter became common. Even the few goods the colonists 'bought' from Spain were traded for wheat flour, pigs, lard, chickens, tobacco, and liquor produced on their farms. Most families lived on isolated farms in the Central Valley, using primitive methods of agriculture. Social and even church life was nonexistent, and the populace lived in a state of grim impoverishment.

The forgotten colony

By now Spain was paying scant attention to its far-off colony and even the colonial governor in Guatemala made very little effort to acquaint himself with the colony's concerns. It was, after all, a three-month trip from Guatemala by horse, and there was little reason to travel to Costa Rica.

Henry Morgan, the Welsh pirate.

Official neglect did have a positive side effect, however. Without large landholdings or plentiful peon labor to work plantations, even Costa Rica's governor and the aristocratic Spanish settlers were forced to work their own fields. Despite the grueling labor, the land at least was fertile, enriched by volcanic ash and irrigated by rivers. Colonists grew wheat, vegetables, and sugar, and raised livestock and poultry. Slowly but surely, the seeds of an economy began to take root.

The birth of commerce

The first export of the Costa Rican colony was mules. They were walked along the Mule Road to Panamá, where they were sold to hardy souls who needed beasts to bear goods from the Atlantic to the Pacific coast. Later came cacao production on the Atlantic coast, and then tobacco, in the Central Plateau. In an attempt to give Costa Rica a product to export and a dependable income that could be taxed, the Crown set up tobacco-processing plants and granted Costa Rica sole rights within the colonies to grow tobacco. But Costa Rican tobacco was of poor quality, and there was not a large market for it.

On the Atlantic coast, piracy and slave-trading were the business of the day. The Atlantic waters were continually plundered by English pirates, including Drake, Mansfield, Morgan, and Owens; and by French, Dutch, and Portuguese buccaneers. They were all attempting to control the territory so they could cross the isthmus, from the Atlantic to the Pacific, and thus avoid the Spaniards in Panamá.

The Miskitos

In 1641 a slave ship was wrecked off the coast of Nicaragua/Honduras, and the black slaves on board escaped onto the Atlantic coast. Well liked by the Amerindians, they intermarried and, over the years, developed an identity and language of their own, called *Miskito*. British pirates joined forces with the *Miskitos*, and together they wreaked havoc along the Atlantic coast of Costa Rica and in the cacao plantations. For the *Miskitos*, the undefended plantations offered little resistance. They sailed in for their biannual raids, took the cacao, captured the black slaves, and set off again.

In 1742, after many years of such devastation, the government built Fort San Fernando in Matina, north of present-day Limón. Only five years later, however, the fort was destroyed by the pirate Owens and the *Miskitos*, under orders of the British-controlled Jamaican governor (the British and the Spanish were by then at war).

Protection money

By 1779 the pirate situation was so out of hand that the government started paying tribute to the *Miskitos* and leaving them 'gifts' of coats made of fine fabric, shiny buttons, or three-cornered French hats, to collect at Matina.

Many years later, in 1841, President Braulio Carrillo refused to continue paying tribute to, or bestowing gifts upon, the *Miskitos* and threatened to bring the resources of the country to war against them. Probably because cacao production had dwindled greatly by then, the *Miskitos* stopped raiding Matina.

Amerindian resettlement

Owing to mountainous terrain and inaccessibility, the Talamanca region of Costa Rica escaped the conquest. Groups of indigenous people, some of them refugees fleeing oppression elsewhere in the country, lived there, undisturbed by the invading Spaniards.

Statue of Juan Santamaría in Alajuela.

However, as more colonists arrived in Costa Rica to clear land, build roads, and farm, the paltry size of the available Amerindian labor force became a serious problem. The solution was to begin raids on the Talamanca region. After numerous forays, attempts to conquer Talamanca proved unsuccessful. There were counterattacks and cruel revenges on both sides. Ultimately, hundreds of Amerindians were 'relocated' to the Central Valley by the Indian Resettlement Policies of 1747.

Meanwhile, in the Central Valley, communities were being established. In 1706, the village of Cubujuqui, which later became Heredia, was founded; in 1737, Villa Nueva de la Boca del Monte, now San José, was

Traces of Miskito influence remain in the Atlantic coast area, where many of the place names come from their language, including Talamanca (Talamalka), Sixaola, and Cahuita.

born; and in 1782, Villa Hermosa, now Alajuela, was settled.

Costa Ricans, living at subsistence levels, were too busy trying to survive to be much affected by the currents of thought and the conflicts that led to Central America's struggle for

Detail of a banknote showing a coffee harvest.

THE OLD CAPITAL

The country's first capital of Cartago was founded in 1561 by Juan de Cavallón as Castillo de Garcimuñoz. The site and name were abandoned when Coronado moved all the inhabitants to El Guarco in the Cartago Valley. Then Perafán de Ribera moved it again, to Mata Redonda, near present-day Sabana. Later, the peripatetic city returned to the Cartago Valley, to its present location. In 1723, Irazú Volcano erupted, covering Cartago in layers of ash. At that time, Costa Rica's capital comprised just 70 houses, a parish church, and two shrines. It had no shops, no drug store, not even a resident doctor.

independence from Spain. The discord that was brewing elsewhere in Central America, fueled by class distinctions and onerous trade restrictions, largely passed them by.

Independence – by mail

Costa Ricans like to tell the story of how they received independence by mail. In fact, a courier aboard a mule arrived in the Central Valley of Costa Rica with the news on October 13, 1821, nearly a month after colonial officials in Guatemala City had declared independence for Costa Rica from the Spanish Empire.

The news aroused ambivalence, confusion, and conflict over what independence meant for the backwater region of Costa Rica. Being the province farthest removed from the colonial capital, Costa Rica came under the least influence of the Spanish Crown, the Catholic Church, the colonial bureaucracy, and the monopolistic Guatemalan traders who dominated colonial life in the rest of Central America. Tucked away in the recesses of the country's central highlands, leaders of the four small communities of San José, Cartago, Heredia, and Alajuela began a lengthy debate over what they should do next.

Rift over independence

Taking their cues from the 1812 Spanish Constitution, written with the participation of a distinguished Costa Rican liberal named Florencio de Castillo, local leaders drafted their first Constitution, the *Pacto de Concordia*, on December 1, 1821. A split quickly developed over whether or not to follow the lead of other Central American countries in joining Mexican nationalist and emperor Agustín de Itúrbide's empire, or to opt for total independence.

Leaders of the towns of San José and Alajuela, inspired by the revolutionary ideas that were then sweeping the world, argued for independence, while those of Cartago and Heredia leaned toward the Mexican Empire. There were even those who argued passionately that Costa Rica should become a part of Colombia, at the time ruled by Simón Bolívar.

The disagreements reflected the basic disparity in the respective characters of the cities. Cartago and Heredia had been founded to create Catholic congregations out of the early settlers: these towns evolved into centers of conservative thought and were more closely linked to the Church and the old colonial bureaucracy. By contrast, San José was founded by settlers who had been banished from Cartago for defying the strict colonial trading laws on smuggling. Alajuela, too, developed into a fringe agricultural center where the smuggling of tobacco flourished. Both towns developed more freewheeling, commercially based liberal attitudes than those of their strait-laced neighbors.

The issue of whether or not Costa Rica would join the Mexican Empire was settled on April 5, 1823. Two armies from the rival cities met in battle on the Continental Divide between San José and Cartago in a skirmish that left 20 men dead. The victorious independence forces, led by a former merchant seaman named Gregorio José Ramírez, took the town of Cartago.

Independence from the Mexican Empire was assured. As it turned out, they need not have bothered: the Costa Ricans belatedly learned that Itúrbide had been declared a traitor several days before the battle, and had been captured and executed. And with him had gone the Mexican Empire.

Farmers and teachers

Gregorio Ramírez set a precedent by relinquishing power in order to return to his farm, an example that would be followed by other victorious Costa Rican leaders. He later returned to put down an army coup, establishing civilian dominance over the military at a very early stage in the country's development.

Statehood was conferred upon a rather ambivalent Costa Rica by the Federal Republic of Central America. This confederation was a noble effort to create a 'United States of Central America' out of the five former Spanish provinces, with a capital in Guatemala City. But it was doomed to failure because of class disparities and the tenacity with which the elite class clung to the local colonial social order in other parts of Central America. Costa Rica, on the other hand, was largely a nation of family farmers. It lacked both an elite class and a well-defined social order, so it offered neither great resistance to, nor enthusiasm for, the confederation. As a sovereign federal state, the country elected its first head of state, Juan Mora Fernández, in 1824. An elementary school teacher, Mora Fernández distinguished himself by

In the mid-19th century, to minimize the rivalries between the four main population centers – Alajuela, Cartago, Heredia, San José – the honor of being capital was rotated among them every four years.

conducting the affairs of state with prudence and humility.

The first printing presses arrived in Costa Rica under Mora Fernández's tenure. By the time his successor, another elementary

Braulio Carrillo was twice Head of State.

school teacher named José Rafael Gallegas, was elected, (against his will) in 1833, several newspapers were in print. One of them, *La Tertulia*, published humiliating attacks on Gallegas. Not much interested in the office to begin with, Gallegas resigned as head of state. One of *La Tertulia*'s major complaints was the social disintegration that had befallen the community as a result of the first modest signs of prosperity brought on by the planting of coffee, near San José. That limited prosperity brought with it prostitution, gambling, and property theft at levels unknown during the more austere colonial era. A strong, no-nonsense authoritarian hand seemed called for, and a San José lawyer, named Braulio Carrillo, was the right man in the right place at the right time.

Braulio Carrillo

Carrillo imposed vagrancy laws, withdrew Costa Rica from the faltering Central American Federal Republic, and enacted liberal reforms such as a civil and penal code. He also outlawed the Church's right to tithes and earned the enmity of Central Valley townships by imposing a tax on rural land, using the revenues to build roads and ports. Carrillo also settled Costa Rica's share of a debt to British bankers

General Morazán.

that had been incurred by the founders of the Central American Federation. Other Central American countries would have that debt hanging over them until well into the 20th century. The payback of the 'English debt' eventually paid dividends in the form of good credit with which to invest in the country's new-found source of wealth: coffee.

Coffee power

Carrillo had, with unabashed autocracy, reorganized public administration to support the demands of the coffee economy. Serendipitously, in 1843 William Le Lacheur, an Englishman on his way back home with a cargo of pelts, put in to Puntarenas, a Costa

Rican port on the Pacific coast, in search of ballast for his ship, which had been battered by storms off the Mexican coast. He loaded some 230,000kg (500,000lbs) of coffee into his hold and the Costa Rica–Liverpool connection was established. Thus were the British Isles and, ultimately, the European continent, opened up as an important new market for Costa Rican coffee.

The economic power that coffee gave to the citizens of San José further encouraged Carrillo's reorganization of the country's institutions around the new source of wealth, but caused resentment from the other townships. In 1837, Cartago, Alajuela, and Heredia challenged Carrillo and San José in the *Guerra de la Liga*. Emerging victorious from the battle, Carrillo moved the capital permanently to San José.

When his term was up in 1837, Carrillo left office, only to return in a military coup the following year, after his successor tried to roll back some of his reforms. Continuing to force the country down the road to a coffee-fueled progress, he proclaimed himself president-in-perpetuity.

General Morazán

By 1842, the new social order created by Carrillo rose up to overwhelm him. Members of the budding coffee oligarchy called on General Francisco Morazán, a hero of the Central American Federal Republic, to free them from what they perceived as Carrillo's despotism. Morazán was welcomed as a liberator when he arrived in Costa Rica, in April of 1842, with an army of 500 mostly Salvadoran volunteers. The head of Carrillo's army, Vicente Villaseñor, met up with Morazán just as the general and his men neared Alajuela on their march from the Pacific port of Caldera, and offered to join forces with him. The *Pacto de Jocote* sealed, Carrillo fell and was forced into exile in El Salvador.

A special assembly named Morazán provisional head of the state of Costa Rica. The general received a hero's welcome in Heredia and Alajuela, but received a somewhat restrained and cooler reception in San José.

Morazán wore out his welcome when he attempted to use Costa Rica as a base to revive his moribund confederation. The general sent missives to the other Central American countries calling for a National Constituent Assembly to revive his dream of a unified Central

American nation. He threatened to impose compliance by force of arms. When Morazán tried to conscript Costa Ricans to enforce his ultimatum, the people of San José revolted. After three days of fierce fighting, Morazán was captured and, on September 15, 1842, he was executed in San José's Central Park.

Less than three years later, Braulio Carrillo, too, was to meet a violent end, assassinated in El Salvador. Today, Costa Ricans have mixed feelings about Braulio Carrillo. He is remembered as both a despot and as a strong, sometimes benevolent, leader who, perhaps, was the right

William Walker invaded Costa Rica in 1856.

man at the right time. He forced Costa Rica to break with its colonial past, placing the country firmly on the path to nationhood.

William Walker

In 1855, a Tennessee adventurer named William Walker took control of Nicaragua. One of his aims was to institutionalize slavery there and in neighboring countries so that he could sell slaves to the United States. Certain US industrialists liked the plan and gave support to Walker. The following year, with an army of 300 mercenaries, called *filibusteros*, he invaded Costa Rica, advancing as far as the site of the present Santa Rosa National Park. Walker and his men entrenched themselves in the fortified

Santa Rosa mansion. Costa Rican President Juan Rafael Mora, a member of the coffee oligarchy, had been monitoring the threat and had already mustered a force of *campesinos* (farm workers) to repel Walker. The Costa Ricans were numerically superior, though many were poorly armed with little more than farming implements and rusty rifles. On May 20, 1856, they engaged Walker in a 14-minute-long battle and forced him to retreat toward the Nicaraguan border.

The Costa Rican army pursued them and, at Rivas in Nicaragua, trapped Walker in a

A victorious Costa Rican army returns to San José.

wooden fort. A young drummer boy named Juan Santamaría volunteered to torch the fort, but was shot dead in the process. With the fort in flames, Walker's men were routed and his Costa Rican adventure was over. Three years later, he met his end in front of a firing squad in Honduras. The name of Juan Santamaría lives on in Costa Rican folklore as a youthful hero and symbol of national freedom, and in the country's main international airport, which is named after him.

President Mora was not such a hero. Despite his victory, his domestic policies were unpopular. He rigged the 1859 elections to win another term in office, was deposed, attempted an unsuccessful coup d'état, and was executed.

Train crosses the bridge at Crucitas, c.1885.

Young coffee picker.

MODERN TIMES

Economic difficulties and the rising tide of reform
came to a head in civil war, but 21st-century Costa
Rica became Central America's peace broker.

In 1889, with the drafting of the country's liberal constitution and the institution of a reliable, quadrennial electoral process, Costa Rica entered an era of bucolic prosperity and political stability. Affairs of state were left in the hands of so-called 'Olympian' political plutocrats who administered public affairs with a laissez-faire assurance.

The coffee coup

It was not all plain sailing, however. The presumed downward trickle of profits in the coffee economy failed to reach enough people, especially in the neglected urban centers. Faced with the closing of European coffee markets during World War I, Costa Rica's first reformist president, Alfredo Gonzáles Flores, instituted a tax on coffee, incurring the wrath of the coffee establishment, which backed the president's own army chief, Federico Tinoco, in a successful coup on January 27, 1917. Tinoco assumed the presidency and named his brother, Joaquín, to head the army.

The warrior priest

Popular reaction to the repressive Tinoco dictatorship brought Jorge Volio Jiménez onto the country's political stage with a dramatic flourish. The pious scion of a Cartago coffee family, Volio studied for the priesthood in Belgium and, heavily influenced by Belgian social Christian thinking, he returned to Costa Rica in 1910 to become pastor of a Heredia parish. No simple parish priest, in 1912 Volio denounced the silence of the Costa Rican government over the intervention of US marines in Nicaragua and backed up his words by leading a group of Nicaraguan revolutionaries into battle. He was

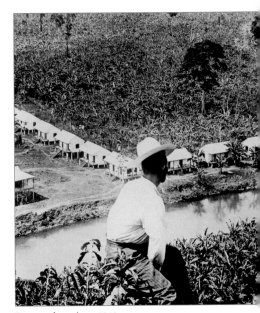

Banana plantation, c.1910.

seriously wounded in the battle of Paz Centro in southern Nicaragua.

For his military adventure Volio was suspended from the Church, but was later reinstated. His passion for social justice led him to more clashes with the conservative local hierarchy, and, in 1915, he left the priesthood to devote himself to working for social change.

As the Tinoco dictatorship became increasingly more repressive, Volio and a handful of other Costa Ricans left the country and formed an armed resistance, but the revolutionary forces were defeated by government troops led by army chief Joaquín Tinoco in battles near the Nicaraguan border in early 1919.

The Tinoco dictatorship was brought down not by this armed resistance nor by a military coup, but rather by outraged school teachers and students who rioted after soldiers marched on them during a demonstration in July of 1919. On August 9, 1919, Federico Tinoco resigned the presidency. The next day, Joaquín Tinoco was gunned down. The gunman was never identified.

¡Viva Volio!

His military defeat notwithstanding, Volio received a hero's welcome on his arrival in San José, and the ready cry '¡Viva Volio!' expressed

Workers at a coffee plantation wash their clothes in a shallow stream, c.1931.

the hope for change in the country's stodgy political status quo. But much to Volio's consternation, the fall of Tinoco meant a return to business as usual in Costa Rica. Volio established the Reformist Party in 1923, which set an agenda for agrarian reform, decent housing, job security, and social protections. During the same year he ran for president on the Reformist ticket against Ricardo Jiménez and Alberto Echandi. Volio came in a close third in a vote that gave none of the candidates a majority. He agreed to join forces with Jiménez, accepting the vice-presidency and a seat in Congress. But, rather than compromising, Volio used his seat to forcefully attack the country's upper classes.

Labor organizer Carlos Luis Fallas immortalized the 1934 'Great Banana Strike' at United Fruit Company in the lowland banana zones in his novel Mamita Yunai.

When the government once again showed indifference to strife in neighboring Nicaragua, Volio commanded a force across the border to intervene. Concerned as to what an increasingly belligerent Volio might do with his force upon his return, Jiménez ordered the general to be intercepted when he arrived in Liberia. After a gunfight that left two government soldiers and Volio himself wounded, he was apprehended and taken back to San José where doctors diagnosed him as suffering from 'nervous hypersensitivity.' Rather than imprisoning the patriot, Jiménez allowed him to be taken to Belgium for psychiatric care. Volio's promising political career came to an ignominious end.

The growth of reform

Volio's brand of reformism collapsed with his party, but the reformist movement was important in giving voice to the aspirations of sectors of society on the margins of the agro-export economy. It also inspired young intellectuals to action, including Manuel Mora, who, in his own words, 'used to follow Volio around like a puppy dog.' Disillusioned with Volio's political flirtation with Jiménez, Mora split with the Reformist Party to eventually form the Communist Party in 1931. The Communists immediately made their presence felt in the lowland banana zones. During a strike in 1934, the Communists won wage guarantees and the right to unionize, but only after a heated battle with both government troops and the United Fruit Company. Meanwhile, plummeting coffee prices during the Great Depression had created additional hardship for a great many Costa Ricans.

Calderón Guardia

The rising tide of reform finally found its champion when, as the economic crisis reached its breaking point, Costa Ricans elected Dr Rafael Angel Calderón Guardia to the presidency in 1939. Inheritor of his father's humanitarian legacy and backed by the coffee establishment, he seemed the perfect choice.

Calderón Guardia, also steeped in social Christian doctrine at medical school in Belgium, carried out reforms beyond the hopes of even the most fervent reformers and the fears of the most entrenched liberal, creating a social-security system, a labor code, and various other social guarantees.

Costa Rica declared war on Germany and Japan following the attack on Pearl Harbor – a day before the United States. But Calderón Guardia added insult to injury for the coffee barons by using his wartime emergency powers to confiscate the lands of German families,

pact feasible – vanished, so too did the wide-based, popular support for Calderón's leadership. As the government clung to power, a disillusioned Mora was paid a visit by an old friend who offered his support. It was the elderly and ailing General Jorge Volio Jiménez.

History has shown that the winners of the ensuing 1948 civil war, led by José (Don Pepe) Figueres, had no intention of rolling back the social guarantees. Instead, they further institutionalized the legacy of nearly 30 years of reformist struggle. It was a legacy summed up by the immortal cry: '¡Viva Volio!'

United Fruit Company banana train, 1916.

some of whom had been in Costa Rica for generations and who had intermarried with the oligarchy.

Having alienated himself from the traditional source of political power, Calderón Guardia made common cause with Manual Mora and his Communist Party, and with the Catholic Church, led by the socially minded Archbishop Victor Sanabria. Together they defied the coffee barons and the economic liberals who had dominated Costa Rica since the end of the 19th century and set about expanding the role of the state in providing for people's needs. Manuel Mora was named head of the country's army.

When the worldwide anti-Nazi alliances – which made this peculiar church-state-party

The grandfather of Costa Rica

José Figueres is best known abroad for abolishing the army, but Costa Ricans remember him for the way in which he lived his life, and for the heritage of democracy that he created and solidified. Don Pepe was born of Catalán parents, and for many, that somehow explained his ego, his opinionated, self-righteous, impossibly principled, obstinate, courageous, unyielding, unpredictable self. He was self-educated, and as a young man he virtually lived in the Boston Public Library, where he became infected with the new and exciting spirit of North American liberalism. He returned to Costa Rica from Boston and New York City in the 1920s with a romantic vision and deeply held belief in the nobility of the human spirit, and hope for social justice for the people of his country.

Until 1942, Don Pepe had no real political experience. Then, on July 2, the *San Pablo*, a United Fruit Company vessel, was sunk by a German submarine in the Port of Limón. All the Costa Ricans aboard were killed. President Calderón responded by imprisoning German and Italian citizens of the Atlantic region. Two days later, 20,000 people rioted after a German-educated medical doctor's window was smashed. Looting followed, and the government not only did nothing to control the mob, but also allegedly encouraged it.

In the aftermath of the riots a climate of fear and suspicion grew. Don Pepe blamed Calderón for failing to maintain public order and safety. He decided to express 'what everyone felt but was afraid to say', and purchased radio air time on 'America Latina'. In strident mocking tones he accused the administration of an inability to govern. His denunciation of the government was interrupted mid-sentence as the director-general of the police arrived and hauled him away. The result was, perhaps all too predictably, the making of a martyr and national hero out of the imprisoned Don Pepe Figueres.

The seeds of revolution

Figueres spent the next two years in exile in Mexico where he forged agreements with exiles, intellectuals, and revolutionaries from other countries, and began stockpiling arms. In 1944, after a particularly violent and discreditable election, Teodoro Picado, Calderón's political successor, was elected president. The fraudulent election, the faltering economy, the Communist presence and widespread official corruption were too much for Figueres. He returned to Costa Rica in May 1944. Determined to do something about Calderón, he jumped into opposition politics, but felt that only a violent revolution would bring about real change.

In the fateful 1948 presidential elections, Otilio Ulate, publisher of the San José newspaper, *Diario de Costa Rica*, ran against Calderón. Ulate won by a substantial margin, but the *calderonistas* maintained control of congress. There were charges and countercharges of fraud, and, in the midst of the violent confrontations, a large number of ballots were set ablaze. The electoral tribunal, which had been entrusted to oversee fair elections, and to which the nation was looking for a verdict, failed to issue one.

With no action forthcoming from the tribunal and no compromise possible between the candidates, the *calderonista*-controlled Congress, in an unprecedented act, annulled the presidential election. Ulate was arrested by Picado's police colonel, and his closest advisor, Dr Carlos Luis Valverde, was shot and died the following day. In San José, businesses were closed and storefronts were boarded up. It felt

Teodoro Picado, president from 1944 to 1948.

LA LUCHA SIN FIN

Eminent political figure, José (Don Pepe) Figueres (1906–90), founded a farm high in the mountains, to the south of San José, and called it *La Lucha Sin Fin* (The Endless Struggle). It was a success, and he used the profits to open schools, libraries, stores, movie houses, soccer fields, and medical clinics for local people. At *La Lucha*, Don Pepe worked at liberating the *campesino* (farm laborer) from ignorance and poverty and attempting to turn some of the Utopian theories he had studied into a workable reality. The day-to-day way of life on the farm provided lessons that in many ways Don Pepe Figueres was later to apply to all of Costa Rica.

as though a bomb were ready to go off. Meanwhile, Figueres was in the mountains near his ranch, *La Lucha Sin Fin* (the Endless Struggle), planning for the coming war.

Civil war

The War of National Liberation began on March 11, 1948. It consisted of a well-planned offensive carried out by men with no formal military background, trained by guerrilla fighters from the Dominican Republic and Honduras, and armed with guns flown in from Guatemala. Forty-four days later, 2,000 men, one in every 300 Costa Ricans, had been killed during the violent, sad war of liberation. Figueres' forces were victorious, despite the efforts of the Nicaraguan dictator Anastasio Somoza, and his invasion of the north of Costa Rica. President Picado, who had never really believed an armed insurrection would occur, and who had no heart for conflict, saw that a swiftly negotiated peace was essential; he announced his surrender.

The Second Republic

Don Pepe Figueres, as both the acknowledged winner of the battle and head of the victorious junta, entered San José five days after the ceasefire and led a triumphant parade. Figueres addressed the people, outlining his goals and fundamental concepts, of what he called his Second Republic: the re-establishment of civic ethics, elimination of the spoils system in public administration, social republic progress without Communism, and a greater sense of solidarity with other nations.

One of Figueres' first acts was to place a 10 percent tax on wealth, a law that was resented, badly administered, and, in most cases, evaded by the affluent. He expanded the social-security system, enacted full voting rights for all women, created a minimum wage, established low-cost national health care services for all, passed legislation on child support, and proposed nationalizing the banks. The firing of large numbers of bureaucrats and schoolteachers, in an attempt to reorganize government agencies, exacerbated his declining popularity. And then the assets of individuals connected with the Calderón-Picado governments were frozen. Don Pepe's extreme – and, to some, arbitrary – politics alienated many. Even the press became hostile to him.

The constitution of 1949 did reflect many of the goals of the Second Republic. It included political and individual freedoms, and added new social guarantees. It established the principle of public regulation of private property and enterprise, and empowered the state to take actions assuring the widest distribution of wealth possible. But arguably its finest social guarantee was to extend citizenship to everyone born in Costa Rica. This was an important issue for Afro-Caribbean residents, who until that time had been treated as second-class people.

José Figueres, the grandfather of Costa Rica.

A BLOT ON COSTA RICA'S IMAGE

Caught between seriously addressing the issue of child-sex tourism or exposing the country's pure ecotourism image to unfavorable publicity, Costa Rican authorities have so far chosen to hide their heads in the sand. A damning US Embassy report on Human Trafficking in 2011 placed the country on its Tier 2 watch list, for failing to condemn or prosecute the practice. Tourists from the US, Germany, Sweden, and Italy are the main customers, but Costa Ricans are also complicit. In 2012, the mayor of the canton that includes Quepos and Manuel Antonio, was arrested on charges of child pornography.

The end of the military

The new constitution also abolished the military. This was perhaps Figueres' most celebrated and memorable achievement, one that he would point to over and over again. In a public ceremony, he delivered the keys of the Bella Vista military fortress to the minister of public education, and told him to convert it into a national museum. Don Pepe knew how to exploit the moment: with photographers standing by, he raised a sledgehammer and symbolically smashed at the wall of the fortress. His supporters considered it a final blow to mili-

Nicaraguan commander in the Sandinista Liberation Front, 1979.

tarism. His enemies regarded the abolition of the military as a clever move: lacking the full backing of the military, he simply decided to get rid of it.

Calm before storm

The 1960s and 1970s were essentially peaceful and prosperous decades. The development of a welfare state and bills protecting indigenous peoples were just two highlights of a progressive regime. But in 1979, the anti-government Sandinista forces in neighboring Nicaragua toppled the Somoza dictatorship. Costa Rica became a fallback area for guerrilla groups and anti-Sandinistas, largely at

the behest of the US, to whom Costa Rica was financially indebted.

Equally bad news, if not worse, was the collapse of both the banana and coffee markets, reaching a peak in the early 1980s. Throughout the decade, debt continued to mount. The silver lining on the cloud was provided by its president, Oscar Arias Sánchez, who was trying to mediate a peace settlement in the escalating regional conflicts. By now El Salvador, Honduras, and Guatemala were also embroiled in various types of war or disputes. Costa Rica, for all its economic problems, was at least an oasis of peace. In 1987, Arias was awarded the Nobel Prize for his efforts to bring peace to Central America. He also accepted millions of dollars of aid from the US, compromising Costa Rica's neutral position.

A family affair

Despite the success of Oscar Arias abroad, his party was voted out in 1990 in favor of Rafael Calderón Fournier, the son of post-war president Dr Rafael Calderón Guardia. Following a lackluster term, he was succeeded by José Maria Figueres, son of Don Pepe, who was, of course, Calderón Guardia senior's arch rival. Sadly, the young Figueres was unable to repeat his father's success and proved to be one of Costa Rica's most unpopular presidents. In 1998 the Social Christian Unity Party (PUSC) won the election under conservative economist Miguel Angel Rodríguez, who pledged to liberalize certain key economic sectors and slash government spending. Despite attracting foreign investment such as the Intel silicon-chip plant, and signing free-trade deals with Canada and Mexico, many Costa Ricans suspected that his privatization plans for the state-run telecommunication and energy monopolies pointed to corruption. Critics accused his government of lack of transparency, triggering the largest street demonstrations since the 1948 revolution.

In April 2002, PUSC retained power with the election of Abel Pacheco, who placed much emphasis on tourism as the country's greatest economic priority. His tenure was plagued by incompetence, lack of leadership, an intransigent, uncooperative Congress, and a plethora of political, financial, and environmental scandals. In 2004 two ex-presidents were arrested on corruption charges, including Rodríguez, who had to step down from his post as the first-ever

Central American Secretary General of the Organization of American States. More arrests followed, and, in the end, five former presidents were under investigation for corruption.

Financial scandals included the collapse of half a dozen unregulated tax shelters and mutual funds, in which the expat community was heavily invested and hard hit. Pacheco's environmental reforms were never passed and the country's national park system deteriorated, with uncontrolled poaching and logging, thanks to lack of funding for park guards.

A political phoenix

The 2006 election was a prolonged showdown between Citizen Action Party (PAC) leader Ottón Solís and the National Liberation Party (PLN)'s Oscar Arias, who had managed constitutionally to overturn the country's ban on presidential re-election. After a recount, Arias won with the slimmest of margins. Some 20 years after his first term started in 1986, Arias returned to the Casa Presidencial to preside over the passing, in 2008, of CAFTA, the US-Central American Free Trade Agreement, which had violently polarized the nation.

The 2010 election made history when Laura Chinchilla, former vice-president in the Arias administration, became the first female president of Costa Rica. History was also made in October 2010 when former President Rafael Angel Calderón Fournier was found guilty on corruption charges, and became the first president to be sentenced to a prison term.

Countrywide, an increase in violent crime and a growing gap between rich and poor today threaten Costa Rica's image as a peaceful, safe country. The child-sex industry has also cast a pall over tourism. On the bright side, Costa Rica has set an admirable goal to become the first carbon-neutral country by 2021. And, despite its social and economic problems, in 2012 the UK-based New Economics Foundation, which ranks countries on the basis of life expectancy and ecological footprint, named Costa Rica the happiest place on earth.

The political domination of the PLN and PUSC ended in 2014 with the election of Luis Guillermo Solís Rivera of the PAC as Costa Rica's president. A well-known political scientist, historian, and academic, he promised to root out corruption, revamp the country's failing infrastructure, shore up public health

care and social security systems, and boost economic growth. However, soon after taking office, Solís suffered a major setback when the US IT giant Intel closed down its microchip plant in San José shedding some 1,500 jobs. The country's fortunes on the international sporting stage fared rather better when, later that year, the national football team (La Sele) made history by reaching the World Cup quarterfinals for the first time. The team returned home to a hero's welcome with Real Madrid goalkeeper Keylor Navas becoming an instant celebrity.

Laura Chinchilla, first female president of Costa Rica.

FICKLE FRIENDS

During his second term of office (2006–10), President Oscar Arias Sánchez unceremoniously dumped Costa Rica's long-standing trading partner and benefactor Taiwan in favor of China. So much for gratitude for the Costa Rica-Taiwan Friendship Bridge, built with Taiwanese funds in 2003 to link the Nicoya Peninsula with the mainland. Local pundits have dubbed the bridge Puente de la Apuñalada (Back Stab Bridge). Apart from wide-open new markets for both countries, Costa Rica's change of heart has been rewarded with a huge new national soccer stadium in San José known as "La Joya" (The Gem), built by Chinese workers.

One man and his horse, Montezuma.

Horseback rider in the northeast.

THE PEOPLE OF COSTA RICA

Costa Ricans, or *Ticos*, come in all shapes, sizes, and colors. 'We are all *Ticos*,' is the proud claim, though some *Ticos* fare better than others.

R acially and ethnically, Costa Rica is not a simple place. Along with the overwhelming majority of Spanish-heritage Ticos, there are four other distinct ethnic groups. The people of Guanacaste have dark skin, and resemble their Nicaraguan neighbors in manner and accent. In the southern, mountainous regions of the country, the Amerindians of Costa Rica, who were here long before the Spanish, belong to six discrete linguistic groups. Though they increasingly speak Spanish, they still debate whether it is more important to retain their indigenous cultural identity or to assimilate more into mainstream Costa Rican culture.

The blacks of the Atlantic Coast are the country's largest immigrant minority; they speak Caribbean-accented English and talk with pride of their Jamaican heritage. Sino-Costa Ricans are called *Chinos*. Descendants of indentured laborers, they own many of the bars, restaurants, and stores, especially in small towns.

Despite the diverse nature of its population, Costa Rica's various ethnic groups were only officially recognized in 2014, when the Constitution was amended as a measure to counter racism and discrimination.

Indigenous people

Archeologists, using very different methods of calculating populations, estimate that anywhere from 30,000 to 400,000 native people lived in Costa Rica when Columbus arrived. Today, about 70,000 native people remain, although it is hard to establish an accurate figure since many indigenous people have had mixed marriages.

The history of the Amerindians of Costa Rica is much like that of other indigenous peoples of the American continent. The Europeans brought diseases to which the native populations had no

Grandmother on babysitting duties in Tortuguero.

immunity and entire tribes were obliterated. In pre-Columbian times, the Chorotegas, cousins of the Nicaro, inhabited Guanacaste and the Nicoya Peninsula. They lived in patrimonial groups, grew corn, and were culturally similar to groups from southern Mexico. These peoples were devastated during the Spanish Conquest by disease and by slave traders who shipped them off to Panamá and Peru. Their surviving descendants are today mostly integrated into contemporary Costa Rican life.

Other native groups spoke dialects originating in Colombia. They were divided into clans, to which the Spanish gave names, and their original names are mostly lost to history: the Guaymí, for example, call themselves Ngabe, pronounced

Nobe. The other clans were named the Terraba, the Boruca, and, in the Talamanca mountains, the Bribri and Cabecar. These people lived in matrilineal societies in clearings in the jungles. With the coming of the Europeans, many of them fled to the almost inaccessible jungle regions of the southern mountains. Much of their culture has been preserved by their descendants, who still speak their original languages and live in the remote regions of the Talamanca mountains.

Despite the influence of Christian missionaries, many native people have not forsaken their animistic religious traditions. The Bribri

Guaymí girl, San Marcos.

call their deity Sibu and trust in shamans, with their vast knowledge of the rainforest's medicinal herbs, to cure a range of illnesses. Farther south, along the Panamá border, the Guaymí continue to live in their traditional areas, which span political boundaries.

Modern temptations

No matter how remote their jungle reserves, the Amerindians are still not insulated from contemporary culture. Battery-powered televisions bring pressure to consume soft drinks and junk food, as well as images of the First World to these people who live for the most part without electricity and running water. Alcohol is another problem, with some migrant workers spending a week's wages

> 'The Costa Ricans are a people of such excellent mettle; ardently patriotic, they are very proud of their independence, their autonomy, and of a prosperity due almost wholly to industry.' A.S. Calvert, A Year of Costa Rica, 1901.

at the local bar while wives and children wait anxiously outside. The cultural imperialism of the airwaves is persistently penetrating the world of people who have resisted the *conquistadores* for some 500 years. Among the young, the temptations of this high-tech world are enticing and the desire to assimilate is strong.

Today, indigenous peoples live on reserves designated for their use in 1971. By law, non-native people cannot own land inside these areas, but this has been difficult to enforce and non-Amerindians have gradually moved into these territories, which just happen to contain a significant proportion of the country's mineral wealth.

Encroaching contemporary society threatens the indigenous peoples' language, their cultural identity, and their way of life. Caught in time between two worlds, slowly relinquishing the old, but not yet embracing the new, native peoples are extremely vulnerable. Many NGOs and humanitarian groups are involved today in building schools and providing medical services in remote reserves to support them. But in the five centuries since the European conquest, little has changed for the aboriginal Costa Rican people. One famous *Costarricense* with indigenous roots is goalkeeper Keylor Navas who plays for the national football team and Real Madrid.

Black settlers

As early as 1825, Afro-Caribbeans came to Costa Rica to fish, hunt turtles, and to market coconuts. These immigrants were part of a migration from the West Indies to the Central American Caribbean coast. From Panamá to Honduras, they came looking for ways to support themselves. Many were transient. One man might harvest cacao in Limón, then find employment on the barges in Nicaragua, and next labor on the construction of the Panamá Canal; they went where there was work.

In 1872, under contract from Minor C. Keith, who later became the founder of the United Fruit Company, blacks from the West

Indies came to work on building the Atlantic railroad. They proved more successful than previous laborers imported by Keith in their ability to tolerate the hazardous working conditions, which included exposure to yellow fever, malaria, and venomous snakes, as well as severe physical labor and oppressive management. The maltreatment of workers in the banana fields of the Caribbean United Fruit Company is well documented. However, the blacks were certainly not invulnerable and they, too, died in their thousands while building the tracks, the endless numbers of bridges,

> After 4,000 West Indians died during the laying of the first 32km (20 miles) of the Atlantic railroad, businessman Minor C. Keith simply imported another 10,000 laborers.

parents to immigrate to the country in the first place: they were again seeking work. Those who stayed behind lived for the most part at subsistence level, producing what they could from small plots of land. They retained their English language and their Protestant religion, remain-

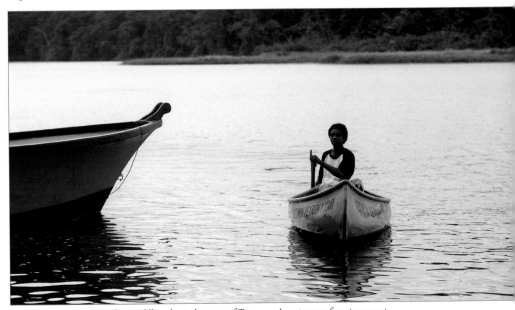

An Afro-Caribbean descendant paddles a boat along one of Tortuguero's waterways for a tour group.

the docks, and the wide, rectangular streets of the port city of Limón.

Other Afro-Caribbeans came to the Caribbean coast on their own, looking for any kind of work to escape the poverty of their native islands. Some ultimately were given land along the railroad right of way, and others, thanks to their command of English, rose from the ranks of laborers to become managers in the banana business and on the railways. Most originally planned to earn whatever they could and then return to their islands.

When United Fruit left the Caribbean region and moved to the Pacific coast, the blacks were left behind, unemployed. Many emigrated for the same reason that had motivated their

ing proudly separate from the Hispanic Costa Ricans and enriching these coastal communities with a distinct Afro-Caribbean flavor. At the same time, they endured racist immigration and residency laws that restricted their movement until the middle of the 20th century.

When the Constitution of 1949 declared that anyone born in Costa Rica had automatic citizenship, doors finally opened for blacks. For the first time they were allowed to travel outside Limón province and they began to attend public schools and enter politics. When, in the 1950s, the value of cacao soared on the international market, many of the squatter-farmers were able to achieve a certain level of prosperity. And, in an ironic reversal of historical patterns, they then hired Hispanics to work their fields. Many members of the subsequent generation of blacks were well educated and, preferring professions to farming, left the Limón area. Indeed, many left Costa Rica entirely to find jobs elsewhere.

Some middle-class, educated blacks who remained in Costa Rica married Hispanics, but their assimilation into Costa Rican society is not total, owing to the curious, two-sided racism that exists. Blacks usually consider themselves more civilized and superior to Hispanic Costa Ricans, while Hispanic Costa Ricans sometimes insist that blacks are racially inferior.

Today, just under 3 percent of the total Costa Rican population is black, and less than 25 percent of the population of the Caribbean coast is of black ancestry. Increasingly, young Afro-Caribbeans attend Spanish-speaking schools and Caribbean-accented English is more often heard among the older generation.

The construction of the railroad to the Caribbean coast brought other waves of immigrants during the late 19th century. Among the builders, managers, and technicians of the Northern Railway Company were English, Irish, and North Americans. But the largest group of

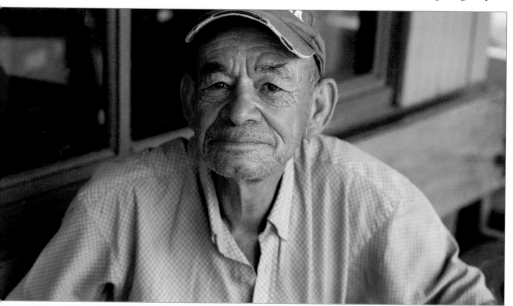

Inhabitant of Santa Elena, Monteverde.

ORIGIN OF THE SPECIES

The national myth holds that most Costa Ricans are descended from Spanish farmers who came from egalitarian stock. In reality, most Costa Ricans are descended from Spanish settlers who intermarried with the local population. Among colonial immigrants from the Iberian peninsula there were also Jews and Arabs, Catalans and Basques, as well as people from the Middle East. In the 19th century, lured by the hope of coffee prosperity, German and English settlers set up import-export trades, while Lebanese, Turks, and Polish Jews became powerful merchants. These newcomers contributed to the demographic mix.

immigrants, apart from the Afro-Caribbean workers, were laborers from southern China, who joined the blacks on the railroad, essentially as slaves, but euphemistically referred to as 'indentured workers.'

Chinese immigrants

The first Chinese to set foot in Costa Rica were 77 indentured servants, in 1855. Almost two decades later, despite the existence of a law against the permanent settlement in Costa Rica of African and Asian races, contractors for the Atlantic railroad imported 'one thousand healthy, robust Chinese of good customs and addicted to work.' These two ethnic groups were to become the founding fathers of the Chinese colony of Costa Rica.

Those contracted by the railroad left as quickly as they could escape, to work as cooks and domestic servants. As their fortunes improved, Chinese immigrants set up small eateries, groceries, and liquor stores. The steady trickle of Chinese immigrant laborers that followed the first railroad workers benefitted from those who were already established. Through work contracts and credit assistance from other Chinese, they set up commercial ventures along the railroad, in the port cities, and in growing rural communities throughout the country. Their small-scale businesses

Among the first generations of Chinese to settle in Costa Rica, many men lived with local Costa Rican white women, while retaining marriages established in China with childhood brides. The money they sent to China was often used to finance family enterprises back home.

In the last century, successful Sino-Costa Rican businessmen traveled to China to oversee their holdings, raise a family and invest toward retirement in the home of their ancestors. During their absence from Costa Rica, their businesses were managed by close younger kin.

A Cahuita resident on the verandah of his wooden house in the traditional architectural style.

required little capital investment, only a minimal acquaintance with the language, and allowed all members of the growing family network to become involved in tending the business. Chinese family traditions upheld the authority of elders and reinforced an already strong generational hierarchy. Well-defined divisions of labor, plus a strong work ethic, ensured that their businesses flourished.

Chinese colonies, headed by businessmen's associations, evolved into strong business groups in the cities and towns of Costa Rica. By the beginning of the 20th century, a number of Chinese immigrants had become wealthy, and were then able to sponsor the immigration of other family members and acquaintances.

With the Communist takeover of mainland China in 1949, return to their ancestral homeland became less attractive, and most Sino-Costa Ricans forsook any hopes of a permanent return to China.

More recent events also reinforced this influx from the East. The prospect of the British colony of Hong Kong being transferred to Chinese hands caused a steady flow of Asian immigrants from Hong Kong as long ago as the 1970s. Today, 1 percent of the total population in Costa Rica is Chinese, and there are more than 250 Chinese restaurants in the San José area alone.

Those Chinese born of mixed Costa Rican-Chinese families consider themselves full members of Costa Rican society, identifying heartily

Chinese participation in the social life of the towns they settled is nowhere more in evidence than at the Limón Carnival, when the traditional Chinese dragon snakes its way alongside flamboyant Caribbean dancers.

with its ways and traditions, while, at the same time, expressing a strong sense of devotion to their immigrant forefathers.

Many among them have married Hispanics, and faced opposition from their parents and

Portrait of a Costa Rican woman from Santa Elena.

ostracism by the Chinese community. Nevertheless, they have retained venerable family traditions that express Chinese values of ancestral wisdom and family solidarity.

Many young Sino-Costa Ricans have now joined the ranks of the professionally educated; although they are doctors, lawyers, engineers, business administrators, and university professors, many also still continue to oversee the family businesses that allowed their ancestors to achieve economic success in Costa Rica.

The most illustrious Sino-Costa Rican is engineer/physicist/astronaut Franklin Chang, a veteran of seven US Space Shuttle missions. Since his NASA years, Chang has spearheaded and encouraged high-tech scientific education

and brought new space-age enterprises to Costa Rica.

The Italians

The Atlantic railroad had serious difficulties retaining Chinese laborers. In an attempt to find an alternative working force, in 1888 the railway managers imported 1,500 'good, humble, thrifty Italians of a superior race.' The disagreeable working conditions soon led the Italians to leave the railroad project. Many remained in Costa Rica, and in the 1950s they were joined by an influx of Italian farmers who settled in a government-sponsored colony, San Vito, in the southern Pacific region of Costa Rica.

Today, San Vito still has a distinctive Italian flavor: there is a Dante Alighieri Society; there are a dozen shoe stores in town, as well as *pasticcerias* serving Italian *gelato* and enticing pastries. More recently, entrepreneurial Italians have come to Costa Rica to open restaurants and hotels all over the country, bringing a dash of style and culinary gusto that is appreciated by Costa Ricans and visitors.

The gringo

They are unmistakable in San José, their heads sticking out above the throng of people crowding the chaotic city sidewalks. *Gringos*, fairer and usually taller than local people, easily catch the eye. A pejorative word in much of Latin America, *gringo* is a much milder term here, applied not only to US citizens but also to Canadians and Europeans. Early in the 19th century, attracted by the promise of wealth from coffee, French, German, and British entrepreneurs, along with teachers, scientists, and professionals, came to Costa Rica. Many married Costa Rican women, and most became thoroughly assimilated into the aggregate of *Tico* culture. Today, many powerful families in the arts and politics bear British or German surnames.

In the 1950s, Quakers from the US came to Costa Rica looking for peace. They found it in the cloud forest of Monteverde, where they formed a community dedicated to a life of harmony with the land. They created a successful dairy and cheese industry, which today supplies much of Costa Rica's specialty cheese market.

Since the 1960s, Costa Rican laws favoring North American and European retirees led to the establishment of a large number of comparatively wealthy *gringos* in the Central Valley area. These retirees, recently estimated at more than 35,000, are officially called *pensionados* or *residentes*, non-nationals living in Costa Rica with a guaranteed monthly income. They come to Costa Rica for the warm climate and for the higher standard of living their dollars afford them.

In 2009, after much debate, legislators passed a law that requires non-nationals to pay into the national social-security system, as well as to pay higher application fees and maintain a greater monthly income in a Costa Rican bank.

With the growing disparity in the country between haves and have-nots, foreigners are some-

A large cadre of biologists, botanists, and scientific researchers has also had a huge impact on both the academic world in Costa Rica, and on research efforts into conservation.

While Costa Ricans are proud to show off their beautiful land, tourism often has a downside: the small landowner may lose his land for a biological reserve; dairy farmers can't afford to buy fresh pasture because property speculation has driven prices sky high; cattle ranchers without enough water for their livestock in the dry season watch as huge resorts build water-hungry golf courses. Profits often flow abroad

Local gentlemen passing a Sunday in San Rafael de Heredia.

times viewed less favourably these days, especially those who come to Costa Rica in order to make a quick buck in sometimes shady or environmentally insensitive property developments.

Effects of tourism

The most dramatic influx of people today is the result of the country's flourishing tourism industry. Environmentally concerned people of all ages come to carry out ecological work. For them the country is a laboratory, a place where the viability of living in harmony with the environment can be demonstrated to the world at large. Their arrival has stimulated major changes in the environmental awareness of the country.

to large hotel groups, and promised local benefits often amount to little more than the modest wages of waiters, hotel maids, gardeners, and pool attendants.

Sustainable tourism, which benefits the local community, has become the watchword of both international conservation organizations active in Costa Rica and the Ministry of Tourism, although in recent years, government policies have vacillated between paying lip service to conservation, and actually putting some teeth into environmental protection. A program that awards 'green-leaf' status, according to the eco-friendliness of hotels, has been successful, along with the Bandera Azul (Blue Flag) program that promotes clean beaches around the country.

Latin American newcomers

More recently, Costa Rica has become a haven for those fleeing violence, wars, and economic problems: during the past couple of decades, onerous political conditions and deteriorating economic circumstances in their home countries have brought significant numbers of South Americans to settle in Costa Rica, including educated Chileans, economically stressed Argentinians, opportunity-seeking Uruguayans, and Colombians escaping drug-war violence. On the whole, these different groups of people have greatly enhanced Costa

much to the North. He should be looking to the South.' But even if he did, the *Tico* would insist that he is different from most Latinos because of what he sees as his 'whiteness,' (fair skin, light hair, and light-colored eyes) or his European heritage.

Just go to Guatemala, Panamá, or El Salvador, and observe the differences. These countries are only short distances away, but the Costa Rican is as different from these other Latin people as, say, the Swiss is to the Italian, or the German to the Dane. Costa Ricans revel in the difference and are unabashedly proud of it.

Young citizens of Tortuguero.

Rica's cultural sensibilities over the past two decades or so.

Absorbing poorer, more desperate illegal immigrants, especially from Nicaragua, has also undeniably caused difficulties. With the arrival of many Colombians in the late 1990s, most of them respectable people, but some criminals as well, drug trafficking, armed robberies, and kidnappings have also increased, on the part of both newcomers and *Ticos*. In general, the country has officially accepted newcomers with a mix of grace and tolerance.

Ticos today

A Latin American writer once observed: 'The problem is that the Costa Rican looks too

Grace under pressure

Costa Ricans have a graceful sense of the universal corruption that surrounds them. They shake their heads, lamentably acknowledging it. They know that almost endless problems beyond easy resolution abound. But despite some skeptical complaining, they express confidence that their government is still the most honest in Latin America.

Travelers to Costa Rica find it difficult to identify just how different Costa Ricans are from people in other Central and South American countries, yet they notice it in subtle ways. There is a certain civility to life here, even in busy San José. People on the streets of the towns and cities are usually well dressed, polite, and quick to help a stranger. Cardboard shanty towns that dominate the cityscape of other developing countries are less evident here. Homeless people are not as omnipresent as they are in other Latin and Asian countries, or indeed, in many large US cities.

Small-town family life

To fly to Costa Rica, leaving behind the numbing babble of Los Angeles or the crowded bustle of Western European cities, and to head for a small town here is like leaping backwards to an earlier time. But it is not an earlier time by North American or even European standards; it is somewhere more idealized and far more precious.

In the villages and small towns of Costa Rica there is a connectedness, a familial unity. On the street, people will nod and say '*Buenos Días*' or '*Adiós*' even to complete strangers passing by. The family is still the main focus in this country. Young people usually live at home until they are well into their twenties and thirties, and some even stay at home after getting married.

The pressure of life in the cities is essentially at odds with this national character. But even for busy city people, the extended family is the focus

Tortuguero elder.

Young man from the north of the country.

HEALTH AND EDUCATION

The standards of health and education in Costa Rica are impressive. In 1920, infant mortality was nearly 26 percent; today it is less than 10 percent. Costa Ricans are healthier and living longer, too. They are ranked higher on the overall health index than Americans, and life expectancy has increased to 80 years. The only cloud on the horizon is the persistence of teenage pregnancies – with ever-younger mothers. The number of mothers under the age of 15 has nearly doubled since 1984 and teenage pregnancies make up to 16 percent of the total.

The general good health of the nation is not due to sheer luck, or the quality of the air. Without the burden of supporting expensive armed forces, Costa Rica is able to invest around 10 percent of its GNP in health care. The public system, accessible to all, is showing lots of wear and tear. But the quality of care is high enough, especially in the private sector, that medical tourism is a booming industry, especially cosmetic surgery and dental work. Many tourists build a vacation around having 'work' done.

Costa Rica is also an exceptionally literate nation, with 97.8 percent literacy across the population aged 15 and over. The country has always been progressive in electing teachers to high political posts. In fact, in 1869, Costa Rica became the first country in the world to make education both mandatory and free of charge.

of their social life, and many city families retain close links with their rural past, spending most weekends and holidays at family *fincas* (farms).

US influence

Because the United States is by far the richest neighbor in the hemisphere, and the most powerful broadcaster of image and ideology, Costa Rica knows a great deal more about the United States than the United States knows about Costa Rica. *Ticos* know the names of sports figures, actors and actresses, television personalities, musicians, and politicians from the US.

And they are aware of the strange collection of fact and fallacy that viewers derive from watching satellite-relayed North American television shows and subtitled Hollywood movies.

Increasingly, a bilingual education is the key to success for the young generation of *Ticos*, many of whom will have careers working for branches of foreign companies and in large customer-care call centers.

Costa Rica welcomes foreign investors. There are duty-free zones, tax-free incentives to foreigners setting up industry, and other incentives to build tourist facilities.

Ticos celebrate an elderly lady's birthday on a beach at Playa Carillo.

THE TICO SPIRIT

Costa Ricans call themselves *Ticos* in a reference to their use of the diminutive ending '*ico*': '*Un momentico, por favor*' (Just a little minute, please) or 'chiquitica' (nice little girl). You'll also hear a lot of '*cito*', as in '*cafecito*', (a nice little coffee). There is a sweetness to the way they speak Spanish. For instance, they will use the gentle verb '*regalar*' (give me, as in a present) rather than the direct '*dar*' (give me) when ordering in a restaurant. *Ticos* are politically temperate, too. Demonstrations protests, strikes, and rallies are common events, yet people behave respectfully and election day has a distinctive party atmosphere.

A fragile world

Costa Rica is a fragile country, sandwiched between politically volatile Nicaragua and Americanized Panamá. Foreign investors are able to buy whatever appears profitable; political and economic refugees come in from other parts of Central America; and drug dealers infiltrate the shores and ports of this relatively violence-free country.

Yet somehow you feel that Costa Rica will endure. Though Costa Ricans may not be perfect, they are essentially a democratic, benevolent, and peaceful nation. After coming to visit, many people from all over the world are inspired to do whatever they can to ensure the survival and intelligent growth of this vulnerable country and its peaceable people.

The Great Immigration Debate

Since the 1980s, Nicaraguans, Costa Rica's major immigrant group, have been blamed for the country's social ills. But that may be changing.

An estimated 500,000 Nicaraguans (although some action groups suggest up to a million) work and live in Costa Rica, many of them illegally. Back in the 1980s, most Nicaraguan émigrés were fleeing the poverty, violence, and upheaval of their own war-torn country. In 1998 two natural disasters – a devastating drought and Hurricane Mitch – prompted a new wave of illegal immigration into Costa Rica.

Most of today's newcomers are economic refugees, swelling the numbers of illegals that make up the majority of the country's growing informal sector, with low wages, under-the-table payments, and no access to the country's socialized health service. Many work as maids, nannies, gardeners, or construction workers, or sell snacks or trinkets in the streets. The sugar cane and coffee industries depend on Nicaraguan workers for their harvests.

Nicaraguan refugees

Not all Nicaraguan refugees are poor, however. Middle- and upper-class supporters of the Somoza regime also came in the 1980s, seeking refuge from Nicaragua's civil war. Many run successful businesses today. Always a troubling issue in Central America, the immigration debate has become more polemic as the country's economic resources have shrunk. Shanty towns of Nicaraguan immigrants ring the capital, and many squat, rent, or own farms in the Northern Zone. *Ticos* are often prejudiced against their northern neighbors, who are stereotyped as 'dirty,' or 'violent,' and are unjustly accused of committing an inordinate number of crimes. '*Nicas*,' as they are known, are often blamed for the perceived social decline of the country and for putting a burden on the health service, schools, and the workplace. Coming from poverty and an unstable society, *Nica* couples tend not to marry, instead finding temporary *compañeros sentimentales* (live-in lovers). Despite their own high divorce and teenage pregnancy rates, *Ticos* are often offended by these social arrangements.

There is also a racial aspect to the low opinion *Ticos* hold of *Nicas*, with their darker skin and their thick accents. The irony that the province of Guanacaste was once part of Nicaragua is lost on most Costa Ricans.

Nicas are generally quieter and less educated than *Ticos*. Most are hard workers and many people prefer to hire Nicaraguans as domestic help, especially since they will work for lower wages. In reality, the immigrants are doing the work many *Ticos* refuse to do, and without them coffee, banana, and sugar production would grind to a halt. On the plus side, Nicaraguans bring with them a love of poetry and music, and a tradition of camaraderie.

Nicaraguan woman and child.

Other immigrant groups

In a strange twist of events, *Nicas* are beginning to move up in the estimation of *Ticos*, as more recent immigrants become the new scapegoats for whatever ails the country. *Ticos* now tend to blame newly arrived Colombians, Ecuadoreans, Salvadorans, and Mexicans for the country's startling increase in violent crime, much of it drug-related. Colombians are the largest new immigrant group, many of them arriving in large family groups that pool resources to invest in legitimate businesses. But money launderers and criminal elements have also arrived and the daily newspapers are full of reports of Colombian drug-gang busts. The sad reality is that more and more Costa Ricans are involved in the drug trade and the violence it brings with it.

THE RISE AND FALL OF SAN JOSÉ

Thanks to the coffee boom, San José enjoyed an architectural golden age in the early 1900s. Remnants of those glory days survive, despite modern urban ills.

In 1737, the authorities ordered the construction of a thatch-covered hermitage on the flatlands of the Boca del Monte. It was to be the centerpoint of a new village to bring together the residents of the area, whose small homes were scattered over the valley. From this humble beginning sprang the city of San José.

For its first 39 years, it was still just a village, with mud-covered streets and miserable little houses. Then an official ordered the construction of a tobacco factory, and it was from here that the country's tobacco industry monopoly was administered. It proved to be an activity that brought a certain degree of prosperity.

The coffee boom

Tobacco was a short-lived success, as was cacao. But then came experimentation with a new crop: coffee. It grew with such ease and bore fruit with such abundance that this small Central American colony soon had the wherewithal to leave behind the squalor it had known.

England was interested not only in buying coffee, but also loaning funds, on account, against the next harvest. The surrounding areas filled quickly with orderly rows of coffee plantations, and the people, with their new wealth, sought the city life, transforming San José into a prosperous coffee-growing center.

Beside the town square there was at first only the Church of Mercy and the Town Council building. But other conveniences, created to serve the foreigners who were beginning to arrive, were soon set up. At the end of the 18th century, the Education Building was erected, as was a cathedral, at the front of which stood a beautiful central park, where

The modern face of San José.

both Amerindians and farmers of Spanish extraction held their weekly fairs. Money was minted at the Currency House, and, to support the nascent militia, military quarters were erected.

Social and cultural life

In 1821, Costa Rica gained its independence from the Spanish Empire and became a republic. The small town of San José soon grew into a commercial city, then a capital city, and the newly installed authorities struggled to improve the streets, build bridges, and open roads to the ports. Guards, armed with rusty muskets, patrolled brick-layered streets that were illuminated at night by kerosene lamps.

In the dance parlors of the bourgeoisie, the quadrille was in vogue. An actor would recite poetry and a young lady would play Chopin sonatas amid conversations concerning the price of coffee in London.

Social and economic life was rigidly defined, limited to the descendants of the Spanish who lived in the central part of town where they built large adobe houses with corridors opening onto enclosed vegetable gardens.

Cultural life centered around the Mora Theater, where fourth-rate companies would perform, along with jugglers and an occasional virtuoso musician. The ladies would sit and listen, dressed in their regal dresses, while the gentlemen stood around, robed in their Spanish capes, smoking and engaging in small talk concerning politics.

Foreign visitors would stay in a rooming house and venture forth to see the town's sights. Some considered the possibility of entering the coffee-export business and others idly took notes for their travel diaries.

The European influence

Earnings from the export of coffee engendered an illustrious bourgeoisie, who traveled to Europe so that their children could be educated in France. When they returned home in San José, the children missed the theaters, the boulevards, the cafés, and the fine architecture of Europe, and as they grew up, they insisted on improving the appearance of their native capital city. As coffee production led to greater prosperity, the leading planter families increased their investments, which inevitably led to rivalries among them, and ever grander plantations were created in an effort to stay ahead of competitors.

Costa Rican architects visited the Universal Exposition of Paris in 1900 and, along with other new and imported ideas, brought back the concept of metal buildings for schools. They imported finely wrought metal plates for walls, steel columns, building crests, and Italian mosaics. The homes of the coffee growers soon began to look like the mansions of the wealthy in New Orleans and Jamaica: French adobe walls; wide, inclined roofs; ornate verandahs with white balustrades, and woodwork cut in the style of gingerbread. Jalousies (louvre shutters) and shades protected the windows made of colored glass through which shone the brilliant tropical sun.

The city's golden age

Toward the end of the 19th century, Monsieur Amon Faiseleau Duplantier, who received the concession to establish the streetcar system, divided his farm on the sunny slopes of the Torres River and there began the business of real-estate sales. The best of San José society fought for the urban lots, building mansions, a few of which still survive in Barrio Amón. Soon the coffee plantations were replaced with tree-shaded streets and stately residences with large gardens. At the same time, Mother Superior Barthelemy Rich was opening her prestigious

Edificio Metálico (Metal Building School), shipped from Belgium in 1892.

girls' high school, the *Colegio de Sión*, where the daughters of the bourgeoisie received their refined education.

On October 19, 1897, the president and a select audience entered the wide doors of the National Theater to inaugurate the building. That opening night featured a magnificent presentation of Gounod's opera *Faust*. The sumptuous building with its four levels and a floor plan in the shape of a horseshoe was financed from the national budget and by a tax paid by the rich coffee growers.

By the early 1900s, the former village had given way to a glowing city, which, even if it did not attain the elegant, urbane layout to which it aspired, had developed a comfortable lifestyle permitted by its growing prosperity.

In front of the National Theater was the elegant Hôtel Français. Nearby, the Petit Trianon was a fashionable coffee house favored by high society, artists, and diplomats; a little beyond, the windows of the Golden Eagle were filled with French wine and liquors and Spanish preserves and fine oils. The *Talabartería Inglesa* and *La Tiendita* satisfied the most demanding tastes in matters of decoration and leatherwork.

The Ford Motor agency exhibited its 1912 model, which was priced at US$975.

It competed with a number of other import agencies, along with booming real-estate businesses that offered farms, lots, beaches, and Victorian residences. The streetcar ran to the limits of the city carrying great numbers of merchants, their employees, and office workers.

The other side of the tracks

Not all members of San José society enjoyed a privileged, rose-colored lifestyle. The city had expanded far too rapidly, with vast, obscure, and sad suburbs encircling older areas. The

The National Palace in 1894.

Ornate mansions in Barrio Amón.

outbreak of World War I and the accompanying fall in coffee demand and prices brought wide-scale unemployment to those who had previously been able to live relatively well, and those who still had jobs worked for salaries that fell well below the poverty level. The Society of Casas Baratas (cheap houses) began the construction of workers' housing units of the type known as *puerta ventana*, where several families would cram into narrow and poorly ventilated rooms.

To the south and near the train station from where trains ran to the Pacific coast, there soon appeared barracks, warehouses, and factories, where soap and candles were manufactured. An industrial zone with beer factories,

> *In 1863, San José officials tripped a switch and turned on electric lights throughout the city. It was the first city in Latin America, and the third in the world, to be electrified.*

ice-making factories, printing presses, mechanics' shops, and lumber mills slowly began to surround and envelop the elegant urban center. With the advent of cement-built structures, the arrival of the new rich, and the industrialization of the city, there also came the desire to

San José spilled over and outward in a random fashion. Car ownership permitted the wealthy classes to move their residences from what had now become the depressed inner city to the more desirable, close-in suburbs of Escalante, Los Yoses, Curridabat, Paseo Colón, Sabana, and Rohrmoser. By the 1960s, several satellite town centers evolved, in the style of the suburban United States.

Certainly San José would no longer win any beauty prizes. Although traffic pollution and congestion are constant irritants, there are some conservation efforts under way, including restor-

A street scene in San José today. Despite modernization, some barrios remain distinctive.

modernize, to create new statements, based largely on North American models, and to destroy vestiges of the past.

End of an era

In the mid-20th century, the city fathers set about 'modernizing' San José. Under the pick and sledgehammer, the magnificent National Palace, the Garrison, the National Library, the Union Club, and many lovely residences disappeared. The inner city lost its sense of identity and was invaded by mediocre commercial constructions. Fast highways opened up, breaking up neighborhoods, and no-nonsense North American architectural influences began to replace elegant European ideals.

ing notable buildings and turning downtown streets into pleasant pedestrian zones. Some barrios still possess a certain charm: Barrio Amón has some grand mansions, many of them now converted into attractive boutique hotels; Barrio Mexico retains an Art Deco ambiance; and Parque d'España is like a tiny, urban rainforest.

You won't find in San José the monumental scale of Guatemala City nor the cosmopolitan quality of Panamá City; yet there is a vital quality to the hustle and sheer movement of the place, along with tangible remains of the coffee-growing bourgeoisie who, in their heyday, enriched the city with neoclassical architecture, European elegance, and whimsical Caribbean-colonial style.

Tortuguero Park's canals and forest.

NATIONAL PARKS

With so much of its land under protected status, Costa Rica is the flag bearer for the forces of conservation. But, while many battles have been won, the war goes on.

An astonishing 26 percent of Costa Rica is designated as national park, biological reserve, wildlife refuge, or some other category of protected area, either private or public. Increasingly, individuals and groups are purchasing tracts of Costa Rican wilderness in order to preserve it. And so, more than a quarter of the country has been set aside in some form or another by human beings to protect it from the potential exploitation and ravages of other human beings.

Guardians and threats

The story of the creation of Costa Rica's parks and protected areas is one of drama, ideals, and sacrifice. One of the first in a long line of international protectors was Nils Olaf Wessberg, who, with his wife, came to Costa Rica from Sweden in 1955 and bought a farm in Nicoya near Montezuma. Fervent naturalists, they built a home of palm leaves, determined to live in harmony with the land.

Yet even in this remote corner of the world they did not escape what many call progress, and they watched, dismayed, as the destruction of virgin forest took place at Cabo Blanco, on the Nicoya Peninsula. Nils became an activist, working ardently to raise money to purchase the land and thereby preserve it.

After three years and 1,000 pages of letters, he raised the US$30,000 he needed to buy the 1,200 hectares (3,000 acres) that constitute the Cabo Blanco Absolute Wildlife Reserve. Today, a plaque inside the park is a memorial to Nils, who, while trying to establish another park in the Osa Peninsula, was murdered by those who had vested interests in preventing his work. In 2004, a new reserve near Montezuma was

White-faced capuchin monkey, Manuel Antonio National Park.

established and named after his wife, Karen Mogensen Fischer.

Another committed individual, Mario Boza, a student of Costa Rican forestry, was able to put his conservation ideas to work in the creation of Santa Rosa, the country's first national park. In 1969, the Forestry Law trumpeted the creation of the Santa Rosa National Monument and established the National Parks Department. But with little funding and few personnel to enforce it, the new law went unrecognized, and the land continued to be used as it had been in the past, as grazing pasture for cattle and as the homesteads of slash-and-burn squatters.

Unable to halt the destruction through bureaucratic channels, Boza went to the press. 'Santa Rosa in Flames; National Park Being Ruined' read the headlines. The public was outraged and park authorities were duly authorized to move out the squatters and protect the land from the encroachment of livestock and agriculture.

Rodrigo Carazo, president of Costa Rica from 1978 to 1982, described the national parks as 'splendid natural laboratories, which we offer to the international scientific community and also to children, young people, and

a frenzied pace. Extensive soil erosion, an effect of the rapid deforestation of the country by the destructive use of land for cattle grazing, causes a phenomenal loss of topsoil.

Threats to the watershed, as well as the nation's extensive hydroelectric system, are another unwelcome result. Uncontrolled dumping of toxic waste from the banana, coffee, and fertilizer industries has contaminated coastal and inland waters. Agricultural chemicals used in pesticides, once employed only on the traditional export crops of bananas and sugar, are now being used by vegetable

Crocodile in the Tarcoles River.

adults who should not be denied the joy of direct contact with nature in its pristine state. All of this represents the contribution of the Costa Rican people to peace among men and goodwill among nations.'

The economy versus the ecology

As admirable as Costa Rica's conservation initiatives may be, the environmental efforts of this Developing World country are counter to its economic development. Parks are, after all, expensive. Urban sprawl – resulting from the concentration of more than 60 percent of the country's population in the most fertile area of the country, the Central Valley – covers the land with concrete and asphalt, and it continues at

NATURAL WONDERLAND

Costa Rica's natural abundance translates into many astounding statistics. In a space that occupies less than 0.03 percent of the earth's surface are 4 percent of all of the scientifically identified plant and animal species on the planet. In total this numbers somewhere around 500,000 species of flora and fauna including: more than 300,000 species of insects (some the size of small mammals!) including thousands of species of moths and butterflies; over 1,200 species of orchids; 800 ferns (more than in all of North America and Mexico); 212 species of mammals; more than 850 species of birds; 200 species of reptiles (half of which are snakes).

and flower growers; pesticide poisoning has resulted in, among other things, the virtual elimination of large species such as armadillos and crocodiles along the Tempisque River. And the crazed rush to feed the demands from North America and Europe for exotic plywood is resulting in the deforestation of the land surrounding the magnificent Tortuguero canals. And so it goes on.

In its understandable attempts to imitate much of North America and the rest of the developed world, the country is experiencing the inevitable conflict between consumption

Walking trail in Monteverde Cloud Forest Reserve, in the country's northwest.

and conservation. Trying to balance these opposing forces are armies of international naturalists. Environmentalists and ecologists from all over the world come to Costa Rica to join the side of 'the good guys.' Today, Costa Rica has environmental experts in abundance, and dozens of international conservation organizations working on behalf of the country's ecological efforts.

Conservation by education

Believing that true conservation can only be accomplished by the will of the people, the national parks system has made a great effort to educate the *Ticos* who are most affected by

the transfer of land into protected parks. The cooperation of these people is necessary for the parks' survival. For example, the traditional custom of hunting species for whom the parks are a refuge needs to be changed. Large animals, such as pumas and jaguars, require an extensive amount of free territory in order to survive. Convincing people not to kill them, or the wild pigs that large cats depend on for food, is an enormous and often thankless task.

Ecotourists and traditional travelers to Costa Rica support the national parks system by coming to visit, paying park fees, and staying at the private reserves, as well as through their work and contributions to the many conservation foundations working in Costa Rica.

Scraping tons of stones out of rivers to build a new highway in the remote Osa Peninsula is killing the goose that laid the golden egg. As river habitats are devastated, the road to bring tourists closer to nature is destroying nature.

Some eco-projects even cross Costa Rica's borders. La Amistad Biosphere is a Unesco-designated reserve that spans the Panamanian border. To the north the *Agua y Paz* (Water and Peace) Biosphere, includes vast tracts of Costa Rica's northern wetlands and Nicaragua's San Juan River. These are just two examples of the potential that national parks have to engender cooperative international relations.

Future perfect?

Yet is this good news good enough? The fact that Costa Rica is thought of as a safe, quiet democratic place is perhaps both the nation's greatest blessing and greatest problem. Ironically the wealthier nations of the world may not be sufficiently moved to donate aid, attention, and media coverage to such a gentle democratic place, when there are so many other, highly visible, demands from places that seem more needy.

It is not clear as yet which side will prevail: the conservationists or the forces demanding economic development at all costs; it is still up in the air whether Costa Rica will become a successful environmental model or just another failed experiment in ecological idealism.

A Tropical Forest Watcher's Guide

To spot wildlife in Costa Rica's dense forests and impenetrable jungles you'll need to walk softly and learn to see in a new way.

Don't be disappointed if, on your first few visits to the tropical rainforest, you fail to see any of the hundreds of bird species, monkeys, and sloths that live there. In fact, your first impression of the forest will probably be of a great green wall of vegetation, not the spectacular variety of colorful animals you had hoped to see. However, be assured that a great diversity of organisms does inhabit the tropical forest, and their very survival depends not least on how successful they are at hiding from predators, which include humans.

Before setting off into the forest, do your homework. Study specialist guidebooks that describe animals living in the area and familiarize yourself with such identifying characteristics as color, shape, and behavior. Determine the time of day or night when animals are most active. A good pair of binoculars is essential; they can also be used backwards as a powerful magnifying glass. Take every opportunity to charter a boat for lake or river trips; they are always worth the investment.

Observe safety tips before proceeding. Remember that even though it may look like Disneyland, it isn't. Here snakes slither, insects bite, and animals may (in very rare cases) become aggressive. Notify someone of your intentions: where you are going, when you plan to arrive, when to expect you back. Take water, insect repellent, flashlight, sunscreen, umbrella or rain poncho, and a hat.

Look before you touch, step, sit, or lean. Scan the trail for slippery rocks, mud, downed trees, ants, and snakes. Then move ahead while you search the canopy for animals. Continually shift your gaze. Don't wander off into the woods following a bird without looking carefully where you step. Snakes are rare but potentially lethal. Antivenin serum is available throughout the country. Try not to panic, and try to remember the snake's colors.

Best viewing times

A general guideline: forest wildlife-viewing is easiest in the early morning and late afternoon, and most productive along habitat 'edges' next to rivers, beaches, open fields, roads, and trail heads. Look for shapes, colors, and behaviors that stand out and do not appear to 'fit' the design of the forest vegetation. In the dry season deciduous forests lose their leaves, opening the canopy for viewing; and shrinking water sources are frequented by thirsty animals.

Know the signs

Seasoned forest-watchers, like legendary animal trackers, are alert to easily overlooked clues that indicate the presence of animals or birds present in the forest. Things rustling or dropping from the forest canopy (especially on a windless day) and unex-

Birdwatchers in Monteverde Cloud Forest.

plained noises are often a sign that an animal is nearby. Seeds or leaves dropping from above are probably caused by parrots, monkeys, or sloths in the canopy. Fruits, nuts, seed husks, or leaf fragments on the trail mean a food tree is nearby and perhaps sustaining feeding animals or birds.

Large, dark shapes in tree crevices might be sleeping sloths, anteaters, or monkeys. Logs on river banks could be crocodiles. Rotten tree sections are often home to amphibians, insects, fungi, and mosses. Holes in trees might contain precious birds' nests.

When you've developed skills in seeing and identifying some of the plants and animals, think about what they eat and why they live where they do. Soon you will begin to understand the complexity that makes the forest so mesmerizing.

A PASSION FOR PLANTS

From the beautiful to the bizarre, Costa Rica's many species of flora offer a vibrant introduction to the kaleidoscopic plant wealth of the tropics.

A 'hot lips' plant in the Monteverde Cloud Forest.

Many visitors' first contact with Costa Rica's spectacular plant life comes at the hotel reception desk, which is often adorned by a vase of heliconias – strikingly angular red or orange flowers, also known as lobster claws, which grow in the country's forests.

Heliconias are typical of the outsize blooms that flourish in Costa Rica's warm and humid climate. As a rule of thumb, the biggest and most robust flowers – including heliconias – are pollinated by birds or bats, while more delicate flowers are pollinated by insects. This second category includes most of the country's orchids – another group of plants for which Costa Rica is justly famous.

Costa Rica has a prodigious number of native plants, including approximately 1,000 different species of trees. To add to this botanical richness, many other species have been introduced from different parts of the tropics, for food or for ornament. Food plants include bananas, which arrived in the early 1500s; coffee, mangoes, and sugar cane; and also the African oil palm, first cultivated on a large scale in the 1960s. Many of the showiest garden and road-side plants are from distant parts of the world. Among the most eye-catching are jacarandas, South American trees that produce a mass of purplish-blue flowers.

Colorful berries nestle inside the elongated bracts of a Heliconia stricta, one of 30 or so native helonica species. Some hummingbird. have bills long enough to reach the nectar deep inside.

The white costus bloom can last up to a month. The plant is also known as "spiral ginger" for the way the stem swirls to follow sunlight – it is, however, a separate species from true ginger.

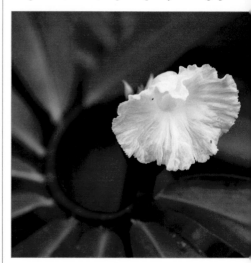

The scepter-like flower of the waxy torch ginger is also called emperor's rod.

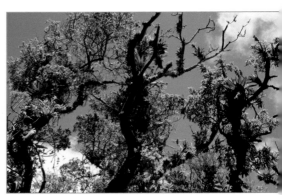

Bromeliad in in the rainforest in Poás Volcano National Park.

THE PLANTS THAT GROW ON PLANTS

Costa Rica's forests are home to an immense variety of epiphytes, or plants that grow on the shoulders of other plants, often far above the ground. Epiphytes manage this remarkable feat by collecting rainwater and by scavenging nutrients from any organic debris that is washed or blown their way.

Of all the country's epiphytes, bromeliads are the most conspicuous. Tank bromeliads collect water by funneling it into a central reservoir formed by their leaves. These plants can measure more than1 meter (3ft) across, and their tanks can hold several liters of water. Other epiphytes, including most orchids, have specialized roots that absorb water and nutrients before they have a chance to evaporate or drain away.

In forests, a different collection of plants – including philodendrons and the *Monstera deliciosa*, also called the Swiss-cheese plant for its huge leaves pitted with a pattern of holes – start life rooted in the ground, but soon head for the sunlit treetops. In the wild, the Swiss-cheese plant and its relatives have a bizarre growth pattern. If the plant climbs up a tree that turns out to be too short, it simply drops back to the forest floor and searches for another likely, taller, host.

Humid, dense forests harbor more than 800 species of wild ferns, ranging from low-lying plants blanketing the rainforest understory, to tree ferns that can soar as high as 25 meters (82ft). Costa Rica also exports a huge number of cultivated ferns, used to adorn flower bouquets worldwide.

Ginger flowers, planted in gardens and naturalized in forests, are truly exotic plants here, originally hailing from tropical Asia.

Kayaking at Puerto Jiménez.

THE SPORTS SCENE

Activity holidays are booming in Costa Rica.
Getting wet – whether by spilling out of a raft or
falling off a board – is usually part of the game.

Sport is a much-loved pastime in Costa Rica, especially the national sport of *fútbol* (soccer). *Ticos* are always happy to have visiting foreigners join them in watching an important game of soccer. Personal fitness is also popular and you will see joggers and cyclists puffing up impossibly challenging hills in the Central Valley in the early morning. On weekends, enormous La Sabana Park, on the west side of San José, is filled with thousands of athletes: soccer teams, basketball players, swimmers, volleyball players, rollerblade teams, and baseball enthusiasts. On the Central Valley plateau, private golf and tennis clubs with complete health spas cater for wealthy suburbanites.

The country's tidal wave of water sports, however, is the main attraction for an increasing number of visitors who come to Costa Rica to surf isolated beaches, to windsurf on magnificent Lake Arenal, and to experience some of the best whitewater rafting in the world.

Beach football.

Whitewater rafting

The brightly colored inflatable raft rushes down a chute of cascading white water, then plunges over and through waves that are nearly 2 meters (6ft) high. Those in the raft gleefully dig their paddles into the frothing water, and then shriek with delight as they maneuver the raft between boulders the size of small cars. After a pulse-racing few minutes, the rafters reach a calm spot on the river, an eddy, from which they can pause and look up from the roaring river course to inhale and appreciate the beauty of the Reventazón Gorge. The scenery along the wide river includes the colossally broad panorama of the canyon, rolling fields of coffee, sugar cane, wild grasses, and radiant flowers blooming unexpectedly in the canopy of trees overhanging the river.

Costa Rica has more accessible whitewater rivers and rapids than any other place in the world. It is, of course, the unique geography of the country that makes it one of the world's great destinations for whitewater rafting. To have the right kind of rapids, you need a river that descends in a fairly steep gradient. The four mountain chains that wind down the axis of Costa Rica provide the perfect conditions. The Talamanca range and the Cordillera Central have many steep, wide, perennial rivers that are regularly supplied with bounteous rainfall.

The variety of these rivers provides an enormous range of wilderness experiences. Some offer idyllic float trips through luscious landscapes with abundant wildlife, while others contain explosive whitewater and raging rapids that challenge the most experienced rafter.

The Sarapiquí River flows through the lowlands of Heredia, providing stunning scenery and exceptional whitewater. About a two-hour drive from San José, the upper portion of the Sarapiquí contains moderate rapids that are suitable for novice paddlers. On the calm, lower section of the river, the jungle closes in and gives rafters the opportunity to relax for a while and view the monkeys, otters, and abundant waterfowl of the area.

The head of the Reventazón River is a 90-minute drive from San José and offers some of Costa Rica's most turbulent whitewater and spectacular scenery. Rafting companies run four sections of the river. The first, which is just below the hydroelectric power plant of Cachí, is steep and contains continuous rapids of moderate to high difficulty. The second section, from Tucurrique to Angostura, is suited to novice paddlers and provides splendid views of the surrounding volcanoes.

The final two sections of the Reventazón, from Angostura to Siquirres, have some of the most challenging whitewater in the world.

Many consider Costa Rica's most famous whitewater river to be the Pacuare. Accessible from the Central Valley via Turrialba, it passes through a deep gorge in dense jungle that contains rich flora and wildlife. Most groups spend two or more days descending this river from Tres Equis to Siquirres, and camping in riverside sites within view of thundering waterfalls and great flocks of birds.

The Corobicí is the gentlest of all Costa Rica's rafting rivers and is ideal for rafters who are also keen birdwatchers. In the adjacent Palo Verde National Park, more than 300 species of birds have been observed, and many can be seen from rafts on the Corobicí. Because the river's perennial flow is controlled by a dam on Lake Arenal, it becomes

Surfers on Playa Grande on the Nicoya Peninsula.

WHITEWATER RAFTING – THE MAJOR PLAYERS

Whitewater rafting, also known as river running, offers anyone in moderately good health an exhilarating way to observe the scenery and wildlife of the country. Several professional outfitters in Costa Rica will provide all of the necessities: life preservers, helmets, and rafts. You can be assured that you are in good hands: guides have been through training in the classroom and on the rivers. Most Costa Rican head guides have been trained at whitewater schools in the US, and many have worked with the world's best.

The first whitewater exploration of Costa Rican rivers was made by a company called Costa Rica Expeditions on the Reventazón River in 1978. The following year the same company pioneered commercial whitewater rafting in Central America. Ríos Tropicales, founded in 1985, started rafting on the Sarapiquí and Sucio rivers, and local graduates of their kayaking school have represented Costa Rica at the World Championships of Whitewater Racing. Aventuras Naturales is the third major company in this field. Others of varying expertise have also sprung up more recently in San José, Turrialba, and elsewhere.

Many of these organizations offer day-trip packages from San José, including transportation, breakfast and lunch, and all the necessary gear, at very reasonable rates. For details of rafting companies see page 272.

an oasis that attracts birds, monkeys, and lizards during the dry season in Guanacaste.

Surfing

Costa Rica's unending beaches are a fixture on the international surfing circuit, and attract hordes of surfers from North America, Australia, and Europe. These aficionados generally concur that the quality of Costa Rica's surf is firmly in the top four – along with California, Hawaii, and Australia. Moreover, they find that the surf here is plentiful and relatively uncrowded, the water temperature is a comfort-

A four-wheel-drive vehicle is often essential, especially during the rainy season.

Popular surf spots

With hundreds of kilometers of coastline, there are, of course, many undiscovered, nameless surfing beaches. But among the favorites are the following:

Jacó, bordering a Central Pacific town southeast of the Gulf of Nicoya, is less than two hours by car or bus from San José. It is a long, silty beach trapped between two rocky points, with waves that are particularly good for body

Almost anyone can experience the adrenaline rush of whitewater rafting.

able 27°C (80°F) throughout the year, and there is still the chance of experiencing the rare thrill of having a wave all to yourself, just offshore from a pristine and empty beach.

Costa Rica is blessed with masses of beaches: there are some 200km (120 miles) of Caribbean coast and 1,000km (630 miles) of Pacific shore, sculpted with sandy beaches, rocky headlands, offshore reefs, and river mouths close to coastal jungles.

There is also a large number of open beaches that are exposed to ocean swells coming from many directions. However, much of the coastline is removed from civilization, so there may be no facilities, food, or emergency services of any kind within many kilometers.

MAKING A SPLASH

Sadly, every year whitewater accidents do happen and even the most experienced rafters, caught in a powerful river eddy, can drown. So choose your trip according to your level of expertise and find an outfitter that sticks to all the safety precautions: life vest, helmets, and accompanying safety/rescue kayaks. Before you enter the water in the raft you should have a practice drill to ensure everyone understands the instructions (often shouted over the thundering water). You should also check your travel insurance policy to ensure that you are covered for rafting. River water is unsafe to drink, so if you do tumble in, keep your mouth closed!

surfing or boogie boarding. The surf is easily accessible, just beyond the patios of many of the high-rise hotels and *cabinas* that line the beach. For non-surfers, however, the beach is overdeveloped, unattractive, and the currents and rip tides are strong.

Just under 3km (2 miles) to the south of Jacó is Playa Hermosa, site of many a surfing competition. It is possible to hitchhike, rent a bike, or take a bus around the point south of Jacó to this beach. South from Jacó to Playa Panamá are many superb unexploited surfing spots. North of Jacó, near Puntarenas, the sandspit at the mouth of the Barranca River produces what is reputed to be one of the world's longest left-breaking waves.

Like Jacó, Dominical is another major surfing beach town, farther down the South Pacific coast. It is much less built up, with a laid-back, funky atmosphere, and a long break with waves to suit all levels.

Far to the north, the beaches of Guanacaste province have some of the best surf anywhere, particularly during the dry season when steady offshore winds help to create the waves. The break near Roca de la Bruja at Playa Naranjo is

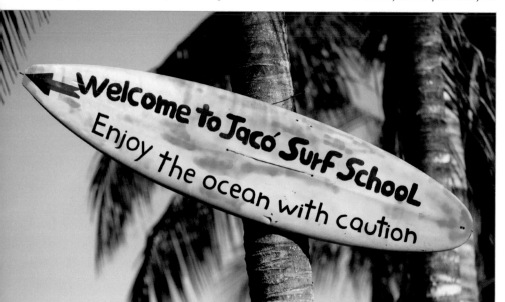

Surf school on Jacó Beach, which is famous for its waves.

SWELLS AND BREAKS

Wave-making conditions are complex in Costa Rica. On the Pacific coast, swells originating from storms in the north and central Pacific Ocean occur frequently from November through March. South swells from distant storms prevail for the remainder of the year.

The beaches of the Pacific are shaped by sediment that is carried to the sea by major rivers. The silt migrates up and down the coast on strong onshore currents. Sandbars produce beach breaks with long and fast right and left rides along much of the coast. Sandspits form at the river mouths, and create long, and often clean, point breaks. But because the sand floor is unstable, bars and sandspits change according to the season. Tides and winds are other factors that will have a strong influence on wave shape.

From December to April, large swells caused by winds and storms originating in the Caribbean arrive at Costa Rica's east coast beaches. The steep, fast-moving waves break over shallow coral reefs, often in shapes and sizes that rival those of the north shore of Oahu in Hawaii. Smaller west swells from trade winds originating in the West Indies prevail from June through August. The only time when there is generally little or no surf on the east coast is September through November.

To check on prevailing conditions before you set out, visit www.crsurf.com

one of the most spectacular waves; the number of surfers is officially limited because it is in Santa Rosa National Park. Surfers need to book ahead with one of the many local surf shops and travel by boat to this surfing spot.

The Nicoya Peninsula to the south of Guanacaste is scalloped with beaches, notably Playa Avellanas and Playa Negra; many of them have rideable waves. Some of the best surfing in the country is found in remote Pavones on the Golfo Dulce coast.

Near Limón, two and a half hours east of San José, Playa Bonita is a good, popular surfing beach. About one hour south of Limón, Puerto Viejo de Talamanca, a tranquil Caribbean village, is the site of the sometimes awesome Salsa Brava, a surf break that has acquired an international reputation. From December through March, consistent, large north swells hit the coral reef with tremendous force.

Windsurfing

Since Costa Rica held its first windsurfing contest on Lake Arenal in the early 1990s, the country has been recognized as an outstanding destination for international windsurfers. With strong trade winds whipping the picturesque lake into a sea of whitewater and waves, it compares favorably with the world's best windsurfing locations, such as the Columbia River Gorge in Oregon and Maui in the Hawaiian Islands (with the only caveat that the waves are sometimes rather choppy).

Almost every other day between January and April, consistent winds of around 20 knots whip the waves to a meter-high (3ft) swell along the length of Arenal, creating excellent shortboard sailing conditions. For the rest of the season, lighter winds predominate and are ideal for longboard sailing.

Lake Arenal is not a suitable place for beginners. Sideshore winds are consistent and blow across the full width of the lake. During high winds, steep swells provide the right conditions to practice acrobatic speed runs, jumps, and loops. The water is a comfortable 18 to 21°C (64 to 70°F) all year round. Volcano Brewing Company Hotel & Microbrewery (formerly Hotel Tilawa) and River Rock Lodge are good places to hire equipment.

If you are looking for the 'funnel effect', try windswept Bahía Salinas, near La Cruz, in the far northwest of the country.

Golf

Golf is a popular game in Costa Rica and new golf courses are popping up all over the country. The Hotel Cariari and Country Club, northwest of San José, was the country's first championship course and hosts many tournaments. A less pricey option in the Central Valley is the scenic Valle del Sol public course, designed by golf architect Tracy May, in Santa Ana, a western suburb of San José. Since the 1990s, other famous golf architects have designed courses in Costa Rica. There are excellent courses on the Nicoya Peninsula,

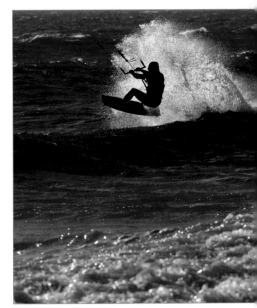

Strong winds at Bahía Salinas bay, close to Nicaragua's border, attract kite-boarders.

including the par-72 Garra de León, designed by Robert Trent Jones Jr in the Westin Golf Resort & Spa, Playa Conchal, and the par-72 courses at Hacienda Pinilla, designed by Mike Young. The newest, and most expensive, course is at the Four Seasons Papagayo Resort at the north end of the peninsula. There is also a Ted Robinson-designed course at the Marriott Los Sueños Hotel in the Central Pacific zone.

There are some fairly good 9-hole courses, too: at Tango Mar, which overlooks the Gulf of Nicoya; the private Costa Rica Country Club in Escazú; and the Los Reyes Country Club in La Guácima, which welcomes guests.

BIG FINS AND FRESH FISH

Costa Rica is a paradise for both fresh and saltwater fishing. It's quiet, too: you will run into other fishing folk only if you really want to.

The king of game fish swims calmly toward Costa Rica's Caribbean coast. At around 70kg (150lbs), he fears no predators, except sharks, as he cruises toward the mouth of the Colorado River. Where the tarpon has come from is a mystery. He could have been off the coasts of Florida, South America, or West Africa. Or he may have been in local waters the entire time.

But now he is with an ocean school of 100 fish of the same size. Suddenly they spot a school of *titi*, a small, sardine-like fish, and chase them to the surface. The tarpon cause an acre of the Caribbean to explode as they churn the water and devour the *titi*. If you are lucky enough to witness this scene, it is simply a matter of casting into the chaos to get into contact with what many consider the most exciting aquatic quarry on earth.

Tarpon enter the river mouths all along the Caribbean coast of Costa Rica, from the Colorado River in the north to the Sixaola River, which forms the border with Panamá. In most rivers, they swim a few hundred meters upstream in search of food, and then return to the sea. Only in the Río Colorado do they keep going upriver, following the *titi*, in an incredible journey of more than 200km (120 miles) to Lake Nicaragua, close to the Pacific Ocean.

Freshwater 'lakes'

As the tarpon begin their long swim, they pass a series of thin fingers of water stretching northward almost to the border with Nicaragua. These freshwater 'lakes' are full of a variety of exotic fish that make great sport on light tackle. One of the most fascinating is the alligator gar, known in Costa Rica as *gaspar*.

Fishing at sunset on the coast.

Looking like a throwback to prehistoric times, this fish has a long, narrow snout as full of sharp teeth as an alligator's. Its coffee-colored body is covered with tough skin and large scales. Its tail is broad and powerful. The meat of the *gaspar* is firm and sweet, not unlike shrimp. But the eggs should never be eaten as they are highly toxic.

The tarpon is not alone in his upriver swims. Snook also make the long journey following the *titi*. And following them all are bull sharks.

The sharks, like the tarpon, continue all the way to Lake Nicaragua. Their presence has led many people to believe there are 'freshwater sharks' in the lake. Actually, they are just visitors from the faraway Caribbean.

Snook are the mainstay of sport fishing in Costa Rica. Large snook are plentiful along all parts of the Caribbean and Pacific coasts, as well as in rivers throughout the country.

All along Río San Juan are lesser rivers flowing into it. At the confluence of the San Juan with the Colorado, Sarapiquí, San Carlos, Infernito, Pocosol, Medio Queso, and Frío rivers there is some excellent angling for tarpon and snook. None of these rivers is heavily fished and all require a bit of enterprise to reach. But those who make the effort are usually well rewarded.

side rivers. This is the case with the Río Frío. Thirty minutes by boat south of Los Chiles is the convergence of the Río Frío and the Río Sabogal. Here tarpon up to 45kg (100lbs) seem to be present at all times.

Every morning and every evening the giant fish, too big to be in a narrow river, leap high into the air, re-entering the water with a thundering splash. It is a sight every fishing enthusiast would love to see. It can also be one of the most frustrating experiences imaginable, because there are days when these fish just won't take a lure. However, just the sight is

A fisherman shows off his catch: a dolphin fish, also known as 'dorado' and 'mahi-mahi'.

The Río Frío

An exception to this rule of relative inaccessibility is the Río Frío, which passes right through 'downtown' Los Chiles – an approximate 3-hour drive, on paved roads, from San José.

The Río Frío is full of tarpon, snook, white drum, gar, and other exotic species. Some people fish right from the municipal landing in Los Chiles; others with boats launch them there and venture north or south. For those who don't have a boat, it is possible to rent a *panga* (barge), driven by a knowledgeable local person who also acts as a guide. These *pangas* can be found at the municipal landing.

Some tarpon, as they swim up the Río San Juan, apparently take diversions far into the

RULES OF ENGAGEMENT

In tarpon fishing, the rules of angling must be suspended or reversed, or there's no chance of success. The first trick is to retrieve the lure with the rod tip low – at water level or, better yet, in the water. That way, when it's time to set the hook, the rod tip can be brought up and backwards in a long arc. The maneuver must be repeated rapidly at least three times with great force. The success rate of experts is to land about one out of every 10 hooked, though try telling that to your friends when you go back empty-handed after a day's tarpon fishing.

well worth the trip – and there is always a good chance of hooking into one of them.

More river fish

The Río Frío, as well as most of the other rivers of Costa Rica, is full of a fish often overlooked by anglers. The *machacha*, a silvery speedster, is an unusual fish in that it is primarily a vegetarian. *Machacha* can often be found under the overhang of *chilemate* trees waiting for ripe fruit to fall into the water. Costa Ricans fish for them using pieces of banana or tomato, but *machacha* will also take small lures or flies, running,

A small tarpon.

ROLLING FOR AIR

Tarpon are one of the few fish that are capable of taking in air directly through the mouth rather than by filtering water through their gills. This ability is necessary for survival because these big, active fish need more oxygen than they can get from the waters that they sometimes inhabit.

This method of direct breathing accounts for the phenomenon known as 'rolling,' when the tarpon come to the surface and flop onto their sides while gulping air. This unusual adaptation also makes it possible for tarpon to swim freely between saltwater and freshwater, and even in oxygen-depleted waters.

You can buy your fishing license, required by law, at most fishing-boat docks. Most sport fishing operators will include it in the cost of a charter trip. The license costs $24 and is good for a year.

changing directions, diving and leaping into the air. They can grow up to 9kg (20lbs) and 1 to 2kg (2 to 5lb) fish are common and offer great sport. Their flesh is bony but tasty.

Up a few of the rivers that feed into the San Juan, particularly the Sarapiquí, you can find the *bobo*, a difficult but rewarding quarry. These fish, which weigh up to 14kg (30lbs), feed in shallow, fast-moving water. They are relatives of the saltwater mullet and are pure vegetarians. They can be taken on small spinners and they offer great sport as they fight hard through the rapids.

In these Atlantic-slope rivers you can also find other exotic species including the *mojarra*, a strong, sharp-toothed, brightly colored pan fish resembling a perch on steroids, and related to the sun fish.

For land-lubbers who prefer to eat fish rather than catch them, the mountains south of San José abound in stocked trout *lagos* (artificial ponds), where you can sink a line baited with *masa* (dough), land your trout in minutes and have it cleaned, scaled, and cooked on the spot.

Sea angling

For most people, fishing off the Pacific coast of Costa Rica means angling for sailfish, marlin, and tuna. All along the Pacific coast there are boatloads of sport fishing operations.

Operators in the Gulf of Papagayo enjoy the most productive sailfishing in the world. Sails here are not the scrawny Atlantic variety. They are hefty, healthy Pacific sailfish averaging over 45kg (100lbs). Fought on a 7kg (15lb) line or less, they offer fantastic sport and a spectacular show full of graceful jumps. Laws require that all sails (except record catches) are released, and fishermen generally respect these rules.

In recent years, marlin have been discovered along most of the Pacific coast. Offshore, *mahi-mahi*, tuna, and rainbow runner are plentiful. Offshore reefs also offer great fishing for snapper, including the prized *cubbera*.

Often overlooked are the fishing possibilities straight from the Pacific beaches. Every beach on the Pacific coast offers the chance to take various types of jack and drum, as well as trophy-sized snook from the surf. Mouths of rivers and streams often attract congregations of snook. Casting from rocks often locates snapper and roosterfish.

Roosterfish abound on Costa Rica's Pacific coast. The colorful, wide-bodied, and powerful fish with the long, spiky dorsal fin that gives it its name, is particularly plentiful in the water surrounding the rocks in Puntarenas or the nearby Pacific port of Caldera. Once hooked, the roosterfish raises its 'comb' and speeds

what a diesel is to a model train; it is not a light tackle fish. Once hooked, it heads for cover with the force of a rhinoceros and if it gets there it will almost certainly cut the line on underbrush.

The *guapote* is a spectacular fish. A breeding male has large bulbous protrusions above the eyes that 'light up', displaying many colors on its flank. *Guapote* in Lake Arenal, the main place where they are fished, weigh up to 9kg (20lbs) or more, although a 7kg (15lb) fish is about as much as most can handle. The *guapote pinto*, or painted *guapote*, can be found in rivers that flow into the San Juan.

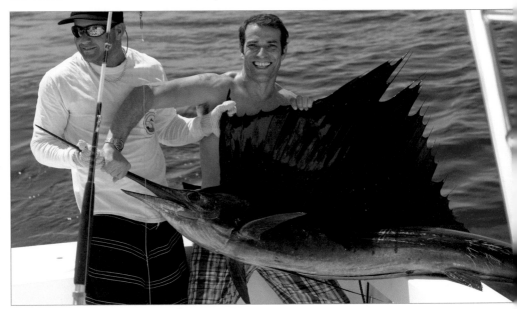

A sailfish caught off the Osa Peninsula, southwest Costa Rica.

away across the surface, offering a unique show and fight.

Neither ocean nor lake, the Golfo Dulce is a deep, tropical fjord in Costa Rica's Southern Zone. Sport fishers here chase marlin and swordfish offshore, and find plenty of snapper, snook, and yellowfin tuna inshore.

The guapote

The star inhabitant of Costa Rica's few lakes is the *guapote*. Some people call this fish the 'rainbow bass', although taxonomically it has nothing at all to do with bass. The only real similarity to bass is in the way it is fished: casting or flipping plugs or spinner baits. Once hooked, the resemblance is soon forgotten. The *guapote* is to a bass

TROUT AND MACHÍN

Wild trout have never done well in Costa Rica (although farmed trout do very well indeed). Despite numerous attempts to stock them in high mountain streams, they have never really thrived. Trout fishing is possible in the breathtaking mountains between San José and San Isidro del General, such as the Río Savegre in the San Gerardo de Dota valley area. Even if the fish are somewhat small, the scenery alone makes a day spent here worthwhile. If you cannot find any trout then a good substitute is the *machín*, a fish that is found in rivers where trout would be expected. It puts up a vigorous fight, very similar to that of a trout.

GOING TO EXTREMES

More and more sensation-seeking visitors are challenging themselves by taking the plunge and trying out thrilling adventure sports such as zip-lining and waterfall rappelling.

If even whitewater rafting seems too tame for you, Costa Rica serves up other out-of-the-ordinary exciting activities that will get your adrenaline going.

The most popular and the most readily accessible adventure sport is zip-lining, also known as a canopy tour. The original canopy tour was built in Monteverde and involved donning a waist harness, climbing inside a huge, hollowed-out *matapalo* (strangler fig) tree up to a wooden platform, hooking your harness onto a wire cable, then stepping off the platform, perhaps 30 meters (100ft) off the ground, into thin air and whizzing along, suspended from the cable, to the next platform in the tree tops. The idea is a refinement of the method used by biologists to get up into the canopy to perform research. Some tours retain that focus on natural history and the chance to get close-up looks at life in the canopy. But most zip-lines today are focused on fun and thrills. Sky Trek, the highest and longest zip-line, also operates in Monteverde, but with the screams of people zipping through the air at up to 48km (30 miles) per hour, there isn't much wildlife sticking around to be observed.

Taking that first step into thin air is quite a thrill. Cables, harnesses, and safety equipment have to meet high government standards, but you are still at the mercy of human error, so choose a canopy tour operator who talks a lot about safety measures and gives careful, complete instructions to neophytes.

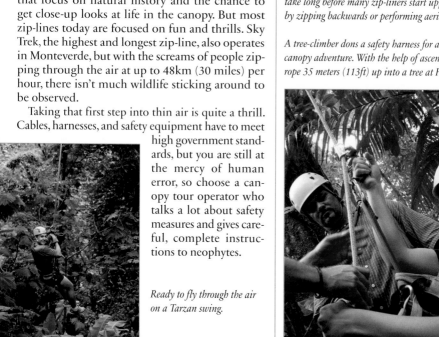

Ready to fly through the air on a Tarzan swing.

A serene zip-liner shows perfect form as she glides through the forest, suspended from a cable. After the initial ride, it doesn't take long before many zip-liners start upping the thrill factor by zipping backwards or performing aerial aerobatics.

A tree-climber dons a safety harness for a different kind of canopy adventure. With the help of ascenders, she will scale a rope 35 meters (113ft) up into a tree at Hacienda Barú Lodge.

Waterfall rappelling on the Osa Peninsula.

WETTER, WILDER, AND HIGHER

For a wet and wild adventure, try waterfall rappelling. Instead of zipping along a cable, you step off the top of a waterfall and rappel your way down, attached to ropes secured by guides at both the top and bottom of the waterfall. It takes a fair bit of courage to take that first step backward, but the thrill is worth it, and you stay cool thanks to waterfall spray.

Other tree-top adventures include climbing 30-meter (100ft) trees, using ropes, or spending a night in a tree-top platform. Hacienda Barú (www.haciendabaru.com) on the South Pacific coast offers both in its 330-hectare (815-acre) nature reserve.

If you are looking to go higher than the tree tops, take a parasailing tour with Aguas Azules (www.costaricaparasailing. com), sailing over the ocean and Manuel Antonio National Park, suspended from a parachute kept aloft by a fast motorboat. Or if you would rather leave the flying to someone else, step into a two-person ultralight, fixed-wing plane and let the pilot take you on a thrilling bird's-eye view of ocean and jungle. Fly Adventure Costa Rica (www.flyadventurecr.com) offers ultralight tours in Uvita on the South Pacific coast and near Samara on the Nicoya Peninsula.

Adventurers with no fear of flying can take to the skies in a piloted ultra-light (microlight) for breathtaking views.

Paragliding gives an exciting bird's-eye view.

Palm peaches at a roadside fruit stall, Dominical.

TICO COOKING

**When you can find Painted Rooster and Married Man
on the menu in Costa Rica's *sodas*, why spend time
at fast-food or international restaurants?**

While it is perfectly possible in Costa Rica to order anything from sushi to tandoori chicken, part of the joy of traveling is sampling local cuisine. The *Ticos'* traditional diet is a simple, healthy one, low in fat, and rich in protein and carbohydrate. Health is increasingly becoming an issue here, and organic markets are springing up around the country. Fruit, fresh vegetables, rice and beans, naturally lean beef from Brahman cattle, and cabbage salads are the trademarks of Costa Rican cooking.

Picadillos are served in every *Ticos* home: diced potatoes, *chayotes* (water squash or vegetable pears) or string beans are mixed with finely chopped meat, tomatoes, onions, *culantro* (fresh coriander), bell peppers, and whatever the cook feels may add flavor to the pot. Leftover *picadillos*, fried with rice, are served for breakfast, usually with hot *tortillas*; this combination is called *amanecido*.

Costa Ricans season their food with a mixture of dry spices called *condimentos mixtos*, which are readily available at the markets. There are many different brands of liquid sauces as well, the most famous being *Salsa Lizano*. Most often these sauces contain cornflour, salt, garlic, black pepper, onion, cilantro, paprika, and a small amount of hot chili.

So-called 'English sauce,' the native version of Worcestershire sauce, is also used, albeit sparingly, by most cooks. Jalapeño peppers, from the mountain towns of Zarcero and Cervantes, are very good, and not as hot as the Mexican varieties. Most Costa Ricans do not like very spicy food, although Tabasco and chili sauce are always on the table in inexpensive restaurants.

Ceviche – raw fish marinated in lemon juice.

Gallo pinto and casado

The classic Costa Rican dish of *gallo pinto* (literally, painted rooster) is rice and black or red beans mixed with seasonings including onion, cilantro (coriander), garlic, and finely chopped bell peppers. Guanacaste, the northwestern province that once was part of Nicaragua, claims to have originated this dish. While predominantly a breakfast dish in the city, rural Costa Ricans eat *gallo pinto* three times daily, accompanied by home-made corn *tortillas*. For breakfast they order it with scrambled or fried eggs and sour cream, or *natilla*.

For lunch, business people, students, and farmers alike usually have a *casado* (meaning husband) – a hearty combination including rice, beans, cabbage salad, fried sweet plantains, and sauced chicken, fish, or beef. An example of *Ticos'* sardonic humor, the name *casado* derives from the ordinary daily fare a man supposedly receives after he is married.

More Tico favorites

Another typical dish is the hearty *olla de carne* (literally, meat pot), which includes a small amount of stewing beef cooked with many vegetables common to the region: often *ñampi* and *camote* (both relatives of the sweet potato), *chayote* (water squash), carrots, and potatoes. It is usually served with white rice – something *Ticos* feel no meal is complete without, along with a side dish of black beans. This dish can be traced back to Cervantes' novel *Don Quixote*.

The *olla podrida* is the great-grandparent of the soup the people in Costa Rica love the most. What gives the distinct flavor to the Costa Rican version is the mixture of vegetables cooked in it: yucca, green plantain, sweet potato, *tannia*, *tacacos*, taro, pumpkin, carrot, *cho-cho*, onion, cabbage, and whatever else comes to hand.

Another interesting soup available at neighborhood restaurants throughout the country is *sopa negra*, made with black beans, onions, and cilantro, with hard-boiled eggs floating on top.

For lunch or dinner, arroz con pollo (fried rice with chicken) or arroz con mariscos (rice with seafood) are filling, inexpensive meals served in sodas (small family-run diners) and hotel restaurants.

Other local favorites include *lengua* (cow's tongue) and *mondongo* (cow's stomach lining). While tongue is tender and often deliciously prepared, *mondongo* has a strong taste and odd texture (think tripe), and is not appreciated by most foreigners.

The ubiquitous accompaniment to most meals is plantains – a relative of the banana. They can be sweet *(maduro)* or green, but they must be cooked before eating and are usually cut into strips and fried in oil or lard (called *manteca*).

Bocas and bebidas

Some bars still serve *bocas* (mouthfuls) with drinks in the same tradition as Spanish tapas. Traditionally they were complimentary, but these days they are increasingly sold separately.

Favorite *bocas* include *ceviche* (raw fish marinated in lemon juice), *carne en salsa* (meat stewed in a tomato sauce), fried cassava, and fried chicken. Beer, rum, and *guaro* (a sugar cane alcoholic drink) are favorite local tipples.

Special occasions

On weekends, Costa Ricans love to eat two versions of *chicharrones* – either deep-fried pig skin (including the layer of fat just below the skin) or tender chunks of lean pork that have been simmered slowly. *Chicharrones* are served with *tortillas* and wedges of lemon.

Gallo pinto for breakfast.

NOUVELLE CUISINE

Costa Rican nouvelle cuisine may sound like a contradiction in terms, but new markets for food exports have stirred interest in the country's vegetables and fruits. New recipes are being created, traditional ones rewritten, and local flavors added to international recipes to create a tropical fusion. Dishes like *pejibaye* soup, a delicate orange creamy broth made from peach palm fruits, and mashed black beans *(frijoles molidos)* seasoned with onions, sweet peppers, and cilantro, are served at formal dinners as hors d'oeuvres. Posh hotel restaurants offer Costa Rica Nights, with delicacies such as plantain soufflé and pork-filled cassava pastries.

At Christmas, everyone eats *tamales*, which are made with *masa*, a corn dough, stuffed with different fillings, then wrapped in banana leaves and steamed. The dish is of Aztec origin and is eaten throughout Central America. It is very rarely the same in any two countries. In Costa Rica, *tamales* are traditionally filled with tender bits of pork, rice, carrots, olives, and sometimes dried plums.

Easter fare

Since colonial times, the Easter meal has been an important and traditional celebration. The Catholic Church's prohibition on eating meat and generally sticking to a frugal diet during Lent explains why fish, pastries, and sweets are popular for the Easter celebration. Since the 19th century, *bacalao con papas* (salt cod and potatoes) has been traditionally prepared for Easter. Huge quantities of salt cod are imported from Europe especially for this occasion. Sardines are also popular.

Just before Easter week, particularly in and around the Cartago area, you will see chiverre, a type of pumpkin, but oval in shape and quite large, sold in the streets. With the pumpkin flesh

Casado for lunch.

Pejibaye soup is made from palm fruit.

THE CHOROTEGA LEGACY

Long before the white man arrived in Costa Rica, the indigenous Chorotega tribe prepared a very thin unleavened cornmeal pancake called a *tortilla*. It is the main ingredient of Costa Rican *gallitos*, an hors d'oeuvre made by wrapping *tortillas* around mashed black beans, spicy meat, vegetable stew, pork chunks or whatever else takes the chef's fancy. The Chorotega also prepared *tamales*, rectangular pieces of corn dough stuffed with deer or turkey meat and a sauce made from tomatoes, pumpkin seeds, and sweet peppers. The sauce, called *pipian*, is still prepared today in a very similar way.

local cooks make a sweet preserve called cabellito de angel (angel's hair), which is eaten during Easter on its own, or as a filling for sweet pastries.

Costa Rican *ceviche* is an Easter speciality, but is also available all year round at any neighborhood *cevichería*. It is prepared by marinating small cubes of fresh white fish or shellfish in a sauce made with lime juice, olive oil, fresh cilantro, onions, and bell peppers, for at least 12 hours. Most Costa Rican cooks believe in keeping the lime juice to a minimum and using cilantro freely to perfume the fish. It is similar to the Peruvian dish of the same name. Salty soda crackers or *patacones* – slices of green plantain mashed, then crisply fried – often accompany *ceviche*.

Fresh *palmito* (palm hearts) are also traditionally eaten during Lent, but can be bought any time, pickled in vinegar. *Palmitos* and rice is an elegant, festive dish served with grated cheese on top. *Flor de itabo* is the flower of a plant often used in the fences of the coffee farms. The plants have large bunches of lily-like, white flowers, which are also eaten for Easter, stewed in butter with eggs and tomato.

Regional cooking

Costa Rica is only a small country, but it still has several clearly differentiated regional cuisines.

The foods of Limón Province on the Caribbean coast are exotically tropical and flavorsome. The area offers dishes influenced by African and West Indian cooking. The names of the ingredients (*haki, yokotaw, bami, calaloo*) echo the beat of Calypso and reggae, as do the names of the dishes themselves (*tie-a-leave, dokunu, johnny cake*).

The trademark of Limón cooking is coconut. Coconut oil and milk are used generously in most recipes, including the traditional rice and beans: rice is cooked in a pot filled with red beans, coconut milk, and aromatic herbs. It is the regional variation of the traditional *gallo pinto*, but in Limón it is usually served on Sundays and on festive occasions. Another local dish is *rondón*, a slow-cooked spicy fish and root-vegetable stew, which is, sadly, getting hard to find amongst all the fast-food pizza and fried chicken now on offer.

From their African background the *Limonenses* have kept the original names of many ingredients and the traditions of using a lot of tubers, such as yams, and adding green leaves to soups and stews. From their ancestors' hard lives in the sugar plantations of the West Indies, the *Limonenses* have inherited many products that were included in the daily slave rations: breadfruit, salt cod, mangoes, cassava, plantains, and a great variety of tropical fruits. And from the demands and preferences of their former British masters, they have retained several recipes for cakes, pastries, and breads, including *pan bon*, rum-flavored fruit cake.

In Guanacaste, pre-Columbian traditions in cooking are very much alive. A larger variety of corn dishes are cooked there than in the rest of the country, including delicious pastries. *Tamales, chorreadas* (cheese-flavored tortillas), *tamal de elote* (sweet corn pudding), and many other

regional delicacies can still be found throughout Guanacaste. Some beach hotels there are starting to include them on their menus.

Since cattle farming is one of Guanacaste's main resources, milk products are often very good. *Bagaces* (a hard, salted cheese, used grated and added to other recipes) has been, since the 19th century, an important part of the salary of the *peones* (farm hands). *Cuajadas* (fresh cheese balls) are usually served at breakfast, eaten with hot *tortillas guanacastecas*, which are larger than the tortillas eaten in the rest of the country. African slave women

Making arepas (maize snacks) at San Raphael de Heredia's Sunday market.

were brought to the region during colonial times to work in the kitchens of the *haciendas*. They also left their mark in the form of the many exotic recipes still cooked in that province. *Ajiaco* and *bajo*, stews made with a mixture of meats and vegetables, maintain their African origins.

On the Pacific coast, Puntarenas specializes in recipes using ingredients from the sea, including *guiso de cambute* (conch stew) and various shellfish dishes featuring different combinations of fresh shrimp, lobster, and *chuchecas* (black clams). Oysters are now farmed on the Nicoya Peninsula and shipped the same day to seafood restaurants in San José.

FRUITS OF COSTA RICA

Whether piled high in the market, served up on
a plate, or whipped into a milkshake, Costa Rica's
rainbow of fruits is a delightful feast for the senses.

Fernández de Oviedo, a Spanish writer who
came to Costa Rica in the 16th century, was
probably the first European to chronicle
the country's astounding variety of tropical
fruits. Enthusiastic at every new discovery, he
pronounced the pineapple the 'best-looking,
most wonderful lady in the vegetable world.'

De Oviedo probably didn't get to taste all of
Costa Rica's different fruits. There are simply too
many, and they are available for every possible
taste preference throughout the year. Get up early
in the morning in San José and visit the Mercado
Borbón, or the dozens of fruit stalls near the
Mercado Central. Or go to the open-air produce
and fruit markets held on weekend mornings, in
almost every town on the Central Plateau, to see
and taste the season's harvest. Along the highways
and main roads will be vendors of all kinds of
fruit and fruit drinks. Herewith, a look at Costa
Rica's A–Z of fruits – from *anona* to *zapote*.

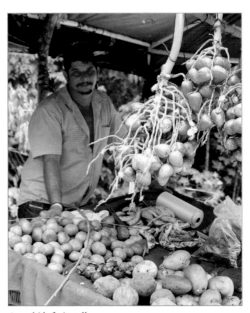

A roadside fruit stall.

Anona

A strange-looking heart-shaped fruit, also called
'the bullock's heart,' the *anona* changes from
green to a dark reddish-brown as it ripens. The
sweet pulp is milk white and contains several
large black seeds. After cutting it in half, eat
it with a spoon, using the skin as a bowl. The
anona is related to the custard apple (*anona chi-
rimoya*) found in the northern part of the country. It has a delicate sweetness and a delightful
fragrance like rose-water. Mark Twain described
it as 'deliciousness itself.'

Breadfruit

Breadfruit, like bananas, are grown in the Atlantic region of Costa Rica. This fruit of Polynesian
origin was introduced to the West Indies by
Captain Bligh of *Bounty* fame, and the Jamaicans
planted it in Limón. An attractive, ornamental
tree with large leaves, the breadfruit is an ingredient in many savory Caribbean dishes.

Caimitos and other stars

The *caimito* or Costa Rican star apple looks
just like a star when cut, similar in taste to the
mangosteen (an exotic fruit found in Malaysia
and Thailand). This glossy fruit varies in shade
from purple to light green. The sweet flesh is
usually eaten fresh, but in Limón you can still
find it made into a mixture called 'matrimony,'
prepared by scooping out the pulp and adding
it to a glass of sour orange juice.

Carambolas (star fruit) are often cut in thin
slices crosswise and used as garnishes for

desserts. This shiny, five-sided pinkish-yellow fruit also makes a refreshing juice.

Cashew fruit

An exotic cousin of the mango, the cashew fruit is best known for the kidney-shaped nut attached to its lower end. The fleshy portion, or apple, varying in color from brilliant yellow to flame-scarlet, is eaten fresh. Its superb color and penetrating, almost pungent, aroma make this one of the most delectable of all tropical fruits. The flesh is soft, very juicy, and zesty. It is also used to make jam, wine, and

species that were almost extinct are now increasing their numbers while feeding on abundant cashew apples. Beware, if the nuts are not roasted before being eaten, they are poisonous.

Granadilla

The sweet *granadilla* (passion fruit) is a favorite all over Central America. It is oval and orange to orange-brown. Within the hard, crisp skin, a bundle of seeds is surrounded by an almost liquid, translucent, and wonderfully tasty pulp. Use a spoon to eat it, or try passion fruit juice.

Breadfruit tree.

Fruit drinks (*naturales*) accompany every Costa Rican meal. A bottled fruit drink called Tropical is also sold everywhere, but try to hold out for the real thing made with fresh fruit or fruit pulp.

a refreshing beverage similar to lemonade, which retains the special aroma and flavor of the fruit. In the late 1970s, the government decided to plant many areas with cashews, for export. The venture was a failure, but the trees are still there.

There was a wonderful side effect, too: parakeets and parrots adore the fruit, and many

Guanábana

Related to the *anona*, the *guanábana* is unrivaled for its use in sherbets and refreshing beverages. Foreigners find the flavor somewhat suggestive of a combination of pineapple and kiwi, but *Ticos* consider that to be heresy.

Guava

A bestselling book by the acclaimed Colombian writer Gabriel García Márquez has the provocative title *The Fragrance of Guava*. You will better understand how the title elicits the Latin American experience if you visit a home when guava jelly is being cooked, and the entire house fills with the aroma. But cooking is not obligatory; you can simply eat the guava raw.

Another fruit, called in English 'Costa Rican guava' (*cas*), is round, yellow, and has soft white flesh. It is acidic, but highly valued for jelly-making and for drinks. If you see it on a menu, try a freshly squeezed *jugo de cas* (*cas* juice).

Loquat

The loquat (*níspero*) is a small, oval-shaped fruit with a large stone, pale-yellow to orange in color. It is also called the Japanese medlar. The flesh, firm and meaty in some varieties, melting in others, is juicy, with a sprightly acid flavor. Although commonly eaten fresh, it can also be used in cooking.

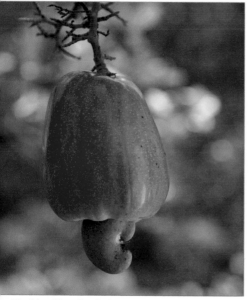
The delectable cashew fruit.

Mango

Alajuela's Central Park is full of mango trees with their tempting fragrance, which is why the town, second in size only to San José, is called Mango City. Alajuela's mangoes are sweet, firm, and delicate. The ripe ones are sweeter and spicier, but smaller and softer than the unripe ones. The aroma is spicy and alluring. Few other fruits have a background as developed as the mango, and few others are so inextricably connected with religious beliefs. Buddha is said to have been presented with a mango grove, so that he might find rest beneath its graceful shade.

Besides eating them as dessert fruits, Costa Ricans make mangoes into chutney, as well as preserves, sauces, pies, and juice.

Mombín

The Spaniards said the *mombín* (or *jocote*) was a type of plum when they first saw it, but it has nothing in common with the plum. This fruit is juicy and spicy, unlike any other. The *tronador* is the best variety. Street vendors sell brown paper bags full of *mombínes* from August through October, the color varying from dark green to bright red, depending on ripeness. The *mombín* is usually eaten fresh, as is its yellow-version cousin. Some refer to the yellow variety as the hogplum because hogs are very fond of them and fatten on the fruit that falls to the ground from wild trees in the forest.

The coco-plum (*icaco*), on the other hand, is never eaten fresh, but its white flesh is made into a sweet preserve, called *miel de icaco*. Another cousin, the *ambarella* (*yuplón*), was brought to Jamaica by Captain Bligh. It came to Costa Rica in the hands of Jamaican immigrants to Limón. It is eaten uncooked, with a little salt, or made into a preserve.

Nanzi

You'll recognize a nanzi (*nance*) by its fragrance. This small, round yellow fruit has been popular among Costa Ricans since pre-Columbian times, but foreigners tend to find its smell too strong. It is used for preserves, wines, and jellies. *Nances en guaro* (nanzis in liqueur) are very good. Left to ferment in liqueur for nine months, they take on an amber-brown color. Nanzi sherbets are also very popular.

Papaya

Papaya (or paw-paw) grows almost everywhere in the country, and most tourists are particularly enamored of a drink called *papaya en leche*, a sort of papaya milkshake. There are two varieties: the huge local papaya and the smaller, sweeter Hawaiian version. Papaya is also excellent as a meat tenderizer.

Pejibaye

More a vegetable than a fruit, this was a treasured food of the aboriginal peoples. You will surely see it on the fruit stands, with its glossy orange skin and black stripes, resembling a large acorn. Cooked and peeled, its yellow pulp tastes very good when a little mayonnaise is added to it to soften the rather dry texture. It cannot be eaten fresh. Cream of *pejibaye* soup is one of the most exceptional dishes of Costa Rican cuisine.

Rambutan

The most exotic sight in a fruit market in Costa Rica has to be the rambutan *(mamon chino)*. The bunches of red and orange fruits, sometimes called 'hairy lychees,' look like gooseberries covered in fleshy spines. To eat them, simply cut the leathery rind with a sharp knife and pull it back from the pulp.

Rose-apple and mountain-apple

The fragrance of the guava is rivaled only by that of the rose-apple *(manzana rosa)*, a beautiful round fruit, whitish green to apricot-yellow oval fruit, white to crimson in color. Its flesh is apple-like: crisp, white, and juicy but not very flavorful. *Ohia* jam is exquisite.

Sapodilla

One of the best fruits of tropical America, from the province of Guanacaste, is the *sapodilla* or naseberry, here called *chicozapote* or *níspero*. It is a dessert fruit, rarely cooked or preserved in any way. The French botanist Descourtilz described it as having the 'sweet perfumes of honey, jasmine, and lily of the valley.'

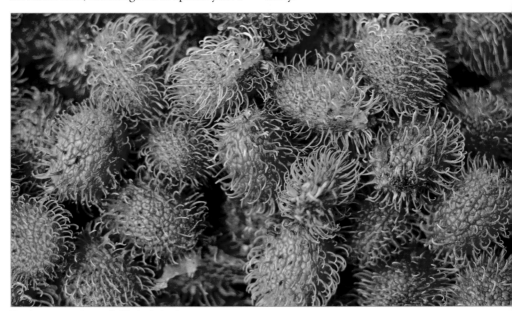

Rambutans, sometimes called 'hairy lychees'.

in color, and perfumed with the scent of the rose. The flesh is crisp, juicy, and sweet. As a preserve or crystallized, it is delicious. If you eat it fresh, don't overdo it because the seeds are poisonous when eaten in large quantities.

A relative of the rose-apple, the *ohia* or water-apple *(manzana de agua)* is a beautiful

> North Americans and Europeans are starting to appreciate the health benefits of tropical fruits. One US health food chain sells tiny papaya pills and touts juice made from noni fruits, common on the Caribbean coast, as a health tonic.

Zapote

A relative of the *sapodilla*, the *mammee-sapota* or marmalade-plum *(zapote)* kept Cortés and his army alive on their famous march from Mexico City to Honduras. The bright salmon-red color of the pulp catches the eyes of tourists walking along the Avenida Central in San José. Street vendors, knowing the sales appeal of the beautiful color, cut the marmalade-plums in halves.

Beware, however, that if you are not used to the very sweet fruits of the tropics you may find the flavor of the tempting *zapote* rather cloying. Very ripe *zapotes* are used to make the most wonderful ice creams and sherbets – try one if you get the chance.

COFFEE

When white coffee blossoms blanket the fields of the Central Valley, filling the air with a sweet jasmine-like fragrance, the *Ticos* call it 'Costa Rican snow.'

You might well surmise that coffee is indigenous to Costa Rica, but it is not. The Spanish, French, and Portuguese brought coffee beans to the New World from Ethiopia and Arabia. In the early 1800s, when seeds were first planted in Costa Rica, coffee plants were merely ornamental, grown to decorate patios and courtyards with their glossy green leaves, seasonal white flowers, and red berries. Costa Ricans had to be persuaded, even coerced, into growing them so the country might have a national export crop. Every *Tico* family was required by law to have at least a couple of bushes in the yard. The government awarded free plants to the poor and grants of land to anyone who was willing to plant coffee on it.

The Central Valley has the ideal conditions for producing coffee: altitude above 1,200 meters (4,000ft); temperatures averaging between 15°C and 28°C (59°F and 82°F); and the right soil conditions. Coffee estates quickly occupied much of the land, except for that needed to graze the oxen that lugged the coffee-laden carts. As the only Costa Rican export, the country's financial resources were organized to support it. By 1840, coffee had become big business, carried by ox-cart through mountains to the Pacific port at Puntarenas, then by ship to Chile and on to Europe. By the mid-1800s an oligarchy of coffee barons had risen to positions of power and wealth, for the most part through processing and exporting the bean, rather than by actually growing it.

Price fluctuations and debt

Despite its early successes, Costa Rica's coffee industry has been a mixed blessing at times.

White blooms of arabica coffee.

The country incurred a heavy debt borrowing US$3 million from England to finance the Atlantic railroad so coffee could be exported from the Caribbean port of Limón. And when coffee hit bottom on the international market in 1900, the result was a severe shortage of basic foods in Costa Rica that year.

This dependency on an overseas market has left Costa Ricans vulnerable on many occasions. Throughout the 20th century, coffee prices fluctuated wildly and the health of the nation's economy varied accordingly.

Traditionally, banana, citrus, and poro trees were planted in the coffee fields to provide nutrients and shade for coffee plants. Later coffee hybrids did not need shade, and treeless fields produced more yield per hectare. These varieties, however, depleted the soil more rapidly and required fertilizer to enrich it, adding to the cost of production. Today, many coffee-growers have returned to the traditional shade-loving plants, pleasing environmentalists who advocate shade-grown coffee.

The coffee plant itself is grown in nurseries until it's a year old, at which time it is transplanted to the field. Two years later it bears harvestable berries and, with care, will continue to bear fruit for the next 30 to 40 years.

presents and new outfits. But today, most coffee is picked by migrant workers from Panamá and Nicaragua.

Costa Rican coffee had been traditionally mixed with other coffees destined for worldwide export. But today, coffee growers are concentrating on producing shade-grown and certified organic beans, along with only the best high-altitude, top-quality specialty coffees from highland regions around Poás, Barva de Heredia, Tres Ríos, and Tarrazú, rated by many aficionados among the best in the world.

Costa Rican coffee is rated among the best in the world.

Coffee plantation in the Central Valley, near Poás.

Since coffee grows best in a mountainous climate, many of the hillsides in the Central Valley are covered with rows of the bright green bushes, reflecting the sun with their shiny, luxuriant leaves. Some fields seem almost vertical and it is difficult to see how pickers keep from tumbling down the slopes as they collect the berries. The answer lies in the ingenious solution of planting the trees directly behind one another so that the trunk of the downhill tree serves as a foothold for the pickers. Coffee is harvested from November to January, during school vacation and Christmas holidays. Traditionally entire families in rural areas picked coffee together, some of the money earned going for Christmas

CAFE BRITT

An entertaining way to get a taste of Costa Rica's coffee culture is to take Cafe Britt's Coffee Tour, in Barva, the heart of traditional coffee country, 1km (0.6 mile) north of Heredia (signposted from Heredia center). This theatrical tour de force takes visitors through the entire process, from growing the coffee cherry to correctly tasting the final product. Combining elements of professional theater, a multimedia show, a farm visit, a processing-plant tour, and tasting session, Cafe Britt whirls the visitor through the world of coffee in about two hours. You must reserve your tour in advance on tel: 2277 1600 or visit www.coffeetour.com.

Tree-top walkway in Selvatura Park, Monteverde.

Surfers on Playa Grande, on the
Nicoya Peninsula

White-nosed coati looking for scraps at a roadside fruit stall, Dominical.

A tree trunk bridge near Rincón de la Vieja.

INTRODUCTION

A detailed guide to the entire country, with principal sites cross-referenced by number to the maps.

Active Arenal Volcano.

Costa Rica may be a small country, but it is packed with things to see and do. Some of its beaches rival the Caribbean; inland, lush forests and towering, active volcanoes attract walkers and nature-lovers. With 28 national parks, 8 biological reserves, and 73-plus wildlife refuges, Costa Rica deserves its reputation as the home of ecotourism. These protected areas provide the perfect environment for observing the country's abundant flora, and spectacular birdlife, including the aptly named resplendent quetzal.

The small but bustling capital of San José is worth staying a day or so to visit some fascinating museums, from the underground Gold Museum and the interactive Children's Museum to the Jade Museum atop a skyscraper. It is also a good base for exploring the nearby mountains, where lodges offer activities from horseback riding to whitewater rafting.

The Central Valley is the country's green and fertile heartland, with traditional market towns, coffee farms, and four active volcanoes. The spectacular volcanic peaks of Poás and Irazú are the focal points of the country's two most popular national parks. From here it is only a short hop to the tropical beaches of the Central Pacific, including famous Manuel Antonio, whose three strands of perfect white sands are bordered by jungle and primary forest.

Taking a break from surfing at Playa Tamarindo.

Many visitors regard the north as the true Costa Rica, with the uncrowded beaches of the Nicoya Peninsula, the vast cattle lands of Guanacaste, and the natural riches of Monteverde and the Sarapiquí region. The Caribbean coast presents Costa Rica's laid-back face: its tall palms, radiant sunshine, and aquamarine waters beckoning visitors to share in its indolent lifestyle.

Costa Rica's south is off the beaten track, amid a wild and wonderful region of vast tropical forests, and Central America's highest peak. The Osa Peninsula and the Golfo Dulce are truly a world apart, often accessible only by boat, small plane, or on foot.

Pack a good map, but don't worry about getting lost – everyone does. Just getting there is half the fun of enjoying this remarkable country.

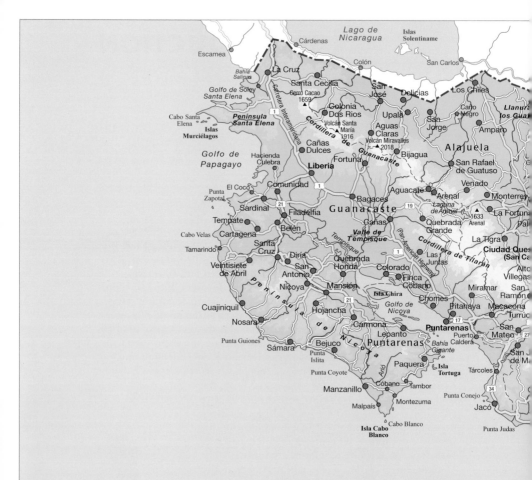

Lago de Nicaragua
Islas Solentiname
Cárdenas
Escamea
Colón
San Carlos
La Cruz
Bahía Salinas
Santa Cecilia
San José
Delicias
Los Chiles
Golfo de Soley
Santa Elena
Cerro Cacao 1659
Caño Negro
Llanur los Gua
Cabo Santa Elena
Península Santa Elena
Colonia Dos Ríos
Upala
San Jorge
Amparo
Islas Murciélagos
Volcán Santa María 1916
Aguas Claras
Alajuela
Cordillera de
Cañas Dulces
Volcán Miravalles 2018
Bijagua
Golfo de Papagayo
Hacienda Culebra
Fortuna
Guanacaste
San Rafael de Guatuso
Liberia
Venado
El Coco
Comunidad
Aguacate
Arenal
Monterrey
Punta Zapotal
Bagaces
Laguna de Arenal
19
La Fortuna
Sardinal
Filadelfia
Guanacaste
1633
Arenal
Pa
Tempate
Cañas
Quebrada Grande
Cabo Velas
Cartagena
Belén
Valle de Tempisque
La Tigra
Tamarindo
Santa Cruz
Cordillera de Tilarán
Ciudad Ques (San Ca
Veintisiete de Abril
Diriá
Quebrada Honda
Colorado
Las Juntas
Alto Villegas
San Antonio
Mansión
Finca Cóbano
Miramar
San Ramón
Cuajiniquil
Nicoya
Isla Chira
Chomes
Macacona
Turrúc
Nosara
Hojancha
Golfo de Nicoya
Pitahaya
San Mateo
Punta Guiones
Carmona
Lepanto
Puntarenas
Puerto Caldera
27
Sámara
Bejuco
Puntarenas
Bahía Gigante
San J de M
Punta Islita
Paquera
Isla Tortuga
Tárcoles
Punta Coyote
Cóbano
Punta Conejo
34
Manzanillo
Tambor
Jacó
Malpais
Montezuma
Isla Cabo Blanco
Cabo Blanco
Punta Judas

PACIFIC OCEAN

Isla del Coco

0   2 km
0   2 miles

Punta Agujas
Isla Manuelita
Isla Pájara
Bahía Chatham
Bahía Wafer
Cabo Barreto
Isla del Coco
Cabo Atrevida
Cerro Yglesias 634
Cerro Jesús Jiménez 430
Cabo Lionel
Isla Muela
Cabo Dampier

Costa Rica

0   20 km
0   20 miles

N

NICARAGUA

Indío

Caño Negro

Deseado

ucitas

San Juan del Norte

San Juan

Punta Castilla

Trinidad

Barra del Colorado

llanura de San Carlos

Boca Sahino

Heredia

Las Medias

Llanura de Tortuguero

Tortuguero

CARIBBEAN SEA

Pital

necia

Puerto Viejo de Sarapiquí

Suerte

4

La Virgen

Las Horquetas

Limón

Cariari

Parismina

Cinchona

Volcán Cacho Negro 2150

Rita

Río Jiménez

Guápiles

Cordillera Central

9

ecia

Charrizal

Alajuela

San José de la Montaña

Florida

Batán

Matina

Siquirres

32

Puerto Limón

Isla Uvita

Santa Cruz

Volcán Irazú 3452

10

Peralta

Petróleo

36

Pavas

Heredia

○**San José**

Turrialba

Pavones

Limón

Finca Banaga

Escazú

arcia

Desamparados

Tucurrique

Cartago

Platanillo

Cahuita

rcedes

Aserrí

San Gabriel

Pejibaye

Punta Cahuita

Puerto Viejo de Talamanca

abanillas

San Andrés

Orosí

Cartago

Vesta

Valle de la Estrella

Punta Uva

Punta Mona

12

San Marcos de Tarrazú

Chirripó

Bribri

Manzanillo

San José

Cordillera de Talamanca

Shiroles

Valle de Talamanca

Bratsi

Sixaola

Parrita de Parrita

San Lorenzo

Telire

I. Colón

Puntarenas

arfita

San Gerardo de Dota

Cerro Urán 3333

Coén

Changuinola

uepos

Naranjito

Río Nuevo

Rivas

3819 *Cerro Chirripó*

Teribé

Almirante

Manuel Antonio

Savegre

San Isidro de El General

General Viejo

Cerro Ena 3097

Matapalo

Cajón

San Pedro

General

Barú

Volcán

Cerro Kamúk 3549

PANAMÁ

Pejibaye

Buenos Aires

Punta Uvita

Djochal

Valle de El General

Térraba

Potrero Grande

Santa Elena

Alturas

34

Colinas

Boruca

Valle de Coto Brus

Chánguena

San Vito

Boquete

Bahía de Coronado

Cortes

Palmar Sur

Puntarenas

Río Sereno

Hato del Volcán

Valle de Diquís

Limoncito

Sabalito

Isla del Caño

Bahía Drake

Drake

Agua Buena

Ciudad Neily

Pueblo Nuevo

Gualaca

Aguijitas

Golfito

Punta San Pedrillo

Golfo Dulce

14

Portón

La Concepción

Punta Llorona

Zancudo

Canoas

Peninsula de Osa

Puerto Jiménez

La Cuesta

David

Punta Salsipuedes

Carate

Cabo Matapalo

Punta Banco

Pavones

Banco

Puerto Armuelles

Peninsula de Burica

Bahía de Charco Azul

I. Sevilla

Yerbazales

I. Boca Brava

Punta Burica

Isla Burica

Mural in San José.

Tobias Bolanos International Airport

CLARET

BARRIO MEXICO

JUAREZ

Avenida 13

Avenida 9

Avenida 11

RINCÓN DE CUBILLOS

Avenida 7

Avenida 7

Pueblo Antiguo

Avenida 5

Avenida Las Americas

PITAHÁJA

PARQUE METROPOLITANA LA SABANA

PADRE CHAPUI

Avenida 3

Avenida 3

CENTRO COLÓN

Avenida 1

Mercado Coca Cola

Museo de Arte Costarricense (Museum of Costa Rican Art)

Avenida Central

Paseo Colón

Laguito

Paseo Colón

Hospital Nacional de Niños

Hospital San Jua de Dic

Avenida 2

Avenida 4

Ministerio de Salud

Avenida Las Americas

Avenida 6

Avenida 6

Castro Madriz

Hospital Antituberculoso

San Rafael

Avenida 10

Avenida 8

Simón Bolívar

Cruz I (Red C.

TOVAR

San Martin

Avenida 10

PASEO COLÓN

CEMENTERIO CALVO

CEMENTERIO DE OBREROS

PERPUETUO SOCORRO

CEMENTERIO ISRAELITA

BOLÍVAR

Av. 24

CEMENTERIO GENERAL

PINO

CORAZÓN DE JESÚS

Av. 26

ALMENDARES

María Aguila

CUBA

Avenida Nosara

PINOS

Avenida 28

Avenida 30

Calle 24

Avenida 28

Avenida 32

N

San José

250 m

250 yds

SAGRADA FAMILIA

UNIÓN

SANTA
TERESA

La Trinidad ↑

Centro Costarricense
de Ciencias y Cultura

H

Museo de Los Niños,
National Gallery

venida 13

Calle 10

Avenida 11

PASO DE
LAVACA

Calle 12

Calle 10

Calle 8

Avenida 9

TOURNON

Spirogyra Jardín
de Mariposas
(Butterfly Garden)

J

Torres

108

AMON

PARQUE
ZOOLÓGICO
SIMÓN
BOLÍVAR

I

Avenida 11

Avenida 13

Avenida 11

Avenida 7

Calle 6

Calle 4

Calle 2

Calle Central

Calle 1

Calle 3

Calle 5

Avenida 9

Av. 11

C. 13

Calle 15

Calle 17 bis

Hospital
Calderón
Guardia

Calle 17

Calle 19

Avenida 5

Avenida 7

Mercado
de Borbón

Avenida 3

Correos,
Museo
Filatélico

Radiográfico
Costarricense

Avenida 5

Galería
Namu

Instituto Nacional
de Seguros INS

Casa Amarilla
(Foreign Ministry)

Calle 11

Avenida 7

Avenida 1

Ferrocarril
al Atlántico

Avenida 5

Edificio
Metálico

PARQUE
ESPAÑA

Fábrica Nacional
de Licores,
Museo de Arte y
Diseño Contemporáneo

K

Biblioteca
Nacional

venida 1

Mercado
Central

G

Banco Nacional
de Costa Rica

F

Club
Unión

Iglesia
El Carmen

Avenida 3

Calle 5

PARQUE
MORAZÁN

Avenida 1

PARQUE NACIONAL

L

Calle 10

Calle 8

Avenida
Central

Banco
Central

Calle 1

Calle 3

QUE
MERCED

Banco
de Costa
Rica

Avenida 2

Teatro
Melico
Salazar

Gran Hotel
Costa Rica

B

Plaza de
la Cultura

i

Musei del Oro
Precolombino

1

Avenida Central

Museo Nacional
del Jade

M

Palacio Nacional,
Asamblea Legislativa
(Parliament)

Museo Nacional
(Bellavista Fortress)

N

San Pedro

Iglesia
La Merced

Calle 12

Avenida 4

PARQUE
CENTRAL

D

A
C

Teatro
Nacional

Avenida 2

2

Mercado Nacional
de Artesanías
(National Crafts Market)

Plaza de la
Democracia

Centenario

Av. 2

Avenida 6

Calle 6

Calle 4

Calle 2

Teatro
Rex

E

Catedral
Metropolitana

Avenida 4

Avenida 6

Archivos
Nacionales

Iglesia
La Soledad

Av. 6

Volio

Avenida 8

Calle 1

Calle 3

Avenida 8

Tribunales
de Justicia

Av. 8

Estación General
de Bomberos
(Fire Station)

204

Alfredo

Iglesia La
Dolorosa

Rep. de Chile

Avenida 10

Calle 7

Paseo de Los Estudiantes

San

Martín

Av. 10

Tomas Guardia

Avenida 12

Paseo

Sarmiento

Paseo

Avenida 12

Avenida 14

BARRIO

CHINO

Sarmiento

C. José Marti

Av. 12 bis

Av. 14

Dr. Moreno Cañas

Av. 10 bis

Av. 12

DOS
FINOS

Calle 12

Avenida 16

Calle 10

Calle 8

Calle 6

Calle 4

Calle 2

Avenida 14

Calle Central

Avenida 16

Calle 1

Calle 3

Calle 5

Avenida 16

Calle 9

Calle 11

Tomas Guardia

Calle 19

Av. 16

Av. 16 bis

Av. 18

Calle 21

CERRITO

Avenida 18

República de Panamá

Av. 20 bis

Ferrocarril
Eléctrico al
Pacífico

214

22

Avenida 18

Estación de
Plaza Viques

Avenida 20

Ministerio de
Obras Públicas
y Transportes

Av. 22

Dr. Carit

Instituto
Geográfico
Nacional IGN

Calle 11

Plaza
Gonzales
Viques

Calle 13

C. 19

C. 19 bis

Av. 18

Calle 23

Calle 25

Avenida 24

Calle 10

Calle 8

Calle 4

Avenida

26

Avenida 24

C. 2

Calle 1

Calle 3

Calle 5

Avenida 24

Calle 7

Calle 9

Calle 11

Avenida 26

Avenida 28

Calle 13

Calle 15

C. 17

Autopista Estado de Israel

209

Desamparados

30

32

214

Avenida 24

Av. 30

Avenida 28

175

LUNA PARK

MONGITO

INVU

COLOMBARI

Calle 7

Av. 32

Av. 34

Av. 34 bis

Calle 15

Avenida 28

Av. 32

SAN
DIMAS

Desamparados

The Correos (Central Post Office) contains a museum.

SAN JOSÉ

With modern high-rises ranked alongside faded 19th-century buildings, Costa Rica's capital may seem a jumble at first. Yet visitors soon discover that it possesses a certain *Tico* charm.

Main Attractions
Teatro Nacional
Museo del Oro
  Precolombino
Mercado Central
Museo de los Niños
Museo de Jade
Museo Nacional

T he growth – some might say the flowering – of San José, began on that day, sometime during the first half of the 19th century, when Europe decided to have its daily cup of coffee.

By the 1850s, San José had been transformed from a humble little village to a boomtown. As the city became wealthy, so its inhabitants, who called themselves *josefinos*, became more refined, more sophisticated, and more worldly.

The golden age

By the end of the 19th century, San José was living high on the profits of coffee exports. The city was third in the world to have public electric lighting and one of the first to have public telephones. It was also the first to allow girls to attend high school. Admittedly, the roads were still unpaved, but most upper-class homes had pianos.

Throughout much of the first part of the 20th century, San José continued to prosper and to build: a national library, schools, banks, parks and plazas, ministries, numerous hotels, theaters, a sumptuous post office, bookstores, hospitals, churches, a magnificent Palace of Justice, and an international airport all spoke of a city with money to spend.

In 1956, Costa Rica's population passed the 1-million mark. By then,

the international focus of influence had shifted. People ceased coveting things European, and became heavily influenced by North American standards and sensibilities.

The modern city

Cars and trucks began to appear where there had only been the gentle horse and buggy, ox-carts, pedestrians, and bicycles. The population doubled over the following two decades.

By the mid-1970s, the air in San José had become noticeably dirty, and

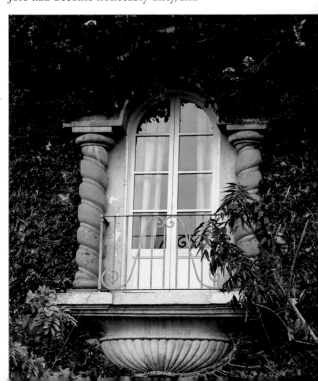

Some of the city's old buildings can be seen in Barrio Amón.

TIP

Theft is a problem in San José. The best way to have a hassle-free day is not to take anything with you that can be snatched. Wear a money belt and leave your passport and other valuables at your hotel.

the once civilized, narrow streets had become overwhelmed with a relentless rush of cars and people. Graceful, ornate old buildings were torn down and replaced with harsh, ugly copies of North American contemporary architecture. San José, the civilized 19th-century city, could not adapt its physical limitations to meet the demands of its consumerist 20th-century inhabitants. And today, in the early 21st century, this conflict has engendered a city that, by most standards, is traffic-clogged and unattractive. The urban conglomeration that is now San José is the shopping and administrative center for the entire Central Valley, with a population of around 333,000.

Fortunately, amid the miasma of diesel fumes, and the hordes of people, there are still some islands of repose. The National Theater is probably the most beautiful building in the country, and its elegant coffee shop is a favorite place to meet. Across the plaza, you can sip a *refresco natural* on the terrace of the Grand Hotel, while listening to *marimba* bands and the burble of 20 different languages.

The domed Temple of Music in Parque Morazán hosts open-air concerts.

Two downtown city parks also offer benches to sit on and a calm port in the city storm. The **Parque Morazán**, across from the Aurola Holiday Inn, has lovely jacaranda trees and a classically columned, open-air Temple of Music where public concerts are held. A couple of blocks to the east, the **Parque España** resembles a mini-rainforest in the middle of the city. Under the dense canopy of tropical trees draped with vines, you will share this cool space with statuary commemorating Spanish heroes, including conquistadors and Queen Isabel.

The National Museum and the Gold Museum are worth seeking out, along with the world-class Jade Museum. Among the souvenir shops, theaters, restaurants, and a few interesting art galleries, there are also some extraordinary remnants of old San José, hints of what a handsome, delightful place this city used to be.

Getting your bearings

Before you embark on the following tour of the city, or indeed go looking for any address within San José, sit

CUTTING DOWN ON CONGESTION

After a 2007 study showed untenably high levels of pollution from car exhausts on busy city streets, the government finally took action and instituted traffic restrictions. Car owners are forbidden to drive into the city on one day of the week – the day depends on the last number of their car's license plate.

There is a move afoot, as well, to rationalize bus routes in the city so that there aren't as many buses from the suburbs duplicating services. A bright spot on the horizon is the revival of train service. Trains now run from west to east through the city (Pavas–Curridabat), between San José and Heredia, north of the city, as well as to Belén, Cartago, Alajuela and the Juan Santamaría International Airport. The services are still fledgling, with two-car trains traveling mostly during rush hours, but they are the best hope for getting people out of their cars and onto public transportation.

To further cut down on congestion and make San José a more people-friendly city, some major avenues are being closed to vehicles and turned into pedestrian zones. To cut down on the visual clutter in the city, unsightly overhead electrical wires are also being buried. San José may never be a beautiful city, but at least it is working toward improving the quality of life for residents and visitors alike.

down with a map and familiarize yourself with the city's grid system of numbered streets (*calles*), which run north to south, and avenues (*avenidas*), which run east to west. The northern avenues and eastern streets have odd numbers; the southern avenues and western streets have even numbers. Confusingly, however, buildings are not numbered and, for the most part, only in downtown San José do any streets have names. Addresses are often given in the following format: Metropolitan Cathedral, Calle Central, Avenida 2–4, meaning that it is on the Calle Central between Avenida 2 and Avenida 4. Alternatively, and more commonly, addresses are given in terms of distance in meters (*metros*), north, south, east, or west from known landmarks. It is as well to know, however, that *Ticos* often equate a city block with 100 meters (3.2ft) – no matter how long or short it is. The end result is that *Ticos* and visitors alike can be seen wandering the city streets perpetually stopping one another to ask for directions. The good news is that people are generally happy to help.

The heart of the city

The Plaza de la Cultura marks the heart of the city. The area around this large square is a popular meeting point for peddlers, artisans, street musicians, in fact just about anybody and everybody. The pride of the square is the **Teatro Nacional** Ⓐ (www.teatronacional.go.cr), without doubt the finest building in San José, if not all Costa Rica. Its construction was financed by 19th-century coffee barons, who, embarrassed that there was no appropriate venue here for the world-renowned opera star, Adelina Patti, to perform, offered to raise money by paying a tax on every bag of coffee exported.

Modeled after the Paris Opera House and neoclassical in style, the theater was opened in 1897 with a production of *Faust*. The four-level floor plan is in the form of a horseshoe, with ornate detailing by Spanish and Italian artisans, and the acoustics are excellent. Ironically, Adelina Patti never did come to Costa Rica, but the country's top-quality National Symphony Orchestra performs here with illustrious international guest artists; their season begins

EAT

On the Avenida Central side of the Plaza de la Cultura is a branch of POPS ice cream parlor, generally agreed to be the best in Costa Rica. It is always crowded.

Ceiling mural in Teatro Nacional.

City Buses

When in San José, do as the *josefinos* do: Hop aboard a public bus to see the city and get some insights into *Tico* culture.

Buses are ubiquitous in San José. They go everywhere throughout the city and its surrounding areas. Many downtown streets are clogged with buses of all kinds. There are shiny new Mercedes models, personalized with their owners' names garishly painted on the rear window; some rusty wrecks emitting thick black smoke – although these have mostly been replaced by cleaner, hybrid buses; and recycled school buses from the United States, scrupulously cared for and graced with fanciful names.

Whether new and slick or decrepit and smoky, the buses have a common trait. They are wonderful windows into everyday Costa Rican life. Almost everyone uses them: students on their way to classes; women in high heels, dressy clothes, and impeccable make-up on their way to work; country folk coming into town to do business of one kind or

Almost everyone takes the bus in San José.

another; young mothers taking children to doctors' appointments at the social security hospital; men with briefcases and neat pants and shirts. They are all on the bus, heading this way or that.

And for a fistful of *colones*, you can climb aboard and join in the great comings and goings of life in the Central Valley. A bus ride in San José is not particularly comfortable, especially during peak hours, but there is no better or more enjoyable way to make quick and often delightful observations on *Tico* life and characteristics.

Courtesy and kindness

For one thing, chivalry is still alive. Or is it just a simple sense of decency, of caring for others? Young men will assist older men, or women with children in tow up the steps; a seated passenger will offer to hold your packages while you stand; someone will always offer his or her seat to an older person or a pregnant woman. The driver will wait for someone making a last-minute dash to catch the bus. A young boy, known to the bus driver by name, boards on Paseo Colón and, for a few stops, takes on the role of the bus's official door-opener.

A wizened old *campesino* (peasant), returning from a trip to the city, takes a long time to board. He carries with him a heavy burlap bag, redolent of coffee beans and *pejibaye*.

A small girl in a rumpled pink dress enters the parked bus, waiting for its scheduled departure at the Coca-Cola bus stop. She speaks briefly to the driver, then stands at the front of the bus, singing a mournful song about love. When she has finished, she moves down the aisle with an open hand, into which the passengers all drop their small change.

Every visitor should take at least one bus ride in San José. Board near the beginning of the line so you can still get a seat, and watch the rush of humanity come aboard, pausing to place their fare in the driver's hand, pushing past the turnstile, greeting friends and neighbors as they make their way down the aisle, more passengers boarding stop after stop, until it isn't possible to squeeze another body on.

Buses marked Sabana–Cementerio will take you on a loop around downtown, past the Central Post Office, the Central Market, Sabana Park, and the vast city cemetery. It's a good idea to take a ride outside the city too. The bus journey to Heredia, via Santo Domingo, will give you a glimpse of San José's prosperous suburbs as well as some of the shabbier parts of town.

in March. There are also daily tours where you can admire the marble, gold, bronze, tropical woods, crystal chandeliers, velvet drapes, and statuary. The ceiling fresco is famous and features an idyllic, if improbable, scene of coffee and banana pickers.

The **Cafe del Teatro Nacional** features changing art exhibits and is very popular, serving excellent salads, snacks, desserts, and specialty coffees. Across from the National Theater is the **Gran Hotel Costa Rica B**, restored to its 1930s glory and renowned as a meeting place for tourists who gather in its outdoor café where musicians often entertain with marimbas.

Gold Museum

Beneath the Plaza de la Cultura is the **Museo del Oro Precolombino C** (Gold Museum; www.museosdelbanco-central.org; daily 9.15am–5pm). On the east side of the square in cool, darkened, cavernous rooms, the collection features more than 2,000 brilliant pre-Columbian artifacts made by the indigenous peoples from the southwestern part of the country. Highlights include tiny half-man, half-bird figures, and erotic statuettes. Located in the same building, the **Museo de Numismática** contains the national coin collection and occasional temporary exhibitions of modern art. On leaving the Plaza de la Cultura, pay a visit to the nearby **Costa Rica Tourist Office** (ICT), 50 meters/yds west on Avenida Central, for news of what's on in town, and to pick up a free bus schedule. Further east, between avenidas 2 and 14 and calles 7 and 11, lies the **Barrio Chino** (Chinatown), the only one in Central America.

West of the plaza

A short walk west of the Plaza de la Cultura along Avenida 2 is the **Parque Central D** (Central Park), another great place for people-watching. The Gaudí-like kiosk in the center of the park was donated by the Somoza family of Nicaragua and sometimes hosts open-air concerts on weekends.

Directly in front of the park is the huge **Catedral Metropolitana E** (Metropolitan Cathedral). Notice the finely carved wood ceiling of the Chapel of the Holy Sacrament and its walls, so carefully adorned with flower motifs that it almost looks as if they have been tiled. A monumental white statue of Pope John Paul II sits in the cathedral garden. The cathedral provides a refuge of peace from the hot bustling city, and the microphone-amplified midday Masses are always well attended.

Due north of Parque Central, along Calle 2, is the **Correos F** (Central Post Office), in a grand old, ornate building that also houses the **Museo Filatélico** (Philatelic Museum; Mon–Fri 8am–5pm) and a pleasant café. Three blocks west of the post office, walking along pedestrianized Avenida 1, you will find the renovated and much brightened up **Mercado Central G** (Central Market; Mon–Sat 6.30am–6.30pm), the city's best market, since 1881.

There are more than 200 stalls selling everything from old kitchen utensils to saddle bags, fresh fish, coffee and spices by the kilo, to religious

Gold figurines in the Museo del Oro.

Fish stall in Mercado Central, one of the most dynamic places in the city.

TIP

At the northern end of the Parque Central, look out for the restored neoclassical facade of the Teatro Popular Melico Salazar.

icons. The prices are some of the cheapest in the city. At the center of the hall are the snack stands, a good place to find real *Tico* food at real *Tico* prices. Keep your hand on your wallet as pickpockets operate here, but don't be deterred from diving into this den to witness gritty *Tico* life at first hand.

Children's Museum

If you have children in tow, you might like to make a diversion a few blocks north to the former Penitenciaria Central (City Jail), now the Centro Costarricense de Ciencias y Cultura (CCSC) that houses **Museo de los Niños** (Children's Museum; tel: 2258 4929; www.museocr.org; Tue–Fri 8am–4.30pm, Sat–Sun 9.30am–5pm), which has interactive exhibits that are entertaining for adults, too. There is a good summary of the country's historical developments, with models of Amerindian huts, Caribbean wooden shacks, and modern housing.

The old prison also houses the modest **Galería Nacional** (National Gallery; Mon–Fri 8.30am–4.30pm; free), which exhibits work by local artists. Teenagers will love Crea+, a

Edificio Metálico.

multimedia center with reading rooms, a digital painting screen, a video game room, and a climbing wall. The CCSC also houses the **Teatro Auditorio Nacional**, a modern venue hosting plays, concerts, conferences, and other major events. The museum complex is in a rough part of town, however, so take a cab, rather than walking there.

Around the INS Building

On Avenida 7, on the north side of the lush Parque España, is the National Insurance Institute, better known as the **INS Building**, a useful landmark that towers over the city.

Opposite is one of the capital's most interesting old buildings, the **Edificio Metálico** (Metal Building School), which was shipped here in 1892 from Belgium to house 1,000 students. A block east of the school on Avenida 7 is the **Galería Namu** (tel: 2256 3412; http://galerianamu.com) which has an impressive selection of indigenous crafts, including ceramics and colorful masks, with an emphasis on fair trade practices. The friendly staff is eager to explain the history behind the items on display and you may even meet the artists who created them.

Next door to the INS, under the shade of a magnificent ceibo tree, is the **Casa Amarilla** (Yellow House). Currently the home of the Foreign Ministry, it was constructed in 1816 as the Court of Justice. You can take a look inside the foyer and also take a peek into the back garden where a piece of the Berlin Wall has been made into a fountain.

Butterfly Garden and Bolívar Zoo

A block north of the INS is the **Parque Zoológico Simón Bolívar** (Simón Bolívar Zoo; http://fundazoo.org; Mon–Fri 8am–3.30pm, Sat–Sun 9am–4.30pm), with a small, sad collection of ill-housed African and Costa Rican animals. The hope is that all the animals will be moved to a larger facility in the countryside west of the city.

For a cheerier view of Costa Rican wildlife, visit the enchanting **Spirogyra Jardín de Mariposas** (Spirogyra Butterfly Garden; www.butterflygardencr.com; daily 8am–2pm) across the river from the zoo. It's not far, as the butterfly flies, but the entrance is a long way off on foot, so you will need to take a cab from the zoo to get to this secret city garden. One of the main aims of Spirogyra is to help rural women find alternative sources of income from field labor, by exporting butterfly cocoons to Europe and the US instead. In addition to the many colorful butterflies, there are gardens to wander through and hummingbirds to enjoy. Go on a sunny day when the butterflies are most active.

National Liquor Factory

Across the street from the INS building is the former **Fábrica Nacional de Licores** (National Liquor Factory), which now houses an arts and cultural center, as well as the Ministry of Culture. Pop into the pretty courtyard and amphitheater (a venue for plays and concerts) which lead to another part of the complex, the **Museo de Arte y Diseño Contemporáneo** (Museum of Contemporary Art and Design; www.madc.cr; Mon–Sat 9.30am–5pm; free on Mon), which mounts changing exhibitions with the latest in avant-garde art, sculpture, and photography. Check the *Tico Times* for what's on.

One block southeast is the **Parque Nacional** (National Park), one of the largest of San José's parks, where lovers drape themselves over park benches and bureaucrats eat their lunches under the shade of the 50 or so species of native trees. It's a very pleasant place by day, and well lit by night, but it is probably not advisable to stroll there alone after dark. In the center of the park a monument depicts victory in the war against the hated *filibustero*, William Walker.

National Museum

Two blocks south of here are two excellent museums. The first one, on Avenida Central, is the **Museo Nacional del Jade** (Jade Museum; http://portal.ins-cr.com; daily 10am–5pm). Located in a modern five-story building, the museum boasts pre-Hispanic masterpieces from all over the country, including carefully crafted *colgantes* (amulets or pendants). Nearby, on Calle 17, is the **Museo Nacional** (Tue–Sat 8.30am–4.30pm, Sun 9am–4.30pm; www.museocostarica.go.cr), housed in the old Bellavista fortress, which still bears the bullet marks from the 1948 Civil War. Constructed in 1870, the building served as a barracks until the abolition of the army in 1949. The collections provide an overview of Costa Rica's history and culture, and include displays on burial ceremonies, a treasury of gold pieces, and rustic furniture from the colonial period. In the courtyard are cannons and some of the mysterious stone spheres found in the south of the country (see page 247). From the terrace of the building there are fine views down over the city and the amphitheater-like Plaza de la Democracia, where open-air concerts are held.

Jade models at the Museo del Jade.

Casa Amarilla in Barrio Amón.

Plaza de la Democracia.

West of the square is the **Mercado Nacional de Artesanías** (National Crafts Market; daily 8am–8pm), one of the best places in the capital to buy souvenirs like jewelry, hammocks, wood products, and bags direct from local artisans.

Sabana Park

The large grassy area of **Parque La Sabana** occupies what was Costa Rica's first international airport. The Spanish-style building that once was the airport terminal has been converted into the **Museo de Arte Costarricense ⊙** (Museum of Costa Rican Art; www.musarco.go.cr; Tue–Fri 10am–6pm, Sat–Sun 10am–4pm). The renovated museum features works by the country's finest 19th- and 20th-century painters and sculptors, as well as international artists.

In the *Salón Dorado* (Golden Room, upper story), French artist Luis Ferrón has immortalized Costa Rican history in a striking-looking stucco and bronze mural. Don't miss the museum's sculpture garden, which has some intriguing, monumental modern works.

A quiet day in Parque Nacional.

Sabana Park is a popular weekend retreat for families who come to picnic, ride their bikes, skate, play, and feed the ducks on the artificial lake. Kite vendors also do a brisk trade on breezy days and it is often the venue for art and music festivals. Sporting facilities include soccer fields, tennis courts, and jogging trails. During the day, this is a relatively safe place as long as you stick to the paths. The park should be avoided after dark, however.

Pueblo Antiguo

A short bus ride northwest of Sabana Park in the district of La Uruca is the **Pueblo Antiguo ⊙** (Old Village; closes for private events, so call first 2242 9200; www.puebloantiguo.co.cr), where actors create an idealized version of 19th-century life in Costa Rica, featuring a model farm and village, set in the **Parque de Diversiones** (www.parquediversiones.com; opening times vary, check website for schedules), a children's amusement park, with rides, costumed characters, and fireworks. Weekend dinner shows feature folklore and folk dancing.

ELEGANCE PAST

To get a feeling for the San José of old, take a walk in Barrio Amón, where some vestiges of elegance survive. Start at the Casa Amarilla (Yellow House), the ornate, Spanish-colonial-style home of the foreign ministry. Walk a block north to Avenida 9 and head west (left). You will pass by some elegant Victorian mansions, complete with gingerbread trim and stone lions guarding walled gardens.

Some of the grander houses have now been converted into boutique hotels, such as the Hotel Don Carlos, which retains a classically Spanish inner courtyard, now used as the lobby bar. Along the Avenida 9 wall of the hotel, look for the charming series of tiled murals that depict *campesino* village life in a folksy, amusing style.

In an effort to reduce congestion and make the city more people-friendly, some of the streets are being pedestrianized.

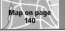

THE CENTRAL VALLEY

The heartland of Costa Rica is home to more than 60 percent of the nation's people. It is the center of government, agriculture, and commerce, and has the oldest cities and many cultural treasures.

The Central Valley (Valle Central), or Central Plateau (Meseta Central), as it is often called, is strictly speaking neither a valley nor a plateau since it contains both kinds of landscape. The Central Highlands might be a more apt name for this area, only 24km by 64km (15 miles by 40 miles), where two mountain ranges meet. You will find rich, volcanic hills and river-filled valleys, with altitudes reaching up to 1,500 meters (4,500ft).

The countryside is beautiful and variable. The climate is salubrious. The air is sweet and soft. The people are generally friendly, dignified, and independent. Volcanoes, some still active, others dormant or extinct, rise up above the hills around the valley. Above them, a big sky is constantly changing – dark, charcoal rain clouds; intense, searing patches of blue; fluffy white cumulus; and rainbows galore. All come and go in quick succession.

There are misty, almost enchanted places such as the Orosí Valley; adobe villages such as Barva that sing of old Costa Rica; and crowded, noisy, relentlessly vital cities, such as Heredia or Cartago. And they are all easily accessible. Day trips by bus or car, or with tour groups, can easily be arranged.

Highlands life

Passing through the small highland towns and villages, you see what in

Central America is the unusual and impressive sight of people living in houses on plots of land that they themselves own and farm. Neighborhoods are often a hodgepodge of larger, fancy homes and smaller, humble ones. Housewives in aprons chat in front yards as they watch their babies. Children in school uniforms walk up the road for lunch at home. Produce from backyard fruit trees is for sale on little tables or stands in front of houses: soft-fruit preserves, homemade cheese and sour cream, oranges,

Main Attractions

Parque Nacional Volcán Poás
Cartago
Orosí
Parque Nacional Tapantí
Monumento Nacional Guayabo
Parque Nacional Volcán Irazú
Parque Nacional Braulio Carrillo
Sarchí

A traditional ox-cart.

candy-stuffed grapefruit, mangoes, tomatoes. Visitors are accepted with a mild, easy curiosity; no one seems especially surprised to have a gringo walk into the local *soda* (neighborhood restaurant) and order *arroz con pollo* (chicken and rice).

San José, Alajuela, Cartago, and Heredia are the largest and most important cities of the Central Valley. Radiating out from San José are towns and suburbs, each with its own flavor and identity: Americanized Escazú; residential, upscale Rohrmoser; exclusive Los Yoses with its lovely old residences; San Pedro, home to many good restaurants, the University of Costa Rica, and one of the largest shopping malls in Central America. There are also four national parks to explore, several volcanoes to climb, and Guayabo National Monument, the country's most important archeological site.

Though most travelers visit the Central Valley between December and March to escape the winter chill of North America and Europe, these months are Costa Rica's dry season, its 'summer.' Frequent travelers to the area know that it is the rainy season in Costa Rica, with its afternoon downpours and dramatic displays of lightning, when the Central Valley is at its magnificent best, lush and colorful. Best of all, the air and San José itself are cleansed by a daily bath.

Poás Volcano National Park

The most developed of all the parks is **Parque Nacional Volcán Poás ❶** (tel: 2482 2165; daily 8am–3.30pm), a popular stop on the tourist trail. It is only 37km (25 miles) from San José on good roads leading through the city of Alajuela. Poás can become crowded and cloudy, so it is best to visit early in the day when views are better and before the throngs arrive. The cool freshness of the air as you ascend the mountain is invigorating, but it can get chilly and rainy, so bring a sweater or a rain jacket.

A map of the nature trails is available at the Visitors' Center, where there are nature exhibits, a gift shop, a cafeteria, and restrooms. If the weather closes in, as it often does up here, at almost 2,740 meters (9,000ft) above sea level, the Visitors' Center is a good place to hunker down and warm up. From a lookout point above the crater, there is an overview of the volcano, which in 1989 shot ash well over a kilometer into the air. The main crater, which is 1.5km (1 mile) wide and 300 meters (1,000ft) deep, is one of the largest in the world. Poás rarely has violent eruptions and is one of the more accessible active volcanoes on the continent (although it was close to the epicenter of a 6.1 earthquake in January 2009. It is active in 40-year cycles and is currently producing acid-like rain and sulfurous gases. It is therefore not advisable to stay for more than 20 minutes near the active crater.

Just a 20-minute hike away, along well-maintained trails through a landscape rich with wild flowers and a multitude of mosses, bromeliads, and ferns, is another crater filled with

An ocelot up close.

La Paz Waterfall.

Fragrant coffee beans from Costa Rica, roasted to perfection and ready for grinding.

a jewel-colored lake, Laguna Botos. Keep an eye out for large-footed finches foraging along the trail, and volcano juncos, sparrow-like birds with yellow eyes and a pink beak.

Descend from the park to one of the nearby restaurants and enjoy the local specialty of *fresas en leche*, strawberry milkshake, or stop at one of the roadside stands to buy strawberry preserves and cookies made by local women. Alternatively, continue to the nearby **La Paz Waterfall Gardens** (www.waterfallgardens.com; daily 8am–5pm) and set off on 3.5 km (1.5 miles) of trails past hummingbird and orchid gardens, a huge butterfly observatory, aviaries and animal exhibits, en route to five impressive waterfalls. To spend more time in the mountain air, consider an overnight stay at Peace Lodge or **Poás Volcano Lodge** (www.poaslodge.com), and enjoy verdant views from your bathtub.

Alajuela and environs

Laguna Botos, a crater lake near Volcán Poás.

As you descend by some 200 meters (660ft) into **Alajuela ❷**, the country's second-largest city, it becomes noticeably warmer. To relax, you can join the old-timers in the central park, amid an orchard of mango trees. Each April work crews use high-pressure hoses to fell the ripe mangos so they don't fall on people's heads.

Alajuela is the birthplace of Juan Santamaría, the young Costa Rican whose courage in helping to rout William Walker and his *filibusteros* from Costa Rica in 1856 is enshrined in national legend. The expanded **Museo Histórico Cultural Juan Santamaría** (www.museojuansantamaria. go.cr; Tue–Sun 10am–5.30pm; free), which occupies a restored former military barracks, one block from the central park, tells his story. A week-long festival of parades, concerts, and dances centers around his birthday on April 11.

From Alajuela take the old highway toward the Pacific, via La Garita. En route is **Zoo Ave ❸** (pronounced zoh-avay; http://rescateanimalzooave.org; daily 9am–5pm), which is primarily an animal rescue and research center, and takes care of more than 100 species of Costa Rican birds, as well as monkeys, deer, crocodiles, giant tortoises, and the occasional puma or ocelot.

La Garita ❹ is expansive and green, mostly a residential area filled with lovely gardens, fields of shiny green coffee bushes and plant nurseries (*viveros*). On the road between Zoo Ave and La Garita, La Fiesta del Máiz restaurant features the near-endless variety of tasty dishes that *Ticos* make from corn.

Coffee country

A day trip to the province of Heredia, the center of Costa Rica's coffee production, quickly takes you away from the heat and clatter of San José. Just 24km (15 miles) from the city, you can walk in an evergreen forest or cloud forest reserve rivaling those of much more remote and inaccessible areas.

En route to Heredia from San José is Santo Domingo, which still retains an historical charm with its low, white stucco houses trimmed in traditional royal-blue paint. Just to the southwest of the center of town is **INBioparque ❺** (tel: 2507 8107;

www.inbioparque.com; Fri 8am–5pm, last entry at 3pm; Sat–Sun 9am–5.30pm, last entry 4pm), a 5.5-hectare (13-acre) coffee estate turned naturalist center that provides an entertaining introduction to Costa Rica's biodiversity. Trails lead through three representative ecosystems, passing a serpentarium, an ant farm, and tarantula and frog exhibits. There are guided tours by naturalists, excellent videos on biodiversity, exhibition halls that give an overview of the national parks' system, a pleasant restaurant, a lakeside café, and an excellent shop with unusual gifts for naturalists aged nine to ninety.

Heredia ❻ (pop. 123,000) lies 11km (7 miles) north of San José, and is known as *La Ciudad de las Flores* (The City of Flowers). The city was first settled in 1706 by the Spanish, long before San José was even thought of. Historically a bastion of coffee wealth, the city today is even more prosperous, fueled by affluent suburbs housing professionals and Costa Rica's burgeoning middle class. Lots of trendy new stores are

An owl butterfly, part of the country's incredible biodiversity.

THE DAY THE EARTH MOVED

On January 8, 2009, an earthquake registering 6.1 on the Richter scale shook Costa Rica from top to bottom. It was the country's strongest earthquake in 150 years. The epicenter of the earthquake was Cinchona, a dairy village just west of Poás Volcano. Entire houses disappeared in minutes, swallowed in a giant landslide that also destroyed the highway from Varablanca heading northeast to Sarapiquí. Almost 100 people were killed or listed missing, and more than 1,200 people were displaced.

As devastating as the quake was for residents, it was also a disaster for the area's tourism, and therefore for local people's jobs. Poás National Park was closed until damage could be repaired. More than 400 people had to be evacuated from the area near the La Paz Waterfall, where the largest landslide occurred. Some were airlifted by helicopter and some hardy tourists hiked out on foot.

The winding, scenic road to Puerto Viejo de Sarapiquí was closed indefinitely, and all traffic re-routed through Braulio Carrillo to the east or San Carlos (Ciudad Quesada) to the west. Part of the road has since reopened, from Varablanca as far as the La Paz Waterfall Gardens. But one of the most scenic drives in the country has probably been lost forever.

popping up, reflecting the global spread of North American brands and the gentrification of the town. **The National University** is located in Heredia; it turns out the nation's teachers and has one of (www.una. ac.cr) the best veterinarian schools in Latin America.

The old town center, with its colonial Casa de Cultura, pitted fort tower, and lovely church, all facing the Parque Central, is a pleasant place to stroll. The **Inmaculada Concepción**, constructed in 1796, is adorned with bells brought from Cuzco, Peru, and its 'seismic Baroque' construction has enabled it to survive many earth tremors.

Alpine scenery

Take the road to **San Rafael de Heredia**, known for its impressive, cream-colored Gothic church, a landmark for many kilometers around, and begin the ascent into the mountains. Driving up the road to Los Angeles, you may get the feeling of having suddenly entered into an Austrian watercolor landscape. Wealthy *Ticos* of earlier

Fruit stall at San Rafael de Heredia's Sunday market.

generations were educated in Europe and returned to their country with a great appreciation for the architecture of Northern Europe, which is highly evident in this cool, mountain area.

Above San Rafael the temperature drops dramatically. About 8km (5 miles) above the town, in wonderfully fresh mountain air at mile-high altitude, **Hotel and Villas La Condesa** (www.hotellacondesa.com) offers horseback riding in the surrounding hills, hiking, an indoor swimming pool, luxury rooms, and a conference center. Along the way you will pass a sign to the private El Castillo Country Club, playground to the established old families that live here. The road beyond El Castillo continues to **Monte de la Cruz** ❼ where a huge, illuminated cross sits in a cloud forest reserve. This is a favorite destination for Sunday hikers.

Costa Ricans like to stroll these mountain roads, especially on Sunday, the traditional day for visiting with family; bus services are reduced on Sunday, further necessitating walking. *Tico* drivers are used to sharing the

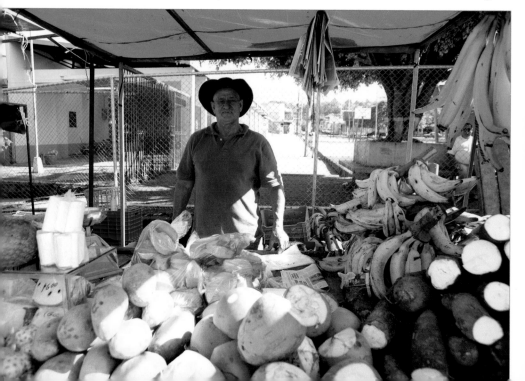

shoulderless roads with pedestrians, but some foreigners in rental cars can find such driving conditions unnerving. There are quieter dirt roads with little traffic and country paths that are perfect for hiking, but you will need a guide to find them. Rich Tandlich (tel: 2267 6325), a longtime local resident and guide, knows them all.

Follow the signs along the road to **Hotel Chalet Tirol** (www.hotelchalettirol.com), driving through a residential area of weekend cottages and retirement homes set in alpine fields. The road leads through a cypress forest where sun filters warmly through branches and dapples meadows of wild flowers. Chalet Tirol sits in the middle of a cloud forest reserve bordering Braulio Carrillo National Park. A fern-choked trail winding under orchid and bromeliad-laden old trees allows visitors to hike for several hours through the cloud reserve to the border of the national park. The hotel's A-frame wooden cottages are set around a miniature Swiss village.

Descending into the warmth of the valley below, the road to San José de la Montaña passes farms growing flowers for export in the wonderfully fresh, cool mountain air.

Barva and environs

In **Barva de Heredia** ❽, founded in 1561, colonial-era adobe houses surround the central park, giving the entire area the atmosphere of a colonial town. If you stand on the steps in front of the adobe **Basílica de Barva**, which dates back to 1767, and look out over the red tile-roofed adobe houses to the mountains beyond, you will get a sense of what the Central Valley probably looked like in the 18th century. The Basílica de Barva was built on an ancient Amerindian burial ground. Close by is the small grotto of the **Virgen de Lourdes** (1913).

In the hills just outside Barva is the lively and entertaining Aventura de Café tour at **Café Britt** ❾ (tel: 2277

1600; www.coffeetour.com; tours daily 9.30am, 11am, 1.15pm, and 3.15pm). Guides at this coffee farm take you through every step of the process, from raw bean to hot, steaming final product, using a multimedia, theatrical approach. If you need it, transport to and from San José is available. Ask to taste the ripe, red fruit that surrounds the coffee bean. It is surprisingly sweet and good, though beware of eating too many at once as they act as a mild laxative.

In **Santa Lucía de Barva**, 4km (2.5 miles) north of Heredia, the **Museo de Cultura Popular** (tel: 2260 1619; www.museo.una.ac.cr; Mon–Fri 8am–4pm organised groups only, booking essential; open to the public Sat–Sun 10am–5pm) has renovated the charming and graceful González house, a 19th-century home, built just around the time that coffee cultivation was beginning to change Costa Rican life forever.

Barva Volcano

There is a steep road to the **Volcán Barva** ❿ that runs just above the

Built in 1797, the church in San Rafael has survived numerous earthquakes.

The attractive central courtyard of Las Ruinas, Cartago.

town of Barva de Heredia, through San José de la Montaña and on toward Sacramento. The volcano is on the western side of Parque Nacional Braulio Carrillo; the approach road is in terrible condition and cars without four-wheel-drive must be left 4km (2.5 miles) from the park entrance. From the ranger station it's an enjoyable hike through cloud forest dripping with moss and epiphytes to the crater lake. An alternative one-hour hike will take you to **Laguna Barva** (2,900 meters/9,514ft), a green lake in an extinct crater rimmed with trees.

If you are still feeling energetic, there is the smaller Laguna Copey to explore, another 40-minute walk away. You may be rewarded by sighting a quetzal there – but don't bank on it. Wherever you hike on Volcán Barva, bring rain gear, a compass, and waterproof shoes or boots – even in the dry season – and be sure to keep to the designated paths. The roads in this area crisscross one another and are not at all well

Basílica de Nuestra Señora de los Angeles.

marked. Even *Josefinos* taking Sunday drives have to stop passersby and ask for directions.

Cartago

Cartago ⑪, 22km (14 miles) south of San José, was the capital of Costa Rica until 1823, when it lost its status to San José. Most of its illustrious colonial past is lost, however, since repeated earthquakes and eruptions of Volcán Irazú have destroyed most of the colonial-era buildings. Today it is both a market town for the surrounding farmers and an education center, with many historical and illustrious *colegios* (high schools) and universities. You will see swarms of students dressed in neat uniforms that identify their school allegiance.

Throughout their history, Cartagans have attempted to build a temple to Santiago (St James the Apostle), patron saint of Spain. The first church, begun in 1562, was finished in 1570, and was one of only two in the entire country. When it was destroyed, a stronger building was erected in 1580 on the same site. This, too, was leveled by the trembling earth. Subsequent churches met the same fate, and when Cartago's massive cathedral, begun early in the 20th century, was toppled by the 1910 earthquake, all efforts to rebuild were abandoned. The roofless cathedral walls with their empty Gothic windows still stand. The site, called **Las Ruinas** (The Ruins), is now a popular and romantic spot with a lovely garden in the center of town.

Cartago, once the center of Costa Rican culture, is still her religious center. The enormous **Basílica de Nuestra Señora de los Angeles** (Basilica of Our Lady of the Angels), a domed, Byzantine structure that dominates the landscape for many kilometers, was built in honor of Costa Rica's patron saint, *La Negrita*, the Black Virgin. It is worth a look inside to see the lovely stained-glass windows and the wood columns painted to look like marble.

Lankester Botanical Gardens

From Cartago it is a short trip to the **Lankester Jardín Botánico** ⑬

(Lankester Botanical Gardens; www.jbl.ucr.ac.cr; daily 8.30am–4.30pm) in Paraíso de Cartago, named, so legend has it, by weary Spaniards moving inland from the Atlantic coast who found its cooler weather and lack of malarial mosquitoes paradisiacal. English botanist Charles Lankester, sent to Costa Rica by a British company to work on coffee planting, arrived in 1900 at the age of 21. The coffee venture failed, but he decided to stay and bought 15 hectares (37 acres) of land to preserve local flora, especially orchids and bromeliads, and to regenerate a natural forest. Today, Lankester Gardens is run by the University of Costa Rica. Hundreds of species of orchids attract orchid fanciers from all over the world, particularly in the peak flowering months of January through April. The garden is also a great bird-watching spot.

The Sanchiri Mirador, 2km (1.2 miles) south of Paraíso, not far from Lankester Gardens, is a good place to stop for a light snack where there are stunning views across the Orosí valley.

Pink torch ginger flower in the Orosí River Valley.

La Negrita, the Black Virgin.

LA NEGRITA

The origins of Cartago's Basílica de Nuestra Señora de los Angeles are rooted in the miraculous. The story goes that in 1635, a young girl walking through the forest that once grew on the site of the basilica discovered a dark-skinned statue of the Virgin Mary. A priest carried the statue, called La Negrita, to the parish church, but it mysteriously returned, twice, to its location in the forest.

In 1926, the Catholic Church built a basilica on the spot to house the statue. Today, in the shrine room, cases full of abandoned crutches, plaster casts, and votive offerings (some made of gold) representing various parts of the body testify to the cures effected by La Negrita, who is Costa Rica's patron saint. Water from the spring behind the church is also said to have healing powers and the faithful fill their bottles from there.

On the patron saint's feast day, August 2, thousands of pilgrims gather at the basilica. Many walk the 22km (14 miles) from San José, the most devoted penitents making the last part of the journey on their knees. So revered is the saint that some of the faithful walk from as far afield as Panamá and Nicaragua. The image of the black Virgin is carried in a solemn procession, through the city and back to its shrine.

EAT

Near Orosí is La Casona del Cafetal (www. lacasonadelcafetal.com), a restaurant set in the hacienda of a large coffee plantation overlooking Lake Cachí. The weekend buffets are extremely popular and lavish, with a whole table of coffee-flavored desserts.

Ujarrás

South of Cartago the landscape becomes green, misty, and magical, especially during the verdant rainy season. At **Ujarrás** ⓭, on a beautiful site in a sea of *chayote* vines, stand the ruins of Costa Rica's oldest church, Nuestra Señora de la Limpia, dating from the 17th century.

The first place of worship constructed in this region was not the church, but a shrine in honor of La Virgen del Rescate de Ujarrás, who, in 1565, it is said, appeared to an Amerindian fishing on the banks of the Reventazón River. The apparition came from inside a small tree. The man carried the trunk to the center of Ujarrás, but by the time he got there, it had become so heavy that even a dozen men could not lift it. The phenomenon was interpreted by the Franciscan fathers as a sign that the Virgin wanted them to construct a shrine on that spot to be used by both the indigenous population and the Spanish, and so it was constructed.

A hundred years later, in 1666, so the story goes, a band of pirates led by the notorious Edward Mansfield and Henry Morgan landed on the Atlantic coast of Costa Rica with the intention of sacking the country. The Spanish governor, Juan López de la Flor, assembled all available fighting men and sent everyone else to the mission to pray. The pirates came inland as far as Turrialba and then, mysteriously, abruptly turned back.

Some say the pirates were tricked by de la Flor: other accounts attribute their retreat to a miracle worked by the Virgin. The grateful townspeople built the church of Ujarrás to commemorate the miraculous event, though it was destroyed 100 years later by an earthquake. Its picturesque remains, slightly marred by the necessary addition of steel girders, stand among gardens and trees draped with Spanish moss. There is a pleasant picnic area beside the church, and clean restrooms nearby.

The Orosí River Valley

A few kilometers beyond Orosí, the **Cachí Hydroelectric Dam** channels waters from a reservoir on the

Luxuriant Lankester Gardens.

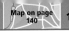

Reventazón and Orosí rivers into an immense spillway. The concrete-dam structure contrasts sharply with the lush natural terrain surrounding it, as does the power of the rushing water with the peace of the river.

Just west of the dam is **La Casa del Soñador** (The House of the Dreamer), a simple two-story cane structure embellished with primitive wood sculptures. Here Macedonio Quesada, a famous Costa Rican primitivist artist, lived and worked until his death in 1995. His two sons work here now, producing melancholy *campesino* (peasant) and religious figures from coffee wood. Visitors are welcome and the pieces can be bought for very small sums.

The town of **Orosí** ⓮ is untouched by the earthquakes that have leveled the colonial structures of Cartago, and it retains the look of an earlier Costa Rica, with wide streets and wooden houses with painted verandahs. Make your first stop the colonial church of San José de Orosí (the oldest church still in use in Costa Rica) and the former Franciscan monastery, now the small but fascinating **Museo de Arte Religioso** (Museum of Religious Art; daily 9am–5pm), just north of the church, which features artifacts from the colonial era. Take a walk around town and have a snack at one of the *sodas* (neighborhood restaurants) or take a dip in the spacious heated *balneario* (pool). Just above the valley there is a lookout site (*mirador*) and park, maintained by the ICT (Costa Rican Institute of Tourism). The large area of sloping, well-trimmed lawns provides spectacular views over the Reventazón River with Cachí to the left and Orosí to the right. It makes a perfect spot for a picnic and a pleasant walk.

Tapantí National Park

The upper part of the **Orosí Valley** is one of the rainiest areas in the country, which renders it unsuitable for agriculture and means that it still has magnificent virgin rainforest. **Parque Nacional Tapantí** ⓯ (tel: 2571 1781; daily 8am–4pm) protects the rivers that supply San José with water and electricity. It also offers excellent birdwatching and hiking. Birdwatchers

FACT

Vásquez de Coronado wrote to the Spanish king of Cartago: 'I have never seen a more beautiful valley, and I have laid out a city between [its] two rivers.'

San José de Orosí, the oldest church still in use in Costa Rica.

will want to get an early start to arrive in Tapantí when the park opens at 8am. The drive from San José is particularly beautiful at dawn, passing misty valleys and lush coffee farms, but the last 10km (6 miles) is over a rough road.

Trails are well marked in the lower part of the refuge. Oropendolas – black, raven-sized birds with golden tail feathers and stout ivory-colored bills – nest in noisy colonies within the park. Clusters of 30 or more pendulous nests hang from branches high in the trees. Visitors will usually hear oropendolas before seeing them, as the males let out a gurgling, liquid-like song, then bow and flap their wings to the females in unusual courtship displays.

The Orosí River runs parallel to the Oropendola Trail, inviting hikers to cool their feet in the water and lie back on the smooth, warm boulders for a mid-morning snooze in the sun. If you are a strong swimmer, you can also jump in, but beware of the fast-running current. Given its reputation as the wettest national park, though, it

The rainforest in Tapantí National Park.

is always advisable to bring rain gear and a change of warm clothes.

Turrialba

Turrialba ⓰ (pop. 70,000) is a busy town bustling with people talking, yelling, buying, selling. The open fruit and vegetable market that lines the sidewalk along the river features some of the freshest and best-looking produce available in Costa Rica, most of it grown in the hills above town. Turrialba's reputation as a whitewater river-rafting center is growing, and rafters and kayakers from all over the world are discovering the Reventazón and Pacuare rivers. Looming above the town is Volcán Turrialba, spectacularly active since 2014, when the first magma eruption in 100 years took place followed by strong eruptions of ash and rocks. In May 2015 the volcano spewed a column of ash 2,500 meters (8,200ft) high and sent large rocks as far as 1km (0.6 miles) away.

Just a few kilometers beyond the town of Turrialba on the highway is **CATIE**, the **Centro Agronómico**

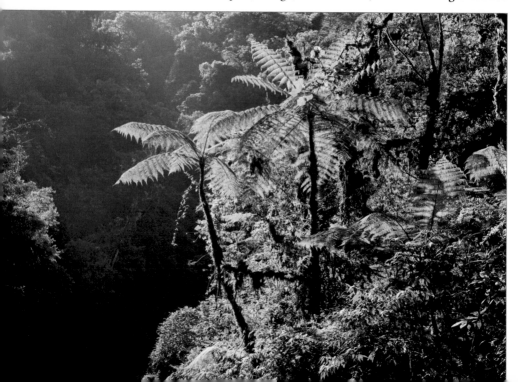

Tropical de Investigación y Enseñanza ⓱ (Tropical Agricultural Research and Higher Education Center). On this 800-hectare (1,975-acre) research plantation, scientists are experimenting with the introduction of more than 5,000 varieties of 335 species of crops with economic potential. More than 2,500 varieties of coffee and 450 varieties of cacao, as well as numerous varieties of bananas and pejibaye palms, are part of the seed bank of CATIE.

Work is being done here on the critical problems of deforestation, overgrazing, and the sensitive ecology of the river basins. Guides demonstrate the cultivation, processing, and care of palms, coffee, cacao, and orchids, and there is also a guided tour of the Botanical Garden. If you are not visiting with a group, call ahead to arrange a tour (tel: 2256 2700).

Visitors to CATIE and the surrounding areas can stay at modest hotels in town or, about 5km (3 miles) out of town on the road toward Siquirres, the luxurious **Casa Turire** (http://hotelcasaturire.com) is a lavish plantation-style hotel in the grounds of a sugar cane, coffee, and macadamia nut plantation. In the mountains above the valley, not far away, is the Turrialtico, which has affordable rooms, some with lovely views of Volcán Turrialba.

Guayabo National Monument

The site of a pre-Columbian city, the **Monumento Nacional Guayabo** ⓲ (tel: 2559 1220; daily 8am–3.30pm) sits on the slope of Volcán Turrialba, 18km (11 miles) from Turrialba. Archeologists are still unclear as to whether this large site was purely ceremonial or a combination administrative and ceremonial center. The ancient stone ruins and the remains of imposing stone roads radiating out to surrounding areas date from 1000 BC to AD 1400, when the site was abandoned for some as yet unknown reason, prior to the arrival of the Spaniards. Speculation suggests disease or starvation.

Visitors can take an interesting guided tour along a forest trail to the excavated area, which contains a

TIP

Braulio Carrillo Park and Volcán Irazú Park both suffer from security problems. Don't leave anything of value in a parked car, and if you intend hiking, check first with the park authorities as to the security situation.

The ruins of Nuestra Señora de la Limpia, Ujarrás.

complex system of stone aqueducts, building foundations, and roadways amid a setting of guava trees, wild impatiens, and clusters of nests. Stone-lined graves, now empty, served as the first indication to archeologists that a cultural site was nearby. In addition, there are several large petrographs, the significance of which remains a mystery.

About 20km (12 miles) north of Guayabo, on the slope of Turrialba volcano, is Volcán Turrialba Lodge, with comfortable wooden cabins and wood-burning stoves to ward off the evening chill. Hikes and horseback rides to the volcano's extinct crater are exhilarating in the clear mountain air.

Irazú Volcano National Park

Easily accessible from Cartago is **Parque Nacional Volcán Irazú** ⓳ (tel: 2200 5025; daily 8am–3.30pm), atop the massive volcano that dominates the landscape on the eastern side of the Central Valley. From the 3,800-meter (11,000ft) summit, it is possible on a clear day to see both the Caribbean and the Pacific. More

often, you will climb above the clouds on your way to the top. Irazú, Costa Rica's highest volcano, also known as El Coloso, broke a 30-year period of silence with a single, noisy eruption on December 8, 1994. The previous eruption, on March 19, 1963, the day of the arrival of President John F. Kennedy in Costa Rica, was even more powerful.

For two years Irazú continued to shower ash over much of the Central Valley. People habitually carried umbrellas to protect themselves. Ash piled up on the Reventazón River, causing it to flood and destroy 300 homes. Roofs caved in from the weight of the ash and San José's air was temporarily turned black.

A visit to Irazú today is a relatively easy half-day tour from San José. Visitors can go to the top ridge, walk along the rim of the main crater, and look across an otherworldly landscape consisting of a brilliant green lake and black and gray slopes, punctuated with plumes of white steam jetting into the air, escaping from fissures in the rock. There are also wonderful

Volcán Irazú.

hiking and birding trails in the Prusia sector of the park.

Braulio Carrillo National Park

Only 45 minutes from bustling downtown San José is **Parque Nacional Braulio Carrillo** ⑳ (daily 8am–3.30pm), a true wilderness. Take the highway to Limón, passing through the Zurquí tunnel, the one and only tunnel in the country.

Occupying 445 sq km (170 sq miles) of mostly primary forest, Braulio Carrillo National Park was founded in 1978 thanks to pressure exerted by environmentalists who feared that the opening of a highway between San José and Guápiles would provide loggers and developers with access to rapidly vanishing virgin forest; deforestation had followed the opening of many other roads throughout the country. A compromise was reached: the road would go through, but the 32,000 hectares (80,000 acres) of virgin forest surrounding the highway would be preserved as a national park. The park thus embodies some ideals of enlightened progress.

Braulio Carrillo contains five distinctly separate forest habitats, dominated by the wet tropical forest. Hundreds of varieties of orchids and ferns, and the majority of the bird species native to Costa Rica, are found here. In order to understand the life cycles, to spot the camouflaged wildlife, and avoid missing hidden spectacular vistas, it is essential to arrange for a guide through the National Parks Service (www.costarica-nationalparks.com) or an ecotourism agency. Although the territory is vast, there are few through trails and many solo hikers get lost for days. The lingering impression of Braulio Carrillo is of vastness: huge canyons, misty mountains, and the ubiquitous broad-leaf plant, called the Poor Man's Umbrella, covering the hillsides.

The easiest way to experience the forest here is to walk the trails at the **Quebrada Gonzales** station, about 17km (11 miles) past the tunnel. The Las Palmas Trail, starting from the parking lot, gradually climbs up from the highway, quickly immersing you in the forest. This is a great birdwatching trail, but you have to get there early. The trails are often muddy, and snakes are sometimes basking on the trails, so be sure to wear sturdy boots, long pants, and mosquito repellent. If you don't have all the right gear, all is not lost, as the birding from the parking lot can also be excellent.

Rainforests made easy

For a bird's-eye view of the forest canopy adjacent to Braulio Carrillo, you can take a ride on the **Rainforest Aerial Tram** ㉑ (tel: 2257 5961; www.rainforestadventure.com; charge includes tram ride, video, and a short hike; reservations recommended). This is an 80-minute, 2.6km (1.5-mile) trip through the forest's treetops, 35 meters (100ft) above the forest floor. The 'tram' is an open, metal gondola, big enough for five passengers and a naturalist guide, equipped with a walkie-talkie to pass along information on wildlife sightings. Visitors can experience the forest canopy up

Dense woodland, Braulio Carillo National Park.

close, breathe the steamy air, and catch the unforgettable tropical smell of damp, mossy tree trunks.

Although it is on every tour company's itinerary, this is not the most exciting experience and the chances of spotting wildlife from the tram are remote. You will have better luck down on the ground, during your short hike to the tram.

Amphibian lovers won't want to miss the **Butterfly and Frog Garden** here, where you can see the famous poison-dart frogs and Costa Rica's iconic red-eyed leaf frog (separate tour). The Aerial Tram is about 5km (3 miles) north of Río Sucio on the road to Puerto Limón, about 50 minutes from San José.

San José suburbs

On the west side of San José lie the prosperous suburbs of Pavas, Rohrmoser, Escazú, and Santa Ana. The largely residential **Rohrmoser** and **Pavas** are chiefly of interest because of the presence of the United States Embassy and the embassies of other countries. Many diplomatic personnel

Sample fresh, locally grown produce and support small-scale farms at farmers' markets.

live along the wide, nearly treeless streets of Rohrmoser, in modern houses protected by wrought-iron grille work.

Escazú ㉒ was originally a crossroads of trails between Amerindian villages. Because water was abundant there, the Amerindians found it a good place to spend the night on their journeys, and gave it the name Escazú, which means 'resting place.'

Spanish settlers were also attracted to Escazú: they settled in the hills and began farming. It was during these early days that Escazú became known as La Ciudad de las Brujas (The City of the Witches). Today, the legends of witches remain, but the old adobe houses, painted blue and white to ward off *las brujas*, are being replaced by high-rise luxury condominiums and shopping centers.

Escazú is an interesting if sometimes chaotic blend of old Costa Rica and a modern, international community, with a large contingent of North Americans. It is often jokingly referred to as 'Gringolandia.' The town center has adobe buildings, an attractive, Ravenna-style church, and, of course, a soccer field. Just outside of town are enclaves of fancy homes owned by North Americans, Europeans, and wealthy local people, drawn to Escazú by the agreeable climate and the superlative views. Unfortunately, this has led to the town's main road being clogged with traffic, and lined with fastfood chains, clothing stores, and tall condominium buildings.

In the hills to the east of the town, in an area called **Bello Horizonte**, are many fine old residences with lovely gardens. It is worth a drive through the hills of Bello Horizonte to visit **Biesanz Woodworks** (tel: 2289 4337; www.biesanz.com), the studio-workshop of Barry Biesanz, an accomplished artist who works with Costa Rican hardwoods. Wooden bowls and boxes, remarkable for their grace and fluidity, are on display in his *hacienda*-style showroom, which is surrounded by an interesting herb garden with an ornamental pond.

San Rafael de Escazú ㉓ is a newer section of town along the highway to Santa Ana. It has several shiny commercial centers where the town's glamorous inhabitants do their shopping. On the old road between Escazú and Santa Ana, across from the Los Laureles shopping center, there is a large walled compound with lights, guards, and surveillance paraphernalia. It isn't a high-security penitentiary: it's the residence of the United States Ambassador to Costa Rica.

Santa Ana

Although condominiums, luxury villas, and shopping centers – the Lindora Road artery road is a traffic-clogged shoppers' mecca – are rapidly urbanizing the town, a rural atmosphere still survives in **Santa Ana** ㉔ a town once famous for its onions, a few of which hang braided on the lintels and eaves of a few rustic restaurants along the road. On the west side of town there are still a few sprawling emporia selling pottery, baskets, and locally grown onions.

Lovely, rustic Santa Ana church, built in the 1870s, reverberates with the sound of chamber music at the Baroque Music Festival, usually held the second week of November. It's an intimate, evocative setting with excellent acoustics.

High in the hills above Santa Ana, you can sit under the stars, overlooking the city lights, and enjoy the balmy breezes at **Rancho Macho**. Or you could come on a weekend afternoon to listen to traditional marimba music. Another romantic spot is the elegant **Mirador Valle Azul**, where you can drink in sparkling city views along with fine wines and Italian food, high above Escazú.

For a taste of modern luxury, the **Hotel Alta** (www.thealtahotel.com), halfway between Escazú and Santa Ana on the old road, is hard to beat. It has an excellent restaurant and sometimes exhibits local artists' work.

If you are in search of more ordinary pursuits, look for **Multiplaza** (http://multiplaza.com), one of the largest shopping malls in all of Central America. It is just off the toll road on the way to Santa Ana, across the road from El Camino Real Hotel.

Ciudad Colón can be reached by back roads from Santa Ana, through

Red-eyed tree frogs are not endangered but their habitats are shrinking.

Butterflies are a common sight around the hedges of Parque Francisco Alvarado.

The craft centre at Sarchí is famed for its hand-painted ox-carts, seen throughout the country.

rolling hills, or by way of the new toll road. It is best known for the **University for Peace** (www.upeace.org), which is on a well-marked road not far out of town. The university, sponsored by the United Nations to study the ways of peace, and to offer a counter to the teachings of war colleges that predominate in many other countries, offers graduate courses to students from all over the world. There are hiking and birding trails throughout the property, as well as popular picnic areas beside a lake populated by geese and ducks.

Returning to Santa Ana via back roads, you will pass the **Hacienda El Rodeo** (tel: 2249 1013; www.haciendael rodeo.com), a popular weekend restaurant where you can hire horses. The *comida típica* food is nourishing but nothing special, but the gently rolling hills above the open-air restaurant are beautiful and perfect for horseback riding.

Sarchí and surrounding villages

For a half-day excursion of craft shopping and sightseeing around typical Central Valley coffee towns,

head north through Alajuela toward Sarchí, stopping en route at **Grecia** ㉕. This little place is renowned for its tidiness, claiming to be the cleanest town in Latin America. Compared to most towns in Costa Rica, it certainly is remarkably well kept. It is definitely worth taking a stroll around the Central Park and visiting the town's unusual, dark-red Church of Our Lady of Mercy, built in the 1890s with metal pieces imported from Belgium.

Just a few minutes' walk away is the popular **World of Snakes** (tel: 2494 3700; www.theworldofsnakes.com; daily 8am–5pm), a serpentarium with 50 snake species from all over the world, plus some other interesting reptiles.

The approach to the mountain town of **Sarchí** ㉖ is unmistakable. Swirling, colorful decorative designs adorn practically every bus stop, bar, bakery, restaurant, and house. In the town's central park in front of the wedding-cake white church, there is a giant painted ox-cart, weighing in at 2 tons and delighting camera-toting tourists.

DECORATED CARTS

Around 1910, as legend has it, a *campesino* (peasant) was crossing the Beneficio la Luisa when it occurred to him to decorate his ox-cart wheels with colorful mandala-like designs inspired by ancient Moorish decoration. The art form caught on and each district in Costa Rica had its own special design. Locals could tell just by looking at the cart where the driver was from. Each cart also had its own *chirrido*, or song of the wheels, by which people could identify who was passing by, without even glancing upward. As late as 1960, the ox-cart was still the most typical mode of transportation, able to handle the rugged Costa Rican terrain. Things have changed, but you will still see the occasional ox-cart on country roads.

Sarchí is a crafts center heavily geared toward the tourist trade, where you can see artisans painting traditional ox-cart designs (see page 158) and creating household furnishings out of tropical hardwoods.

There are pleasant little roadside stalls on the outskirts of Sarchí selling homemade candied fruits, honey, and fudge. In comparison to the large commercialized furniture shops that predominate in Sarchí, a visit to these small stands is extremely friendly and personal, like stepping into a Costa Rican home for a chat.

About 15km (9 miles) up the road is the town of **Zarcero** ㉗. Should you arrive on a day when the highland clouds are swirling through the town, famous for its cheese and fruit orchards, or when a drizzling fog is bathing everything in soft, diffused light, you might feel that you have just walked into a dreamland.

Parque Francisco Alvarado

Unique in Costa Rica, and possibly the world, is the **Parque Francisco Alvarado** in Zarcero, a topiary extravaganza created by Evangelisto Blanco, a local gardener, who clipped and pruned cypress bushes and hedges into a whimsical garden of amazing shapes and creatures: birds, rabbits, oxen, dinosaurs, a monkey riding a motorcycle, an elephant with light bulbs for eyes.

Evangelisto has been sculpting the hedges for more than four decades, and the energetic compulsion of his work has been compared to the creations of modernist architect Antonio Gaudí, in Barcelona. Unable to afford marble or stone, Evangelisto works with the plants as his medium of self-expression, creating extraordinary sculpted shrubs.

About 8km (5 miles) after the turnoff for Sarchí, along the Inter-American Highway, is the exit for the 200-year-old colonial town of **Palmares**. This lovely area used to be a tobacco-growing center. Unaffected by the vicissitudes of modern tourism, it is a model town through which to stroll and view typical Tico life, except in mid-January when it hosts a huge, noisy music festival that attracts thousands of revelers.

Parque Francisco Alvarado, Zarcero.

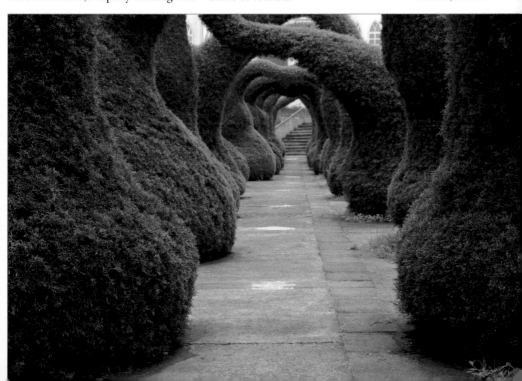

POTTERS, SCULPTORS, AND GOLDSMITHS

The Amerindians of Costa Rica left behind many gold, jade, pottery, and stone artifacts. Sadly, most of their traditions were destroyed by the *conquistadores*.

Because Costa Rica was a cultural and commercial meeting point for ancient American civilizations, native Costa Ricans absorbed and modified known techniques in ceramics, gold and jade work, weaving, and stone carving. Early inhabitants, especially in the pre-Columbian port of Nicoya (in the province of Guanacaste), traded with travelers from as far away as Ecuador and Mexico. They also developed their own style of decorating pottery: beasts that are half-bird, half-man; and people with exaggerated genitals, suggesting a fertility-rite culture. Examples of the pottery can be found throughout Central America. Visitors to the Gold Museum, the Jade Museum, and the National Museum in San José can see early pieces and learn more of their history.

While the Spanish never found the gold deposits that inspired the name 'Rich Coast,' early Costa Ricans worked with both gold and jade to make decorative pieces. Although these traditions have been all but lost, pottery and the more modern craft of ox-cart decoration have been revived by the tourist dollar. For pottery, visit Guaitil and Nicoya; for other crafts, try Sarchí. Other examples of Costa Rica's crafts are found in the south of the country: *molas* (hand-sewn appliqué) pieces are produced around Drake Bay, and both grotesque and beautiful balsawood masks are made by the Boruca people.

Vestiges of Chorotega culture linger on in pottery produced in Guaitil, where the entire village is an open-air workshop and showroom.

Inexpensive vases and pots, decorated with whimsical animals and other pre-Columbian images, are for sale at roadside stands in Guanacaste.

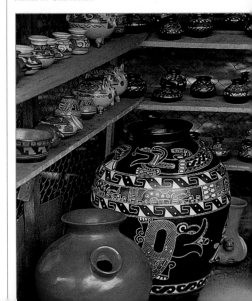

Reproduction pre-Columbian jewelry and figures are popular souvenirs.

In a Sarchí workshop, an array of paint cans stands ready to transform traditional ox-cart wheels into colorful kaleidoscopes. In the town's central park, you can snap a photo of the world's biggest painted ox cart.

ORNAMENTED OX-CARTS

Used exclusively to transport coffee and other agricultural products until well into the 20th century, wooden ox-carts are unmistakably Costa Rican, and symbolize the self-reliance of the small farmer. The father of two-time president Oscar Arias made his original fortune hauling coffee by ox-cart to Puntarenas.

Ideally suited for the country's mountainous conditions and rutted dirt roads, ox-carts are still common in many parts of the country. The carts, which come in all sizes (including a miniature about the size of a toy car), are made in Sarchí, the wooden crafts capital of the country. There, master carvers began painting the carts in the early part of the 20th century. Originally adorned with bright colors and geometric patterns, these days ox-carts are being decorated with jungle scenes, wild animals, flowers, and other non-traditional designs.

Visitors to Sarchí can have a go at painting the carts themselves with fine-tipped brushes, or alternatively they can leave it to the experts and order a custom-painted cart; these are often used as home bars or as decorations at hotels and the country estates of the wealthy.

…de figurine.

A family tradition of whittling lives on in the charming, wooden 'House of the Dreamer,' carved by sculptor Macedonio Quesada in the Orosí Valley. His sons now create fascinating figures out of coffee-tree roots, for sale at very reasonable prices.

Traditional Ox-cart, near San Isidro, Central Valley

Playa Espadilla Sur, Manuel Antonio National Park, Central Pacific.

THE CENTRAL PACIFIC

The Central Pacific beaches are among the best in Costa Rica, and there is a host of natural wonders to see en route. Manuel Antonio National Park is the stuff of tropical dreams.

Main Attractions
Crocodiles at Tárcoles Bridge
Parque Nacional Carara
Parque Nacional Manuel Antonio
Surfing at Playa Hermosa
Playa Espadilla

When the chaos of San José becomes a bit too much, get away from it all and onto a Pacific beach. A toll highway to the Pacific has put Playa Jacó, one of the country's most developed seaside destinations, less than two hours' drive of the capital. If you prefer something a little less hectic, some of the country's finest beaches, in and around Manuel Antonio National Park, are just an hour's drive farther south of Jacó.

The road to the coast

If you go by car, and want to take the scenic route to the coast (as opposed to the new highway), turn off the highway toward Atenas, past the Juan Santamaría International Airport, then head through La Garita de Alajuela. One of the first lowland towns that you will approach is Orotina, festooned with fresh fruit stands. The road to Orotina winds through coffee plantations built on precariously steep slopes. Driving along the ledges of these mountains, you will be treated to views of rich green farmland and undulating valleys.

As you approach the **Río Tárcoles bridge ❶**, you will notice tourists clustered at the railings, cameras and binoculars aimed downward. The fascination here is **crocodiles** – gray, primordial behemoths, some as long as 7 meters (20ft), basking on the muddy banks or stealthily patrolling the brown river, with only snouts and crenelated spines showing above the water line. Most crocodilians in Costa Rica are the smaller caiman species. This is the easiest place to spot as many as 20 of these larger American crocodiles or *Crocodylus acutus* lurking here at the river's mouth.

The **Parque Nacional Carara ❷** (tel: 2637 1054; daily 8am–4pm),

Iced drinks for sale on Playa Espadilla, Manuel Antonio National Park.

one of the country's smallest reserves but richest in wildlife, borders the highway between Playa Jacó and Puntarenas just south of the bridge. Because Carara lies in a transitional zone between humid and dry forest, it sustains wildlife from mountainous terrain, primary and secondary forests, lagoons, and marshlands of the Tárcoles River. The vegetation in Carara covers a similarly broad range: from shady evergreens to towering rainforest giants draped with epiphytes and strangling vines.

Among the birds most commonly spotted here are toucans and araçaris (similar to toucans, but smaller) and endangered scarlet macaws. Squirrel, howler, white-faced, and spider monkeys are often seen, and, very, very rarely, wildcats such as margays, jaguarundis, ocelots, and jaguars. There are also sloths, coatis, and agoutis, as well as a variety of reptiles, and lovely, blue morpho butterflies. Guides are invaluable in interpreting the ecological complexity of this reserve; they are available right at the park entrance, or by advance request (contact the National Parks Service; tel: 8383 9953).

In the evenings, when the lowlands cool, pairs of macaws fly down from their daytime feeding areas in the mountains. At sunset, park your car near the bridge over the Tárcoles River along the highway outside of the park entrance and listen for their raucous squawking as they fly to their roosting areas in the nearby coastal mangroves. Also watch for shorebirds and waders that frequent the estuary. Roseate spoonbills, with their startling pink plumage, are spectacular at sunset. Crocodiles bask on the river banks, apparently comatose, but they are waiting for a prize, such as a careless spoonbill.

Crocodile tours run along the Tárcoles River, but stay well away from irresponsible operators who encourage their clients to feed the crocs with pieces of meat. Once a crocodile associates a person with food, it is one dangerous animal.

Several kilometers from the Jacó–San José highway, 17km (10 miles) before Playa Jacó, you come to **La**

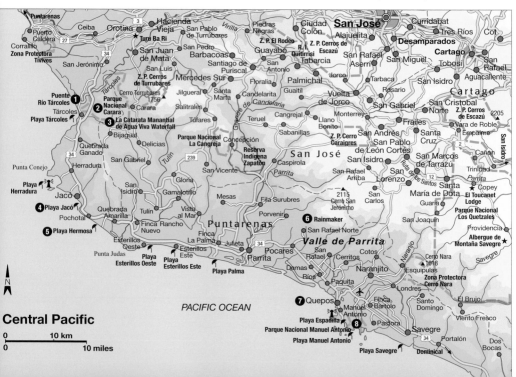

Central Pacific

0   10 km

0   10 miles

PACIFIC OCEAN

Catarata Manantial de Agua Viva Waterfall ❸ (daily 8am–3pm), a 200-meter (650ft) -high waterfall, one of the highest in the country. You can hike the 3km (2 miles) up to the falls if you are in good shape – take plenty of water with you – or you can drive up the dirt road 5km (3 miles) south of the entrance to **Villa Lapas Rainforest Resort** (www.villalapas.com), which offers hikes along suspension bridges, a canopy tour and comfortable rooms in an all-inclusive resort hotel.

The beaches

If you are anticipating the white-powder beaches washed by gentle, clear waters of tourist brochures, then the beaches of the Central Pacific could be something of a disappointment (Jacó sand is a dirty gray). The lure of these places is their proximity to San José, their big waves for surfers and their lively nightlife, not their picture-postcard perfection. Still, with a bit of exploration off the main road, away from the density and hustle of the central beach scene, you will find some clean and appealing beaches. **Playa Herradura** lies five minutes' drive north of Jacó, its waves are gentle, and there are trees for shade and for stringing hammocks on the public end of the beach. The other end is dominated by the huge Marriott Los Sueños resort and marina. **Playa Esterillos** is a long 11km (7-mile) stretch of mostly deserted beach, about 10km (6 miles) south of Jacó, but beware of strong riptides. Best to avoid Playa Tárcoles, which is polluted.

Jacó Beach

Playa Jacó ❹, once famous for its year-round surfing waves and raucous, party-time ambience fueled by plenty of cold beer, has morphed into a concrete collection of high-rise hotel chains, condominiums, and outposts of trendy San José sportswear shops and restaurant chains. There are still a few inexpensive *cabinas* to rent near the beach, but most accommodations are in hotels, with swimming pools, bars, air-conditioning, and tour packages to other points of interest in this

Exotic plumage of the scarlet macaw.

SAVING THE MACAWS

Scarlet macaws are the great glory of Carara National Park. These enormous red, yellow, and blue parrots mate for life and live for more than 30 years. They nest in December, and in January the young are still in their nests, easy prey for thieves who sell them on the black market. Public-education campaigns to discourage people from buying macaw chicks, along with checkpoints along the highways to search cars during peak vacation times, have had some effect in lowering the number of scarlet macaws in captivity. But it is impossible to estimate how many of the birds are still kept as pets by Costa Ricans. Thanks to conservation programs, there are more scarlet macaws in the wild than there were 10 years ago, but there are still fewer than 2,000 in the entire country.

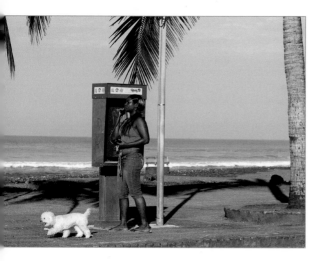

Making a call at Playa Jacó.

Nesting scarlet macaws, Carara National Park.

slightly more sophisticated venue than the raunchier but very popular Los Amigos across the street. Men should be aware that the companionship of a local girl may cost them more than the price of a few drinks, and thieves and drug-dealers add an unsavory note to the night scene.

A haven of relative elegance amid the honky-tonk Jacó atmosphere is Hotel Poseidon in the center of town on a quiet side street. The restaurant serves sophisticated fare with an Asian-infused take on fresh fish. At the far southern end of the beach, Hotel Club del Mar Resort offers another enclave of sophistication, comfort, and tranquillity.

Along the coast some 3km (2 miles) from Playa Jacó is **Playa Hermosa** ❺, a world-class surfing spot with very strong beach breaks. It's the venue for many national and international surfing competitions. It is an easily accessible place where there is also a variety of wading birds to observe: great white herons and snowy egrets; and great blue, little blue, tricolor, and little green herons. You may also see

coastal province. Perhaps the hotel pool is the best place to swim in Jacó since the water is not very clean and there are dangerous undercurrents. Jacó has no shortage of amusements: horses, bikes, scooters, and kayaks are available for rent. Chuck's W.O.W. Surf Shop (tel: 2643 3844; www.wowsurf.com) rents and sells surfboards, gives lessons, and posts a daily surf report. For dancing, try the Monkey Bar or Le Loft, a jacanas, walking on lily pads on their huge yellow feet; and black-bellied whistling ducks.

Head east on the coastal highway for 40km (24 miles) to the bustling plantation town of **Parrita**, dominated by an enormous African oil-palm development, which was established in 1985. Oil palms do very well here. Palm-oil workers live next to the highway, in plantation villages of two-story, brightly painted homes, set in a 'U' around what is the focal point of every *Tico* village: the soccer field.

Around 10km (6 miles) east of Parrita is the tiny village of Pocares from where you should turn inland and continue for around 6 to 7km (4 miles) to reach **Rainmaker ❻** (tel: 2777 3565; www.rainmakercostarica. org; Mon–Sat 7.30am–4pm), an exciting, 610-hectare (1,500-acre) private nature reserve and eco-project. Visitors can explore the rainforest canopy with the minimum of environmental disturbance, walking on boardwalks that link six suspension bridges; one bridge spans 90 meters (300ft), and at the highest point of the trail you will be a dizzying 25 stories above the jungle floor. Visits must be booked in advance with operators in Quepos and Manuel Antonio.

Manuel Antonio National Park

Once an important banana-shipping port, **Quepos ❼** is now something of a dormitory town and business center for Manuel Antonio, 7km (4 miles) away. There are some good accommodations, restaurants, shops, banks, and nightlife, a regular bus service, and the flavor of an old-time fishing and banana town. The sport fishing here is excellent. Hotel reservations are essential during the vacation season at both Manuel Antonio and Quepos.

The **Parque Nacional Manuel Antonio ❽** (tel: 2777 5185/5155; Tue–Sun 7am–4pm) encompasses three long strands of magnificent white sand, fringed by jungle and the Pacific Ocean, along with 7 sq km (3 sq miles) of forest. The beaches are clean and wide. Above them are tall cliffs covered in thick

Lizards abound in Manuel Antonio National Park.

CALDERA HIGHWAY

After 35 years in the planning stages, the much-anticipated 77km (48-mile) Caldera Highway finally opened in January 2010. The new toll road was designed to cut back on travel time to the Central Pacific beaches. Unfortunately, by the time it was finally built – with only two lanes most of the way and not enough passing lanes – the road could not actually cope with the prevailing amount of traffic. Long lines at toll booths have added to the congestion. If you do leave early enough on a weekday morning, though, you may just be lucky and sail through to Caldera in an hour. Note that at certain times on busy weekends, both lanes are dedicated to vehicles either heading out of San José or coming back into town.

Enjoying the beach at Manuel Antonio.

White-faced capuchin monkeys in Manuel Antonio National Park.

jungle vegetation. This park is one of the few places in the country where the primary forest comes down to the water's edge in places, sometimes allowing bathers to swim in the shade. In order to protect the ecosystem of the park, rangers allow a maximum of 600 visitors on weekdays and 800 on weekends. It's best to avoid weekends when the beaches can be crowded; early morning is the best time to visit when tourist groups are fewer and animal sightings easiest. There are always licensed naturalist guides available at the entrance to the park; hiring one will greatly increase your chances of spotting wildlife.

Playa Espadilla is the very popular public beach just outside the north end of the park. It is beautiful but it has unpredictable riptides. From Playa Espadilla, you enter the park across an estuary, which at high tide often requires a boat ride. To get to **Playa Espadilla Sur**, the first beach in the park, follow the jungle path across a long sandspit called a *tombolo*. **Playa Manuel Antonio** and **Playa Puerto**

Escondido require more hiking but the latter, accessible only at low tide, is less crowded. All provide relatively safe swimming, but watch out for rocks hidden by high tides.

There are excellent trails for hiking and wildlife sighting. Keep an eye out for all four of Costa Rica's monkey species – the aggressive, white-faced (or capuchin) monkeys that may steal your picnic (or bite you, so don't feed them); the larger, acrobatic spider monkeys *(colorados)* that keep their distance; the sedentary leaf-eating howler monkeys *(mono congo)*; and the tiny squirrel monkeys *(titís)* that tumble through the tree tops.

Birdlife encompasses more than 350 species, including boobies, frigate birds, pelicans, and terns. Snakes and iguanas abound, and if you are sharp-eyed, you may be able to distinguish a sloth from a heap of vegetation in a *cecropia* tree. You can sunbathe, body surf, swim, and snorkel (if you bring your own gear), and picnic (if you bring your own food – there is no food service in the park). There are very rudimentary restrooms and cold-water showers at playas Espadilla Sur and Manuel Antonio.

Activities outside the park

Outside the park, you can rent horses from **Brisas del Nara** (tel: 2779 1235; www.horsebacktour.com) for a ride up in the cooler mountains to a waterfall and swimming hole; or you could go on a sunset sailing cruise, offered through **Iguana Tours** (tel: 2777 2052; www.iguanatours.com). Other options in areas outside the national park include mountain biking, whitewater river rafting or sea kayaking tours, available from **Ríos Tropicales** (tel: 2233 6455; www.riostropicales.com). For excellent assistance and information on the area, as well as books and papers in English and local handicrafts, drop in at **La Buena Nota** shop (tel: 2777 1002) at the north end of the village of Manuel Antonio, near the beach.

Just outside the park to the north, in the hills that rise up from the beach, there is a garish profusion of signs advertising an ever-growing number of hotels, restaurants, and *cabinas*.

With rare exceptions, most accommodations on the ocean side of the road are built on the cliffs above the beach and offer views of the ocean rather than direct access to beaches. One of the best views is from **Hotel Sí Como No** (www.sicomono.com), a luxury eco-hotel that has won international prizes for its sustainability in both design and services. For access to secluded beaches, the eco-hotel **Arenas del Mar Beach and Nature Resort** (www.arenas delmar.com) is unbeatable.

You can get to Manuel Antonio by car, bus, or plane. The road is paved all the way to Quepos, and new bridges have replaced the rickety old wooden ones. You will pass through some beautiful countryside, although the flat coastal section runs through endless green corridors of palm plantations, which can soon become monotonous. It's about a three-hour trip by car, some four hours by bus, and 20 minutes by plane. SANSA and NatureAir both fly daily to Quepos. Be sure to book your plane tickets well in advance, especially during the peak 'dry season,' January through April.

Boa constrictor in the Serpentarium of Manuel Antonio.

Playa Espadilla on a rare quiet day.

Playa Samara, in the Guanacaste province.

*Cascading water in Monteverde
Cloud Forest.*

THE NORTHWEST MAINLAND

Almost all of Costa Rica's natural attractions are
represented in this large and rewarding region: miles
of deserted beaches; acres of tropical dry forests,
interspersed with cattle ranges and cowboy towns;
and misty cloud forests rife with wildlife.

The province of Guanacaste
includes both the northern
part of the Nicoya Peninsula,
attached to the mainland, and a huge
tract of mainland set between mountains draped in cloud forest and the
Pacific Ocean. This is Costa Rica's Big
Country, where vast grasslands are
punctuated by huge spreading guanacaste trees and bony, white Brahman
cattle. During the rainy season, the
landscape is a sea of green, but in the
dry season, the savannahs become
sun-baked tracts of gold. Traditionally
cattle country, Guanacaste is better
known nowadays as the gateway to
controversially large hotel resorts.
Thousands of sun-starved visitors from
northern climes arrive at the Daniel
Oduber International Airport south
of the province's capital, Liberia, the
majority of them on all-inclusive, package beach holidays. Overdevelopment
in some areas has even engendered a
new word: *Guanacasteficación*, signify-
ing unsustainable development.

The Guanacastecos

The *Guanacastecos*, as the residents of
this province are called, are self-reliant
people. You may spot a bumper sticker
on a local car, declaring (in Spanish,
of course) 'Thank God I was born in
Guanacaste.' Many are descended from
the Chorotega Amerindians, with skin

the color of tortoise shell, eyes a warm
brown, black wavy hair, and an easy,
friendly grace.

Democratic decision

In 1787, the Captaincy General of
Costa Rica, which then governed the
country from Guatemala, decided that
Guanacaste should be part of Nicaragua. There it stayed until 1821 when
the Captaincy General was dissolved
and the people of Guanacaste were
asked to decide their own national
identity. Opinions were divided: the

Main Attractions

Main Attractions
Parque Nacional Palo Verde
Park Nacional Rincón de la
    Vieja
Parque Nacional Santa
    Rosa
Monteverde Cloud Forest
Reserva Santa Elena

*Huge guanacaste trees punctuate the vast
grasslands in the country's northwest.*

FACT

Founded 20 years ago by a Swiss animal-lover, the Las Pumas wildlife refuge provides a haven for rescued wild cats and other animals. Since the death of its founder, it has been run by the non-profit Hagnauer Foundation; donations are welcome.

Northerners around Liberia wanted to be a part of Nicaragua and the Southerners on the Nicoya Peninsula wanted to revert to Costa Rica. A vote was held and the majority elected to be a part of Costa Rica.

The Interamericana northbound

The Interamericana Highway, route C1, cuts northwest straight through the heart of Guanacaste, bisecting its capital, Liberia, and heading northward to Nicaragua.

At **Cañas ❶** you first get the sense that immense Guanacaste is more like a separate country than it is a province of Costa Rica. Cañas, which was named for the fields of white-flowered wild cane that used to cover the countryside, is a cowboy town, with a frontier feeling, not unlike a village in Mexico.

Four kilometers (2.5 miles) north of Cañas on the highway you reach **Las Pumas ❷** (www.centrorescatelaspumas. org; daily 8am–4pm), a private wildlife refuge that provides shelter for some of Costa Rica's large cats that, for various reasons, are not able to live in the wild. For most visitors, this will be the only chance to see – and photograph – a jaguar or a puma, if not in the wild, at least rescued from the wild.

About 4km (2.5 miles) north of Cañas, **Safaris Corobicí** (tel: 2669 6191; www.nicoya.com) offers guided 'floats' down the Corobicí River on its 6-meter (17ft) Avon rafts, a wonderful opportunity to observe the river habitat, especially the birds – laughing falcons, herons, trogons, wood storks, motmots, parrots, osprey, and, of course, egrets. Howler and white-faced monkeys all make their homes along the shores of the Corobicí. Plan for an early-morning trip to enjoy the best birding.

Palo Verde National Park

Parque Nacional Palo Verde ❸ (tel: 2695 5908; daily 8am–4pm) is one of Central America's largest protected wildlife areas, occupying 198 sq km (76 sq miles) near the mouth of the Tempisque River. To get there, take the road from Bagaces to the west, off the Interamericana Highway. Four-wheel-drive is recommended, especially during the rainy season.

Palo Verde encompasses lakes, swamps, woodlands, grasslands, and forest, and is a major sanctuary for migrating waterfowl in Central America. Tidal fluctuations and seasonally overflowing rivers attract around 300 species of terrestrial and water birds, including herons, whistling ducks, ibises, and the immense Jabirú stork with its distinctive red neckband. Large mammals and reptiles are also abundant and can be seen especially well during the dry season when they gather at water holes. Coatimundis, armadillos, iguanas, and crocodiles measuring up to 5 meters (16ft) long are not uncommon here. You can stay in dormitory-style lodging in the park or in the slightly more comfortable lodge, with air-conditioning, run by the Organization for Tropical Studies (tel: 2524 0607; www.threepaths.co.cr).

Only 25 years ago, currents and sediment run-off from Guanacaste formed a sandbar, which then became stabilized as an island in the middle of the Tempisque River near the head of the Gulf of Nicoya. Today, it is known as **Isla de Pájaros ❹** (often confused with the Isla Pajáros Biological Reserve farther south in the gulf). From the park, you can charter a boat

Woman in traditional costume, Liberia.

GUANACASTE CULTURE

Since the annexation of Guanacaste in 1824, its traditions have formed an important part of *Tico* culture. Annexation Day is celebrated as a national holiday on the Monday closest to July 25 throughout the country and particularly in the northwest. In honor of the late-comer province, the country's national tree is the wide-spreading Guanacaste tree that rises up out of many northwest cattle pastures. And whenever a national cultural event needs folk dancers, organizers call on Guanacaste dance troupes, the women dressed in colourful swinging skirts and the men in the traditional costume of white trousers and shirts, with red bandanas and straw hats. But Guanacaste's most pervasive contribution may be *gallo pinto*, the national dish of rice and beans which *Guanacastecans* claim to have invented.

and guide to take you to this tiny sheltered islet. While the white ibis and a species of egret make up most of the birds that regularly nest here, roseate spoonbills, wood storks, and anhingas also make their homes on Isla de Pájaros. The noise during nesting season, when chicks are squawking for food, is deafening.

Past the Palo Verde turnoff from the Interamericana, watch for the road sign for **Llanos de Cortés ⑤**, a gem of a waterfall, about 3km (2 miles) north of Bagaces. The dirt road will take you about 2km (1 miles) to a large parking area. Then it's a scramble down a steepish rocky trail to an idyllic, 15-meter (50ft) -high, wide expanse of waterfall, emptying into a sun-dappled, natural swimming pool. Idyllic, that is, when it isn't crowded with weekend day-trippers. Try to visit on a quieter weekday and do not leave any valuables in your parked car.

Directly across the river from Palo Verde National Park is **Rancho Humo** (tel: 2233 2233; www.ranchohumo.com), a private wetlands preserve of more than 800 hectares (2,000 acres) that offers excellent day-long tours in quiet electric carts around a water wonderland teeming with wading birds and wildlife. Access is via the Friendship Bridge and backroads, starting from Honda Quebrada, on the Nicoya Peninsula; tours are by reservation only.

Liberia

The capital city of Guanacaste province, **Liberia ⑥** was established more than 200 years ago. It is also known as Ciudad Blanca, the White City, owing to the traditional whitewashed adobe houses, built in the *Puertas del Sol* – 'Doorways of the Sun' – style, designed to let both morning and afternoon sunlight into north-facing corner houses. A few of these lovely old adobe homes can still be seen, along the city's narrow streets. Many of the houses have classical courtyards and grand rooms with high ceilings and 19th-century murals. The kitchens, to the rear of the house, open onto courtyards, where corn and other grains were once dried. The easiest way to get a first-hand look at one

Testing the skin-nourishing benefits of warm mud at a hot spring.

BACK IN THE SADDLE

Before tourism arrived with a bang in the 1990s, Guanacaste was cowboy country, and Liberia was literally a cow town, with dusty dirt roads. As late as 2000, you were as likely to see horses parked on the streets as cars.

There are still some working cowboys around – in Costa Rica they are called *sabaneros* or *vaccaros* – and the best way to see them in action is at a rodeo. Many towns hold rodeos as part of their annual saint's day fiestas: for example, Santa Cruz, which mounts the biggest rodeo during its early January festival. At Finca Santa Alicia, a horse ranch just 20 minutes south of Liberia, there is often a rodeo on Saturday nights. But most rodeos these days are traveling shows, so watch for posters along the highway.

of these grand houses is to drop into the Café Liberia (http://sdevenelle4.wix.com/cafe-liberia) on Calle Real. It's an excellent café/restaurant in a beautifully restored mansion with painted cupids cavorting amongst flowers on the ceiling mural in the main dining room, and a garden courtyard that doubles as an art gallery.

Early morning is an ideal time to take a walk through the center of Liberia. Visit **Agonía Church** (located at the end of the main street), an adobe structure built in 1852 and one of the oldest Catholic churches in the country. Stroll down Paseo Real, the last remaining, intact colonial-era street, running east from the Central Park. Apart from these few colonial remnants, Liberia is starting to resemble a giant shopping mall, with two shopping centers at either end of town, a plethora of US-style fast-food eateries, and a multiplex movie theater, the only one in the province, on the outskirts of town. More usefully for travelers, there are also many bank branches with automatic cash machines.

Rincón de la Vieja Park

About 5km (3 miles) no along the Interamerica you will reach the turno **Nacional Rincón de la** 2666 5051; Tue–Sun 7a spectacular park contai ing volcanic peaks, the s one reaching a height of (6,286ft), plus four complete ecosystems within its 14,000 hectares (35,000 acres). The name, which applies to both the park and the volcano it protects, derives from the legend of an old woman who once lived on its slopes. Her house was referred to as 'the old woman's corner' – hence Rincón de la Vieja. The volcano is intermittently quite active now and some hiking trails are off limits, owing to noxious gas emissions. Check current conditions with the park office before heading to the park.

Las Pailas

The road to the Las Pailas entrance, via the small community of Curubandé, once very rough, slow-going for 17km

Tumbling waters at La Cangreja Waterfall, one of the hiking destinations in Rincón de la Vieja.

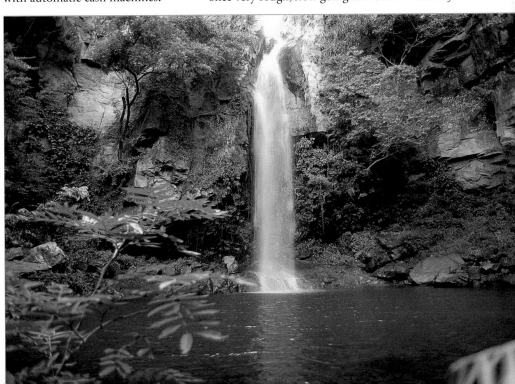

0 miles), has been widened but it still appears to be covered in snow. It's actually chalky limestone, the same rock that was used to build the early adobe houses in Liberia. Unfortunately, the reason the road was widened was to improve the access to a new geothermal power plant, almost at the entrance to the national park. You will see huge above-ground pipes snaking around the hillsides leading to the park. Not a pretty sight, but it is one of the costs of otherwise clean energy. There are still spectacular views to be had, including the green slopes and towering cone of the volcano to the north and, to the west, a verdant valley with grassy coastal plains edging the Pacific Ocean, which you can see on a clear day glistening far below. Be prepared to pay a small toll, unless you are a guest of the Hacienda Guachipelín lodge (www.guachipelin.com), which owns the land the road passes through.

At the Las Pailas ranger station, you sign in and pick up a map of the park and the hiking trails. Just steps away is the park's most spectacular volcanic area, **Las Pailas**, Spanish for 'the

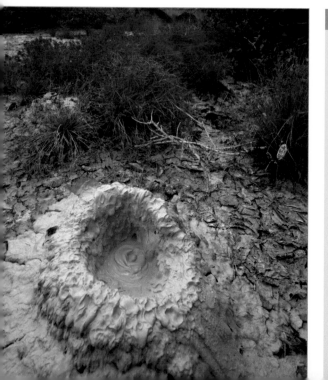

A bubbling mud pot in Rincón de la Vieja National Park.

kitchen stoves.' There is a well-marked, 3km (2-mile) self-guided loop tour of hot springs, boiling mud pots, sulfur streams, and vapor geysers that color the surrounding rocks red, green, and vivid yellow.

Researchers announced the discovery of a new organism that thrives here in the boiling mud and that may prove useful in helping plants adapt to higher temperatures with global warming. Your nose will also be tingling with the strong aroma of rotten eggs (sulfur). The warm mud from the so-called *sala de belleza* (beauty salon) makes an excellent facial mask. Visitors must exercise extreme caution, however, and stay on the trail. Breaking through the brittle surface of the area or getting a face full of steam can result in severe burns.

La Cangreja waterfall

From the Las Pailas entrance you can hike for about two hours to the **La Cangreja Waterfall**. The waterfall is 40 meters (132ft) high and cascades down to form a blue pool. Take a dip in the refreshing swimming hole edged with pockets of contrasting thermal waters. If you tread softly, the wildlife viewing here can be very good. Listen and look for the park's famous resident, the long-tailed manakin, a red, blue, and black bird whose song sounds like 'toledo' (the bird's name in Spanish). Again, check with the park office before you head in this direction, to make sure the trail is open.

The two closest lodges to the park are Rincón de la Vieja Lodge, a collection of rustic cabins and more comfortable bungalows with good hiking trails to nearby hot springs and an excellent canopy tour; and Hacienda Guachipelín, a more upscale lodge with comfortable rooms and excellent food. It is also a working ranch, with first-rate horses and many kilometers of hiking and birding trails and adventure activities, including canopy tours and river tubing.

To the Nicaraguan border

At the end of a day in this region, consider making a short trip east to the village of Santa Cecilia to watch the sun set over **Lake Nicaragua**, or, as the Nicaraguans have named it, 'the Sweet Sea.' You may be fortunate enough to see the so-called 'freshwater sharks' (in fact it is believed that they have swum upstream from the Caribbean). A rise in the bumpy road about 8km (5 miles) beyond the center of Santa Cecilia brings the vast inland sea that is Lake Nicaragua into view. The infamous William Walker planned to conquer Nicaragua and to use the Nicaraguans as a labor force to build canals from Lake Nicaragua to the Pacific. He envisioned a waterway to transport goods by boat across the isthmus from the Pacific to the Atlantic. Although wealthy investors in the United States backed this plan, Walker's defeat first by Costa Rica, and later in Honduras, put an end to the venture.

A trip to **Puerto Soley**, on Salinas Bay, passes through the small town of La Cruz, a stopping place for those traveling north through Central America, and for migrant laborers from Nicaragua crossing back and forth, seeking work in Costa Rica.

From La Cruz, there are wonderful windswept views of the valley and

Strolling on one of Santa Rosa's remote beaches.

Sunset over Lake Nicaragua.

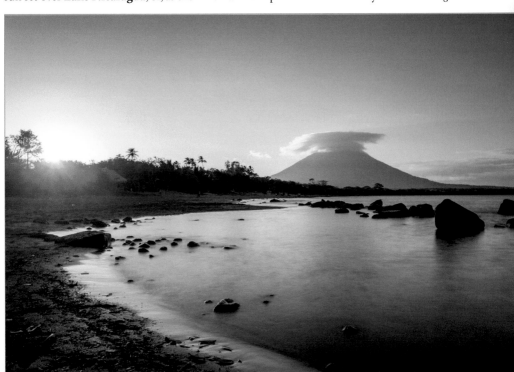

TIP

In Parque Nacional Santa Rosa there are fine views from the lookout point at the Monumento a los Héroes – a large concrete arch that commemorates those who fell in battle at Santa Rosa in 1856.

Salinas Bay below. Winding down the hill, you will pass a ranch established by Anastasio Somoza, the ex-dictator of Nicaragua, before reaching Puerto Soley, a windy beach with a new villa complex. The wind is so strong here that the wind-surfing conditions rival Lake Arenal.

Kite-surfing has become very popular here, on **Playa Copal,** where two schools offer lessons: the Kite Surfing School operates year-round (tel: 8826 5221; www.bluedreamhotel.com); Cometa Copal Kite Surfing Centre (tel: 2676 1192; http://kitesurfingincostarica.com) operates from November through April.

Guanacaste National Park

The **Area de Conservación Guanacaste** ❽ (tel: 2666 5051; www.acguanacaste.ac.cr) was created in 1989 with foreign funds donated to Costa Rica's Neotropica and National Park foundations in order to protect the migratory paths of animals living in Guanacaste National Park and the adjacent protected area of Santa Rosa National Park.

The Guanacaste Conservation area encompasses a wide band of largely deforested land that extends from the Orosí and Cacao volcanoes to the Pacific coast. Although it covers only 2 percent of Costa Rica, it contains an astonishing 65 percent of the country's biodiversity. Dry tropical forest dominates this vast land, but habitats ranging from mangrove swamps and beaches to rain and cloud forest are also within the park's boundaries. Over the past several hundred years, complex patterns of cutting, grazing, burning, and farming have dissected Guanacaste's landscape into a complex mosaic of life zones. Forest fires have also taken their toll on huge tracts of regenerating forest.

Despite setbacks, the American visionary ecologist, naturalist, and conservationist, Dan Janzen, whose life work has been the preservation and reforestation of Guanacaste, feels that this park will ultimately be restored to its original state. 'Dry forests have been destroyed,' Janzen says, 'but they are tough, able to withstand six months of drought a year and are very regenerable.' In 200 or 300 years, full-grown tropical dry forests may again dominate Guanacaste. For the moment, most of the park is restricted to researchers, but you can arrange a stay by reserving in advance (tel: 2666 5051).

Santa Rosa National Park

Parque Nacional Santa Rosa ❾ (www.conozcacostarica.com/parques/santa rosa.htm; 8am–4.30pm) encompasses virtually all of the environmental habitats of the region. An almost infinite system of trails takes visitors through zones of deciduous tropical hardwoods to arid mountains with deserts of cactus and thorny shrubs, and along rivers lined with forests to mangrove swamp estuaries near the beach. Two of its remote beaches, Nancite and Naranjo, are important turtle nesting sites. Elsewhere, many mammals, including monkeys and peccaries (wild pigs), plus more than 20 species of bats, live in the national park.

During more than 20 years of scientific work at Santa Rosa, biologist Dan

Santa Rosa Park is home to white-faced capuchin monkeys.

Janzen has taught two generations of local people an intelligent appreciation of the forest. Through his work, residents of Guanacaste now have experience and expertise in firefighting, maintaining horses, and managing cattle, identifying plants and dealing with 'biotic challenges' like ticks, diseases, thirst, and wounds. Jobs as research assistants, guides, and reserve caretakers provide many with skills and a stable, long-term source of income.

Much of the park is quite difficult to access and requires strenuous hiking. An easy and very accessible trail is the short **Naked Indian Path**. As with many of the park's trails, you pass through forest that, during the dry season, loses many of its leaves, making wildlife viewing easier for the naturalist. Huge multicolored iguanas are commonly seen in the trees bordering the trail. Hiking toward Duende Creek and the bat cave, look for them sunning on tree branches.

Santa Rosa's historical significance as the location of the battle against William Walker was a primary factor in the government's decision to make it a national park. A decisive battle against Walker took place at the hacienda called **La Casona** (The Big House; daily 8am–4pm; entry included in national park admission charge). By coincidence, on the three occasions that Costa Rica has been invaded, it has been here that the invaders were eventually turned back.

Today, a different kind of battle is fought in Santa Rosa: park rangers versus hunters. Though hunting is outlawed in the park, the law is virtually unenforceable due to the inadequate number of rangers. Armed hunters are frequently met by unarmed rangers who often must engage in fights with them to remove them from park boundaries. The low-paid rangers often risk their lives in these skirmishes.

The long-running battle between rangers and poachers reached a terrible climax in May 2002, when a pair of disgruntled hunters set fire to La Casona, the historic farm estate, and burned it to the ground. The house, a landmark in Costa Rican history, has since been rebuilt and once again provides a window into the life of Costa Ricans during the colonial period.

A trail leads from the house to a memorial to the heroes and martyrs of the battle. President Juan Rafael Mora's famous speech, in which he exhorted his countrymen to defend Costa Rica against William Walker, is preserved on an historic plaque.

Expropriated land

Back in the 1970s, during the Nicaraguan Civil War, the Costa Rican government was interested in expanding Santa Rosa Park to help stabilize population levels for some of the park's species. Just to the north of the park, on the border with Nicaragua, former dictator Anastasio Somoza lived on his family ranch, conveniently located so he could move easily and clandestinely back and forth across the border.

Costa Rican leaders felt that the country's best interests were not

The humid environment of Monteverde Cloud Forest.

The Vampire Bats of Guanacaste

Most bats are beneficial, pollinating plants and eating insects. But there is one that inspires fear and dread, along with spooky legends.

There are 105 species of bat in Costa Rica. That number represents more than half of all the mammals found in the country. They are everywhere. Peek under a heliconia leaf in a forest and you may spot a sleeping bat dangling from the spine of the leaf. Look up, under the overhang of a lodge roof, and you may spy more bats. Hang around the entrance to the deep caves of Barra Honda in the early evening, and you may hear the shrill flutterings of millions of bats rising up. As night falls, wherever you are, you will spy winged shapes swooping through the air.

Bats are the only mammals that can fly. Most are benevolent, if curious looking, animals that feed on nectar, fruit, and insects. They are highly beneficial, even necessary, as significant pollinators and

The much-feared vampire bat.

disseminators of seeds, especially in deforested areas in Costa Rica. Bats also control insect populations; it is estimated that a colony of 1 million bats can consume more than 4,500kg (10,000lbs) of insects a night.

Within Santa Rosa Park in Guanacaste, however, inside a cave near the Naked Indian Path, lives a group of *Desmodus rotundum*, the much-feared vampire bat. Only three bat species in the world drink blood, and all of them are native to the neotropics.

Vampire lore

Victorian novelists, followed by Hollywood, have done their part in creating the myth of the vampire who lives on the blood of innocent human beings. The Irish author Bram Stoker (1847–1912), creator of Dracula, was the first to link Transylvanian vampire legends with the scientifically studied habits of neotropical vampire bats.

There are other factors that contribute to the legends that surround these creatures. They are not attractive: the vampire bat has large thumbs that protrude from the wings, appendages used for stealthy crawling toward its prey. It has a flat pig-like nose, large eyes, prominent teeth, and small pointed ears, making it one of the least appealing creatures of the night. They are also the only mammals in the world that feed exclusively on blood.

Among the misinformation and myths, it is true that this species feeds mainly during the darkest hours, quietly alighting upon a sleeping victim and making a painless incision with razor-sharp teeth. Contrary to the myth, though, bats don't suck out the blood of the victim; instead, they lap it up.

A bat does not drink its victim dry. Instead, the real harm comes from rabies and other infections, introduced through the wounds. Sleeping humans are sometimes prey as well, but only rarely.

Cattle ranchers, in particular, strike back against the vampire bat by dynamiting, and gassing their caves with toxic substances. Such methods, often born of an irrational aversion to the bat, do not specifically target the vampire variety, and other misidentified, beneficial bats are also killed. Anything and everything in the area is also harmed or destroyed. Ironically, before forests were cleared and livestock introduced, vampire bats had far fewer animals to feed on.

On the positive side, recent research into bat saliva, which is so effective at preventing blood from clotting, may one day lead to advances in preventing heart attacks and strokes.

served by the presence of an ousted military dictator near its border. So, in 1979, the Hacienda Murcíelago, owned by the Somoza family, was expropriated and made part of the national parks system. The hacienda, which lies on Santa Elena Bay with access to Playa Blanca and its untouched white-sand beach, is now a part of Santa Rosa Park.

A more recent addition to the park includes land that was once occupied by the formerly secret Santa Elena Airstrip, used to bring in supplies to aid rebel efforts to overthrow the ruling Sandinistas. Built with the blessing of ex-president Alberto Monge, in violation of Costa Rica's neutrality law, the airstrip was torn up under the administration of Oscar Arias in 1986.

Santa Rosa beaches

A rugged 13km (8-mile) hiking trail, or a road accessible by four wheel drive during the dry season (impassable during the wet season), leads from the Santa Rosa ranger station to **Playa Naranjo**. White sand and clear water with excellent surf breaking near Roca de la Bruja (Witch's Rock, a stone monolith 2km (1 mile) offshore, make Naranjo a popular but remote surfing destination. Boats can be chartered from Playas del Coco to Naranjo. Alternatively, there is camping at Playa Naranjo (tel: 2666 5051).

Playa Nancite, one of Costa Rica's most pristine beaches, is northwest from Naranjo. Each month, usually on a waxing three-quarter moon, turtles come ashore here to nest. Tens of thousands may participate in the event, called an *arribada*, one of Costa Rica's grandest natural spectacles (see page 236). Exact times are unpredictable, as they are with most biological phenomena. Even though a full-scale *arribada* may not be taking place, solitary turtles can sometimes be seen nesting on Nancite and Naranjo beaches. Access to Nancite is mostly limited to researchers, so ask first at the park office at the entrance if you can visit.

Monteverde Cloud Forest

From lowland, dry tropical forest to the misty, mountain cloud forests of **Monteverde** isn't far as the crow flies. By road, you turn off the Interamericana Highway at the Rancho Grande exit at Km 133, heading for Sardinal. Monteverde sits atop the Continental Divide, and, despite some road improvements, the last 37km (21 miles) are still challenging, allow up to an hour to make the slow, winding ascent up a mostly unpaved road.

Despite the ordeal to get here, every year tens of thousands of people make the climb, primarily to visit the **Reserva Biológica del Bosque Nuboso de Monteverde ⑩** (tel: 2645 5122; www.reserva monteverde.com; daily 7am–4pm; night tours by reservation). In order to protect the flora and fauna and the trails of this popular preserve, visitors are limited to 220 at any given time – which means you may have to wait your turn. You should book at least one night's accommodation in advance; to get the best out of the area you need to stay three days.

More visitors are attracted to the Monteverde Cloud Forest than to any

'Hot lips' flower, Monteverde Cloud Forest.

Bright pink berries, Monteverde Cloud Forest.

TIP

The resplendent quetzal is the national bird of Guatemala, not Costa Rica. That honor goes to the yigüirro, or clay-colored thrush.

other forest reserve in Costa Rica, and usually for one purpose only: to sight the resplendent quetzal, the most colorful and spectacular bird in the tropics. Be warned, however: it is a difficult bird to spot, and increasingly so with more and more visitors hiking the same trails here. Pick up a trail map at the park entrance and strike out on less-traveled trails and you may have better luck. With the exception of their almost luminous crimson breast, they are cloaked in radiant green plumage and easily disappear among the rich colors of the cloud forest. The best time to spot them is January through September and especially during the mating season, which runs from March through June.

Monteverde is much more than an opportunity to spot a quetzal, however. This misty, verdant, high-altitude cloud forest is home to a multitude of diverse creatures: 448 species of birds identified so far, about 700 species of butterflies, 3,000 species of plants, and 130 species of mammals, of which 70 are bats. Pick up a checklist and map at the Visitors' Center. Tours with excellent naturalist guides, are available. Before leaving the

forest, visit the **Hummingbird Gallery**, across the road from the entrance, to observe the hummingbirds that buzz around a group of feeders and to see an exhibition of the remarkable photos of Michael and Patricia Fogden, biologists and pre-eminent nature photographers, who spent two decades recording the fauna of Monteverde.

Monteverde's Quaker community

The community of **Monteverde** ⓫ was established by a group of Quakers who moved here from Alabama in 1951. To support themselves, the Quakers began making cheese from milk brought to their primitive processing plant each morning by *Tico* dairy farmers. Today the Quakers produce tons of cheese daily; Monteverde cheese has become a proud Costa Rican specialty and can be found in markets throughout Central America. En route to the reserve, stop in at their cheese-processing plant, **La Fábrica de Queso** Ⓐ (The Cheese Factory; http://monteverdecheesefactory.com), to watch the production through windows in the plant. Better still, order a

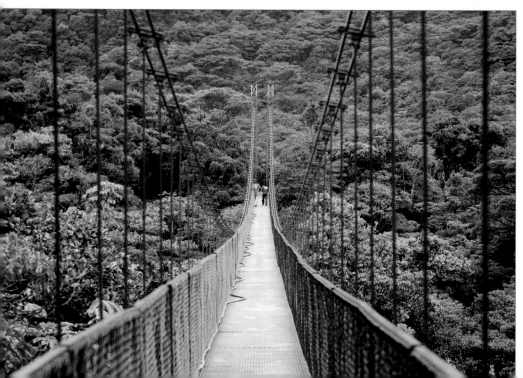

A tree-top walkway in Selvatura Park.

milkshake made with their excellent ice cream. Don't expect to see too many Quakers elsewhere in Monteverde, however. They generally avoid the commercialized town that Monteverde has now become.

Just north of here look in at **CASEM** 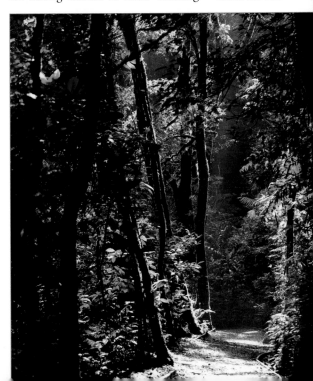**B** (Comité de Artesanías Santa Elena-Monteverde), an arts and crafts cooperative founded by eight women in 1982. Today, more than 140 artisans contribute their work, which is on sale at less-than-downtown prices at the CASEM shop (tel: 2645 5190). At the entrance to CASEM, there is a large fig tree. When it is fruiting, it is the easiest place to spot monkeys and many species of birds feasting on the figs. Across the road is the popular coffee shop, **Stella's Bakery**.

Other Monteverde attractions

Adjacent to Monteverde Cloud Forest preserve are two much smaller private reserves. There is usually good wildlife viewing at the 81-hectare (200-acre) **Reserva Sendero Tranquilo C** (Quiet Path Reserve), which is open for small-group guided tours, led by expert, bilingual nature guides. You must book ahead by contacting the Hotel El Sapo Dorado (tel: 2645 5010; www.sapodorado.com).

Opposite the Hotel Heliconia, on the road to Santa Elena, follow the signs to **El Jardín de las Mariposas D** (Butterfly Garden; tel: 2645 5512; daily 8.30am–4pm; www.monteverdebutterflygarden.com), which exhibits all the butterfly species of the region. Guided tours take you through the various stages of a butterfly's life and into a screened garden where hundreds of species flutter freely. The best time for a visit is a sunny morning. There is also a leaf-cutter ant colony exhibition. Reptile-lovers won't want to miss the **Serpentarium of Monteverde** (tel: 2645 6002; www.monteverde-online. com; daily 9am–8pm) where you can safely observe more than 40 species of reptiles and amphibians.

More frogs are on view at **The Frog Pond of Monteverde** (tel: 2645 6320;

www.monteverdethemepark.com; daily 9.30am–7.30pm), on the south side of Santa Elena. The best time to visit is toward evening when the frogs become more active. An alternative adventure is a visit to the **Bat Jungle E** (tel: 2645 7701; daily 9am–7.30pm; tours available; http://the-bat-jungle.blogspot.com) across from CASEM, where you can learn all about these fascinating nocturnal mammals.

Skywalkers and artists

One of the most popular Monteverde attractions is the Monteverde Park with its **Sky Walk F** (tel: 2479 4100; www. skyadventures.travel), a 2.5km (1.5-mile) series of trails and five hanging bridges suspended Indiana Jones-style from platforms in the tree canopy. It's a wonderful way of getting a bird's-eye view of the forest, up to 41 meters (138ft) above the ground. For the truly adventurous the same company also offers **Sky Trek**, a high-speed, high-adrenaline canopy tour that involves donning mountain-climbing harnesses and zipping through the trees suspended on strong cables. A more relaxing

Monteverde trail.

FACT

The Santa Elena Airstrip was financed by a bogus Panamanian company set up by Oliver North, then a member of the US National Security Council, to aid the Sandinistas' opponents, known as the Contras.

experience is offered by the **Sky Tram** gondolas which take visitors smoothly up into the rainforest for amazing views accompanied by and informative commentary from a knowledgeable guide. An interesting **Herpetarium** houses over 30 species of venomous and non-venomous snakes, poisonous frogs, toads, lizards, and turtles.

Monteverde is also famous for its artistic community, with many resident painters, sculptors, and textile artists. An international music festival is held every spring where local and international musicians perform programs ranging from jazz to classical to Latino. Proceeds benefit local school music programs.

Santa Elena Reserve and around

Around 5km (3 miles) northeast of Monteverde village is an outstanding local initiative, the **Reserva Santa Elena** ⓬ (Santa Elena Rainforest Reserve; www.reservasantaelena.org). Comprising some 310 hectares (766 acres) of mixed montane and elfin forest, the reserve was created in 1992 as a local high-school project and includes several kilometers

Tarzan swing in Selvatura Park.

of well-kept paths and a visitors' center. On clear days, you are treated to views of magnificent Arenal Volcano to the north. Tours are well organized and cheaper than Monteverde, yet the flora and fauna (including quetzals and howler monkeys) are every bit as impressive as those of its famous neighbor. There are four principal trails, all short enough to be done in a day. You also avoid the crowds here, plus you will feel good that a proportion of your admission charge will go toward the funding of Monteverde's schools.

The most exciting way of exploring the forests around the reserve is on a canopy zip-line tour. **Selvatura** (tel: 2645 5929; www.selvatura.com), a private park just south of the Santa Elena Reserve, provides an 18-platform canopy tour within a cloud forest, as well as hanging bridges, a reptile exhibit, a butterfly garden and an excellent insect museum, billed as the world's third-largest.

Orchid fanciers won't want to miss the **Jardín de Orquídeas** (Orchid Garden; tel: 2645 5308; www.monteverde orchidgarden.com; daily 8am–5pm), where more than 450 orchid species live. At first glance, it appears rather small and may even look flowerless. But once the attendant equips you with a jeweler's loop, you can start to see a world of miniature orchids opening up, including the world's smallest orchid.

East of Monteverde Cloud Forest, on the Atlantic slope, is the vast **El Bosque Eterno de los Niños** (Children's Eternal Forest; tel: 2645 5003, www.acmcr.org). Back in 1987, a group of Swedish schoolchildren raised and donated enough money to purchase 6 hectares (15 acres) of forest. Now, with support from young people from all over the world, they have bought more than 22,000 hectares (54,000 acres), covering a range of forest types including cloud, rain and seasonal evergreen. The most easily accessible section of the forest, called the **Bajo del Tigre trail** (daily 8am–4.30pm), is just south of CASEM. A self-guided tour takes you along a 1.5km (1-mile) trail dotted with information panels.

The Resplendent Quetzal

Costa Rica is a delight for birdwatchers, many of them in search of one of the most beautiful and sought-after birds in the world.

The resplendent quetzal is rightly acclaimed as the most magnificent bird in the western hemisphere. Some 40 species of the trogon family, to which the quetzal belongs, inhabit the tropics worldwide, and 10 of those are found in Costa Rica. But the quetzal is the star, regarded as one of the country's greatest natural treasures.

The pigeon-sized male owes his elegance to the intensity and brilliant contrasts of his colors, the sheen of his plumage, the beauty of his adornments, and the great dignity of his posture. The rich crimson of his underparts contrasts with the iridescent green of his head, chest, and upper parts. His head is crowned with a narrow crest of upstanding feathers that extends from his small yellow bill to his nape. The pointed tips of the long, loose-barbed coverts of his wings project over the crimson of his sides, creating a beautiful scalloped edge. Most notable of all are his central tail coverts, which stretch far beyond his tail and, like two slender green pendants, undulate gracefully when he flies.

The quetzal is a fruit eater, its diet almost entirely reliant on wild avocados, but when these are not available, the birds will eat insects and even frogs.

Symbol of freedom

As witnessed by ancient sculptures and paintings, the long tail coverts were highly valued as personal adornments by the Aztec and Maya nobility. Mayan kings prized the green tail feathers of the quetzal more than gold itself. They also believed the bird could not live in captivity, and it was therefore the supreme symbol of freedom. This belief persisted for some time, but modern aviculturists have learned how to keep them alive in captivity – a hard negation of a beautiful myth.

The quetzal's song is eminently worthy of a bird so splendidly attired. Fuller and deeper than those of any other trogon, their songs are not distinctly separated but slurred and fused into a flow of soft, mellow, and unforgettably beautiful sound.

Nesting habits

Monogamous pairs of quetzals nest in the holes of trees located in mountain forests or in nearby clearings. The hole, like that of a woodpecker, extends straight downwards from the opening at the top. Usually it is deep enough to conceal all of the sitting birds except the ends of the male's train. On the unlined bottom of the chamber, the female lays two light-blue eggs. She incubates through the night and in the middle of the day. The male takes a turn on the eggs in the morning and in the afternoon. His train projects through the doorway, fluttering in the breeze. On an epiphyte-burdened trunk, the ends might be mistaken for two green fern fronds.

'Very-good, very-good'

Sometimes, when his partner arrives to relieve him of his spell in the nest, he soars above the tree tops shouting a phrase that sounds almost like 'very-good very-good.' At the summit of his ascent he circles, then dives into sheltering foliage. These 'joy flights' seem to express the bird's great vitality.

Resplendent quetzals are still abundant in Costa Rican tracts of unspoilt mountain forests. So long as such forests are preserved, they are in no danger of becoming extinct, but if they are destroyed, then Central America will lose its most magnificent bird.

The resplendent quetzal is protected in four national parks and two cloud forest reserves.

THE NORTHWEST: NICOYA PENINSULA

Miles of sandy beaches draw visitors to this sunny peninsula jutting into the Pacific Ocean, where you will also find the country's best surfing, diving, and sportfishing.

y far, the most popular beach destinations in Costa Rica cluster round the shores of the Nicoya Peninsula. The outer, western beaches rim the Pacific coast, while the inner beaches face the Gulf of Nicoya. This boot-shaped peninsula straddles two provinces: the northern part branches out from the Guanacaste mainland, then morphs into Puntarenas province in the south. In the days before there were any roads on most of the peninsula, the mainly coastal communities were accessible only by boat from the nearest port, Puntarenas. So, rather anachronistically, the Nicoya Peninsula remains part of Puntarenas province today.

Puntarenas

Puntarenas is the jumping-off spot for car ferries to the Southern Nicoya beaches. So it's not surprising that many visitors think **Puntarenas ❶**, the capital and the largest city of the province of Puntarenas, is simply a place to pass through to get to somewhere else. But the town, stretched along a narrow spit of sand – *punta de arenas*, or point of sand – still has a lot of character and is worth exploring. When it was the country's main port, before the Atlantic railroad was built, Puntarenas was a mini-Marseilles, bustling with longshoremen, sailors on leave, prostitutes, and merchants and day-trippers

from San José who traveled by train to escape the city heat and conduct their import/export businesses. The growth of the Caribbean port of Limón and the more recent opening of the deep-water port at nearby **Puerto Caldera** put a major dent in the commercial viability of Puntarenas.

Today, fishing is the main industry of Puntarenas and a visit to the busy fish market is the best entertainment in town. Go early in the morning and watch expert shellfish shuckers and fish gutters at work. Perch on a stool at one

Main Attractions
Puntarenas
Montezuma
Cabo Blanco Absolute
 Wildlife Reserve
Playa Tamarindo area
Playa Nosara
Playa Sámara

Horseback riding on the beach at Montezuma.

TIP

Take a trip into the glorious waters of the Gulf of Nicoya aboard the luxurious, 21-meter (71ft) Manta Ray catamaran (www.mantaray sailing.com), which sails from the Calypso dock in Puntarenas.

of the food counters in the market and sample a *ceviche* (fish marinated in lime juice) or a fillet of fish just off the boat, part of a catch that will soon be making its way to the fish-packing plants at the entrance to Puntarenas or to Central Valley markets in refrigerated trucks. Tourism in the town is boosted by the arrival of huge cruise ships at the town's modern dock. There are some comfortable beachfront hotels, including the vintage Hotel Tioga, reminiscent of an Art Deco ocean liner.

With its views of the long, arching coastline of the Nicoya Peninsula to the west, the beach along the gulf is beautiful, and the sunsets over Nicoya are quite spectacular. The downtown section of the beach is pleasant and clean, and flies the Bandera Azul (blue flag), denoting an eco-friendly, clean beach inspected by government officials. Swimming in the estuary and rivers, however, should be avoided.

If you want to see what's under the water, visit the **Puntarenas Marine Park** (tel: 2661 5272; Tue–Sun 9am–4.30pm) at the east end of town, where 28 large aquariums showcase the marine life of the Gulf of Nicoya.

Downtown

The crowded center of Puntarenas, three blocks back from the beach,

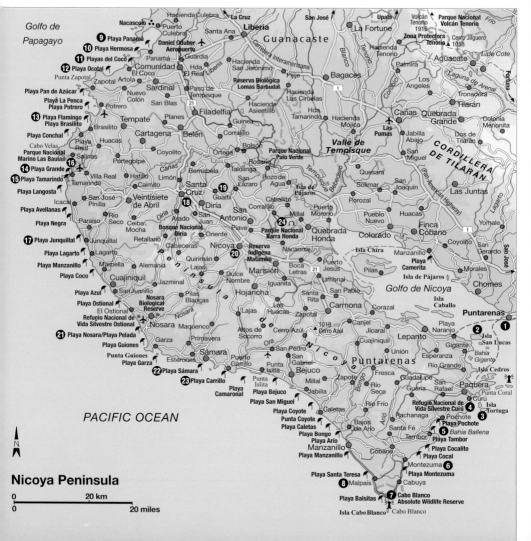

Nicoya Peninsula

PACIFIC OCEAN

0   20 km
0   20 miles

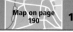

bustles in the morning as the towns-folk, called *porteños*, conduct busi-ness, often getting around on bicycles. Everyone seems in a hurry, perhaps to accomplish what they need to do before the onset of the afternoon heat. Though it is, like San José, an archi-tectural victim of excessive concrete, Puntarenas still retains many of its older buildings: plank structures with latticework below the roof to permit the breeze, and 'gingerbread' detailing reminiscent of Victorian mansions. The wooden buildings are painted in bright color combinations, and, together with the few remaining man-sions of the merchants, a smattering of Art Deco buildings, and the magnifi-cent stone church, they convey the fla-vor of Puntarenas in its prime.

Evening is perhaps the best time to catch Puntarenas. Enjoy a late after-noon *refresco* at one of the *sodas* (cafés) on the long, broad **Paseo de Turistas** fronting the beach and watch the sun sink below the mountains of Nicoya across the bay. The *sodas* offer a chance to try some native Costa Rican fruit drinks. This is perhaps the only place in the country to get *maté*, a type of milkshake with a lingering, nostal-gic aftertaste. Or try a cold, creamy 'Churchill,' an achingly sweet, but surprisingly refreshing icy fruit drink that includes two kinds of milk – pow-dered and sweetened condensed milk.

Seafood restaurants and hotels line the ocean front. Most are air-conditioned or are sited to catch the gulf breezes. On the estuary that runs parallel to the town, the profession-ally managed Yacht Club is well pro-tected, and is one of the very first stops a transoceanic yacht makes on the first leg of a trip from the West Coast of the US to more distant ports of call.

Just to the south, down the coast from Puntarenas, is **Playa Doña Ana**, on a cove well situated between two spectacular rocky headlands. Costa Rica's second-largest surfing wave is just offshore. A few kilometers along the road toward Caldera is a turn-off for Mata de Limón, where you can sit at a lagoon-side table and enjoy some of the tasty seafood and fish specialties for which Puntarenas is famous, at the **Restaurante y Marisquería Leda** (tel:

When in Puntarenas, try a 'Churchill' sundae, a sweet, icy fruit drink with condensed milk.

Fisherman mending his net on Paseo de Turistas, Puntarenas.

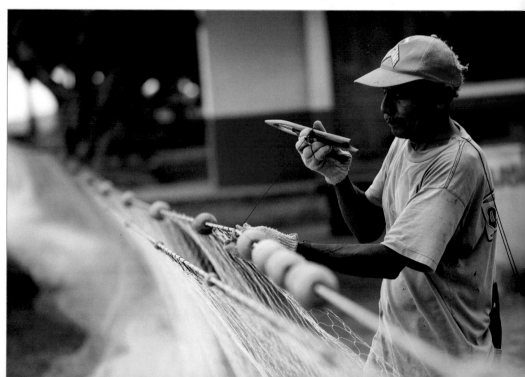

*Selling kebabs on
Paseo de Turistas.*

2634 4087; http://restauranteleda.com). If
they are listed on the menu, try the
local *chuchecas*, black clams sautéed in
lots of butter and garlic.

The Gulf of Nicoya

Car ferries, as well as a smaller, pas-
senger-only *lancha* (launch), cross
from Puntarenas to Paquera on the
Nicoya Peninsula. The one-hour trip
across the gulf passes by 40 or so
islands, including **Isla San Lucas ❷**,
Costa Rica's former prison island. The
prison was closed in 1991 and the
island deserted, except for the guards
posted there to prevent vandalism.
There are no restrictions preventing
visits to the island, however, and visitors who are so inclined can view dis-
turbing reminders of the life prisoners
endured here.

Calypso Tours offers a cruise on its
21-meter (71ft) catamaran *Manta Ray*,
outfitted with two on-deck pools,
to the islands in the Gulf of Nicoya.
It crosses the waters of the Gulf and
visits **Isla Tortuga ❸** (Turtle Island),
where, in an idyllic setting of white
sand and turquoise waters, you can

enjoy a seafood buffet served with
white wine. There is also adequate
time for swimming, snorkeling, or
optional kayaking and pedal boat
rides, and, of course, for sunbathing.

Calypso, one of the oldest tour
operators in Costa Rica, also offers
other excellent tours, including fishing and diving trips (tel: 2256 2727;
www.calypsocruises.com).

The South Nicoya Peninsula

The ferry ride across the Gulf of
Nicoya will bring you to a different
world of seasonally dry grasslands,
gigantic spreading trees, rolling cattle
ranches, memorable bays, and, most
of all, scenic beaches, ideal for surfing, nature walks, turtle-watching and
beachcombing. Bring binoculars on
the ferry to focus on sea birds flying
in the wake of fishing boats, plus the
odd sea turtle floating by, or dolphins
cavorting in the usually calm gulf.

From the ferry landing at Paquera,
Tambor is just a short drive, and Montezuma is about an hour away. Buses
wait to meet the Paquera ferry to head

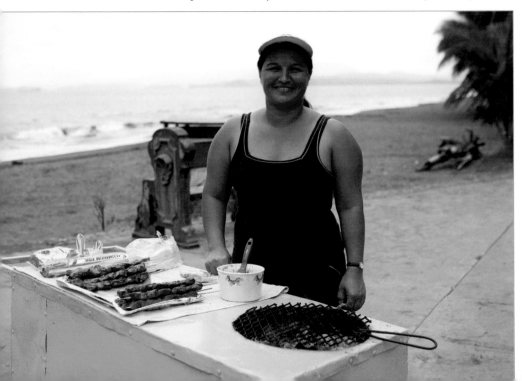

south to Montezuma, but there are no such direct services from the other ferry landing farther north at Playa Naranjo. If you are driving south from Paquera, the roads are only partially paved, with few road signs, but the local people are used to giving visitors directions.

The drive along the peninsula, although rough, is rewarding. It traverses many kilometers of pasture land, through small towns and villages, past people on foot or on horseback, and dwellings of every description – and every now and again reveals views of the blue bays of the Pacific.

Some 7km (4 miles) south of the town of Paquera lies the **Refugio Nacional de Vida Silvestre Curú 4** (Curú National Wildlife Refuge; tel: 2641 0100; www.curuwildliferefuge.com; daily 7am–3pm). Although small, the park encompasses five habitats and offers sanctuary to a surprisingly large and diverse number of plants, animals including the white-faced monkey and a healthy group of reintroduced *mono colorado* (spider) monkeys, and more than 230 species of birds. It has three beautiful beaches, ideal for swimming and diving. There are basic accommodations available, along with horseback tours and sea kayaking to nearby islands. The hiking is also excellent. The refuge is private property, owned by the eco-minded Schutt family; it's a good idea to call in advance to arrange accommodations and tours.

Bahía Ballena

Bahía Ballena 5, which means Whale Bay, is an expansive bay of serene beauty and tranquility. The waters are gentle and warm, with large flocks of pelicans diving for fish. January is an especially good time for sighting whales here. The bay shelters two beaches, **Playa Pochote** and **Playa Tambor**, with shallow water ideal for wading. In the 1990s, however, its tranquil face was irrevocably and controversially transformed by the construction of the enormous, Spanish-owned resort, Hotel Barceló Playa Tambor, followed by a huge residential project and golf course. The project inspired a passionate debate about what kind of tourism is best for Costa Rica: mammoth projects such as this, which involved

TIP

If you like a game of golf or enjoy horseback riding, there are resorts on the Nicoya Peninsula that specialize in both activities.

Tourists playing football on the beach at Puntarenas.

*Guanacaste tree,
Nicoya.*

the removal of mangroves to create a beach, or small enterprises that reflect the character of their communities. In the end, big business won.

In the village of **Tambor**, inexpensive lodgings and good local-style meals can be found, and you might just get a sense of life as it was before the arrival of big-time tourism. Continuing southeast through the town of Cóbano, the road leads to Montezuma.

Montezuma

Montezuma ❻ in many ways feels like the end of the line. The partially paved road rolls down a steep hill (sometimes with actual gaps in the road) and ends abruptly in front of a row of funky hotels, trendy restaurants and bars, and *cantinas* (snack bars) on the beach front. Here, young North American and European travelers far outnumber the local people, who have accepted them with seeming good grace. Hotel rooms fill up quickly everywhere in Montezuma during the dry season and peak holiday times, including November during the annual film festival, so reserve well ahead.

*Horseback riding on
the beach is popular
with tourists.*

Lodging and dining in Montezuma range from the basic to the luxurious, and the beach-going is exceptional. To the north of town there are wide, sandy beaches, with beautiful clear water. A scenic footpath leads north for 6km (4 miles) to a dramatic waterfall that spills into a pool right on the beach. To the south, the surf crashes against volcanic rock – and, just a short hike away up a river, there is another waterfall with a pool for swimming. Although it's tempting to dive in, don't; in recent years there have been some tragic accidents here when Tarzan-emulating young men have plunged head-first into the rocky pool. The first couple of rocky bays north of Montezuma have strong currents, but Playa Grande is safe for swimming.

You can rent bikes and boogie boards and horses at agencies in town. But most visitors to Montezuma seem to spend their time swimming, sunning, or simply hanging out in this laid-back place that seems expressly designed for the youthful, low-budget traveler, as well as for more experienced travelers who appreciate its off-the-beaten-track casual atmosphere. Off in a world of its own, a 15-minute walk north along the beach, **Ylang Ylang Beach Resort** caters to nature-lovers, with accommodations ranging from comfortable tents to charming bungalows in a lush garden setting complete with pool and spa services.

Perhaps the most romantic restaurant in all of Costa Rica is tucked away on a rocky cove, a few minutes' walk south of town. Since 1994, husband-and-wife team Nicola and Daniela, from Rome, have been serving up dramatic, seaside atmosphere and superb Mediterranean seafood at **Playa de los Artistas** a totally alfresco restaurant with driftwood tables perched on rocks, illuminated at night by lanterns and starlight. On weekends they fire up a huge barbecue to grill seafood and meats. The fish carpaccio here is not to be missed, nor the homemade chocolate tart, a deep, dark satisfying finish to a memorable meal.

Cabo Blanco

It is almost 11km (7 miles) from Montezuma to the **Cabo Blanco Absolute Wildlife Reserve** ❼ (tel: 2642 0093; www.nicoyapeninsula.com/caboblanco; Wed–Sun 8am–4pm) along a little-used, unpaved road that runs parallel to the beach. En route, there is a cluster of small *cabina*-hotels in the town of Cabuya. The reserve, established in 1963 through the inspiration and tireless efforts of Swedish immigrant and national parks pioneer Nils Olaf Wessberg, is Costa Rica's oldest protected wildlife region.

Originally, Cabo Blanco meant what its name said (*blanco* in Spanish means blank as well as white), and there was no public access. All life there was to be protected, without any interference from humans. Today, however, visitors can see approximately one-third of the 1,200-hectare (3,000-acre) reserve, encompassing a wet, tropical forest on the tip of the peninsula. It is one of the most scenic spots along the whole Pacific coast. It is also one of the hottest, so bring plenty of drinking water. There is a large population of marine and shore birds here as well as mammals. In addition, there is a ranger station with rest rooms and picnic tables,

Montezuma's beaches attract backpackers and those looking for an off-the-beaten-track atmosphere.

Enjoy a romantic dinner under the trees at Playa de los Artistas, Montezuma.

Spiky agaves grow in Cabo Blanco.

well-maintained trails, and a lovely remote beach, where you can wade in to cool off.

To drive to the reserve you must cross two small streams – for which a four-wheel-drive vehicle is recommended; it's essential in the rainy season. Remember that, as noted above, the reserve is closed on Monday and Tuesday to reduce the impact of tourism.

Beyond Cabo Blanco, the road heading up the Pacific coast is rough and unpaved. During the rainy season it is extremely muddy and some of the rivers and creeks without bridges are only passable in a four-wheel-drive vehicle. During the dry season things don't get any more comfortable either as vehicles churn up a fine, brown dust that coats travelers and plants along the roadway.

Surfers and nature-lovers gravitate to **Malpaís ⑧** and Santa Teresa, two beaches about 6km (4 miles) north of Cabo Blanco, as the pelican flies. But most visitors drive the 12km (7.5 miles) along the paved road that runs southwest from Cóbano. A cluster of

Palm-fringed Playa Flamingo.

hotels and restaurants has sprung up to cater to an international, young surfing crowd, along with a few luxury retreats aimed at well-heeled travelers who value creature comforts in a really remote setting.

Papagayo to Playa Ocotal

And now for something completely different... If you like a beach holiday with lots of action, the Pacific beaches to the southwest of Liberia are extremely popular. This coast is the hub of tourism in Guanacaste, largely owing to the expansion of the Daniel Oduber International Airport just 45 minutes away. Huge, all-inclusive resorts cater to masses of winter-weary tourists arriving in Liberia from the north, in search of sun, surf, and sand.

The Papagayo Peninsula project already has an 18-hole golf course and an ultra-expensive flagship hotel, the Four Seasons Costa Rica Resort, with more hotels and private villas planned. Around **Playa Panamá ⑨**, half a dozen all-inclusive resorts are packed in the high season with budget-minded

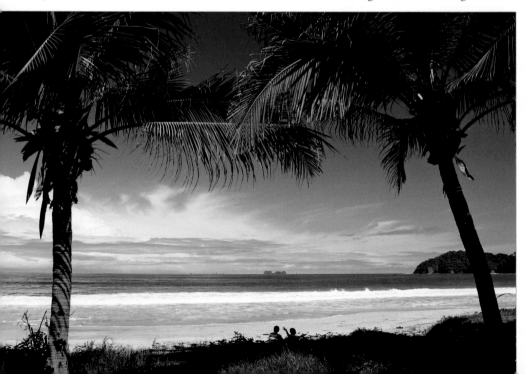

package travelers who rarely leave the manicured hotel grounds.

To the south is **Playa Hermosa** ❿, a sparkling half-moon cove with gentle surf. Despite some large-scale development at the northern end, this beach still has some charm and some excellent small restaurants and hotels. It is also a major diving center, with the long-established Sirenas Diving Costa Rica (www.sirenasdivingcostarica. com) based here. **Hotel El Velero** (tel: 2672 1017; www.costaricahotel.net) is an affordable, laid-back, small hotel right on the beach, steps from the warm, shallow ocean waters, perfect for swimming. It sits directly across from the posh Four Seasons, whose lights you can see glittering at night.

Nearby **Playas del Coco** ⓫ is a working beach town with a large fishing fleet. A new boardwalk has beautified the beach area considerably. The swimming isn't great, but Coco is the launching point for myriad diving, surfing, and sport-fishing trips. The town itself has lots of character, albeit a little honky-tonk, with plenty of open-air bars, discos, and tacky

souvenir stalls. But there are also some excellent seafood restaurants to suit every price range. In town on the main street, **Papagayo Seafood** (tel: 2670 0298) has reliably fresh seafood daily. For romantic, oceanfront dining, check out **Donde Gloria & Claudio** (tel: 2670 1514), a breezy, alfresco terrace restaurant serving Spanish-Catalan and Peruvian seafood specialties.

The north end of the beach caters to a more sophisticated crowd with small bed and breakfast establishments and the stylish, Italian-owned **Hotel La Puerta del Sol** (tel: 2670 0195; www. lapuertadelsolcostarica.com).

Just a couple of kilometers south of Coco lies dramatic **Playa Ocotal** ⓬, a black-sand beach fringed with steep cliffs. Dominating the highest point is **Ocotal Beach Resort** (tel: 2670 0321; www.ocotalresort.com) overlooking the sandy coves, rocky capes, and islands off the Nicoya coast, and rightly famous for its spectacular views and first-rate dive shop and sport fishing operation. You can take a boat trip to a nearby island to find great swimming and snorkeling, or arrange a diving

Playa Flamingo in all its glory.

A glorious sunset over the Nicoya peninsula.

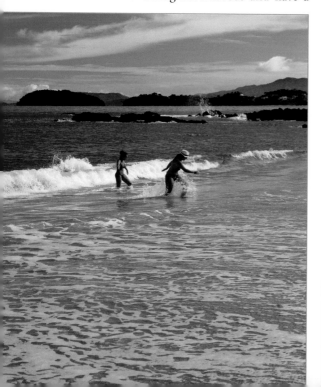

Swimmers at Playa Conchal.

expedition either in local waters or as far away as Isla del Caño.

Playa Flamingo

If you are driving south from Liberia, head south on the highway toward Belén. From there it is a short distance to **Playa Brasilito** and the Playa Flamingo area, which includes **Playa Potrero**. In the dry season, if you are feeling adventurous and have a four-wheel-drive car, you can negotiate the bumpy Monkey Trail short cut that starts near Sardinal and emerges near **Playa Pan de Azúcar** (Sugar Loaf Beach). Ask local people for directions.

The Tempisque River Bridge, formerly called the Taiwan Friendship Bridge, is the most direct route for visitors heading to these beaches and points south.

Playa Conchal, once a deserted slice of beach composed of bottomless drifts of pink, orange, mauve, and sunset-colored seashells, lies just south of Flamingo. Although it is an ideal place to snorkel and beachcomb, the huge **Westin Golf Resort & Spa** looms over the beach, blocking access from the main road. But you can still reach the public beach by walking south for a kilometer (0.6 miles) along the shore from **Brasilito**, a bustling little town with a few interesting restaurants and the vintage **Hotel Brasilito** (tel: 2654 4237; www. brasilito.com), which has modest rooms in an old wooden building close to the beach. Good seafood restaurants here include **El Camarón Dorado** (tel: 2654 4028) practically on the beach.

WET AND WILD IN TAMA

Along with its surfing renown, established in the classic 1960s surfer movie *Endless Summer*, Playa Tamarindo is famous as a party town, starring in its own episode of Entertainment Television's *Wild On* international party-scene series.

The hot clubs come and go, along with the transient surfers who arrive in town, stay long enough to get a night-spot hopping, and then depart in search of the next wave. Barbecues and dancing on the beach around a bonfire are highlights for the 20-somethings, along with dance clubs and atmospheric lounges; just ask around to find out where the latest action is. Older beach-goers may enjoy the Friday-night beach barbecues with folkloric music at the elegant Hotel Capitán Suizo at the south end of the beach.

About 7km (4 miles) north of Brasilito you will find **Playa Flamingo** ⓭ one of Costa Rica's loveliest, longest, white-sand beaches. The natural harbor formed by Flamingo Bay is home to a huge charter boat fleet. For almost a decade now, the marina has been closed while local authorities make up their minds about granting a new concession, but the fishing boats and pleasure sailboats are still moored out in the bay.

One of the best restaurants in town is **Coco Loco** (http://cocolococostarica. com), known for fresh fish and seafood, and exotic cocktails. Located right on the beach it also offers unforgettable views of the setting sun.

To the north is **Playa Potrero**, a cove of coconut palms and calm water, which is an excellent place for a picnic and a dip in the ocean. A cluster of new hotels, from modestly comfortable to extravagantly luxurious, dots the beach. Elegant **Bahía del Sol** is the cream of the crop, right on the beach, with the best sunset views and excellent service. The views get better, although the roads get worse, as

you continue north along this picturesque coastline toward **Playa Pan de Azúcar**, Sugar Loaf Beach. When you arrive at Pan de Azúcar, it is obviously the last resort. Stop in at the **Hotel Sugar Beach** (tel: 2654 4242; www. sugar-beach.com), the only hotel on the beach, for incredible views and enjoy a drink, lunch, or a swim in the cove.

Playa Tamarindo area

From the Flamingo area, go through Brasilito to Huacas and continue for 13km (8 miles) south, where you will need to make a right turn for **Playa Grande** ⓮ and **Playa Tamarindo** ⓯. Tamarindo does have a national wildlife refuge, though you would scarcely realize it. The wildlife seems more concentrated in the town's many bars and clubs than it is in the nearby estuary. The lush and lovely Hotel Capitán Suizo, at the south end of Playa Tamarindo, is still the most luxurious hotel in town and has the best location, right on the beach. Some relatively inexpensive lodging is still available in the village of Tamarindo, but over the past 10 years, Tamarindo has

Lifeguard station at Playa Tamarindo.

Tamarindo town.

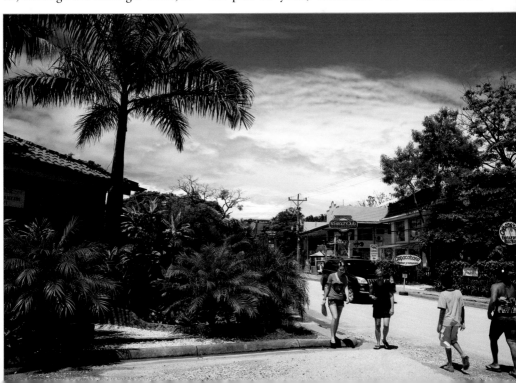

experienced such major growth that it seems to resemble a construction site more than a tourist town. Commercial centers and condominium developments have popped up everywhere. On the plus side, there is a lot more to do in town, including dining at a plethora of international restaurants.

Tamarindo is a favorite surfers' haunt, so there is no shortage of surf shops, including **Witch's Rock Surf Camp** (tel: 2653 1262; www.witchsrock-surfcamp.com), which has it all: surf shop, rentals, and lessons, along with a hotel and restaurant popular with the surfing crows. The well-run **Iguana Surf** (tel: 2653 0148; http://iguanasurf. net), has a beachfront location where you can rent boards and snorkeling equipment, and also offers tours: one of its most popular is a two-hour guided paddle through the San Francisco Estuary – a great way to see birds and wildlife.

Playa Grande is just a 5-minute boat ride across the Tamarindo estuary; by car it's a 40-minute drive from Tamarindo, on a paved road from the Huacas turnoff. Famous for its surfing

Small boats ply the estuary between Playa Grande and Playa Tamarindo.

waves by day, Playa Grande is a major leatherback turtle nesting habitat by night, and the site of ongoing environmental conflicts between conservationists and developers. The developers appear to be getting the upper hand but the beach itself is still protected.

Las Baulas National Marine Park

Parque Nacional Marino Las Baulas ⑯ (tel: 2653 0470; daily 6am–6pm, night tours in turtle season; free during the day), which incorporates Playa Grande, was created in 1991 to protect the world's most important leatherback turtle (*la baula*, in Spanish) hatching area, and was expanded in 1995. It was estimated at that time that there were only about 35,000 leatherbacks left in the world and approximately 900 of them came to Playa Grande to lay their eggs each year. Sadly, the population has subsequently fallen into a dramatic decline despite concerted efforts by the National Park Service and scientists to protect them.

During the long nesting season from August to February, if you are lucky, you may see one or two turtles struggling up the beach to dig a nest. Visitors must join a guided group since beach access is strictly limited, and flash photography of the wildlife is forbidden.

On the beach at Playa Grande is **Hotel Las Tortugas** (tel: 2653 0423 www.lastortugashotel.com), a congenial, turtle-friendly hotel, with low lighting at night to avoid disorienting nesting turtles. Catch the Guanacastecan breezes from a comfortable hammock near the turtle-shaped swimming pool, chat with the garrulous owner of the hotel, Lewis Wilson, who was instrumental in establishing the marine park, or take a guided tour of the mangrove estuary in a kayak, which ensures a quiet trip for riders and the birds they observe.

South of Tamarindo

Playa Langosta, immediately south of Tamarindo, is separated on the ocean side by a rocky headland that is impassable at high tide, but connected by the dirt road that runs south from Tamarindo. This beach is also frequented by surfers who ride waves just in front of the estuary at the southern end. The shore is rockier here and the surf crashes dramatically, sending sprays high into the air. More sedate than its noisy neighbor, Playa Langosta is home to two lovely bed and breakfast establishments and to the excellent **Playa Langosta Beach Club** (tel: 2653 1127; www.langostabeachclub.com), a French-run restaurant where you can lunch on lobster and fish carpaccios on the beach or dine in romantic splendor, poolside under palm trees twinkling with fairy lights.

Directly south from Tamarindo, along a bumpy, dusty road, **Playa Avellanas** and **Playa Negra** are popular surfers' turf. So far, these two beaches have escaped the over-development of the Tamarindo area, although there is a huge, Marriott Hotel next door to the popular **Hacienda Pinilla Beach Resort and Golf Club**, (tel: 2680-3000; www.haciendapinilla.com), 10km (6 miles) south of Tamarindo, where golfers can tee off with ocean views, on a par-72, Mike Young-designed championship course.

At Playa Avellanas, there is an idyllic beach café called **Lola's on the Beach** (tel: 2652 9097) where you can lounge under palm trees. Or you can take a nature walk in the mangroves in front of **Cabinas Las Olas** (tel: 2652 9315; www.cabinalasolas.co.cr) a favorite with surfers. Even if you're not a surfer, the **Hotel Playa Negra** (tel: 2652 9134; www.playanegra.com), a little farther south, is a charming place to stay, with round, thatched-roof cabins overlooking the ocean and a circular pool.

Head inland from Tamarindo for some 18km (11 miles) and, at the junction of the village called Veintisiete de Abril, turn toward the coast and proceed for approximately 12km (8 miles) to lovely **Playa Junquillal** ⑰, a paradisiacal, wide beach with high surf that gives you the sense of having found a secret place. The Swiss-run **Guacamaya Lodge** (tel:

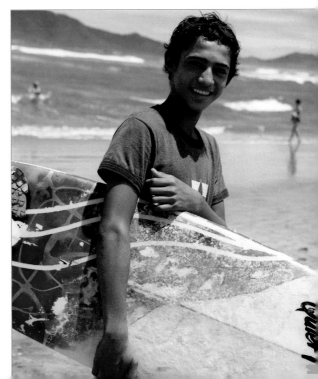

Playa Tamarindo featured in the cult surfer flick Endless Summer.

2658 8431; www.guacamayalodge.com) is the best place to stay, on a hill with a view over the ocean and a beautifully landscaped pool.

Inland to Santa Cruz

Heading inland from the coast at Paraíso, few populated areas disturb the unbroken beauty of the rolling hills and valleys. An occasional cluster of three or four houses indicates a village. Here chickens, ducks, and the occasional cyclist claim the road. The kilometers are marked by the infrequent passage of herds of noisy Brahman cows, turning traffic into a cattle drive, followed in their leisurely journey by *sabaneros* on horseback. These *Guanacasteco* cowboys don't direct the animals out of the road; they let the automobile wend its way through them. The cattle, with their sensitive faces, seem neither concerned nor particularly curious.

Santa Cruz ⓲ is a busy market town and administration center. You'll know you are approaching it by the unattractive *tallers* (auto workshops) that line the highway. In the

central plaza, the modern church stands beside the original colonial clock tower of the old church that was destroyed by an earthquake in 1950. The central park is a quiet, shady place for sitting and viewing the life of a Guanacaste town.

Santa Cruz is most famous for its popular folklore festival held in mid-January, featuring bullfights (the Costa Rican kind where the bull is teased but not killed), rodeos, folk dancing, and traditional marimba music.

One of the main visitor attractions in this part of Guanacaste is the village of **Guaitil ⓳**, which specializes in re-creating ceramic pots in the style of the pre-Columbian inhabitants of this part of Costa Rica. After the Conquest, pottery-making died out here, possibly because the images adorning pots were considered pagan by the Catholic Church. The craft has been revived in recent years and today the popularity of these giant ceramic pots is obvious from their presence in the lobbies and dining rooms of many hotels in Guanacaste. Almost every house in Guaitil has a kiln and pots for sale in the yard. The widest selection, however, is next to the soccer field in front of the church.

Nicoya

From Guaitil it is a scenic 20-minute drive on a smoothly paved highway to the town of **Nicoya ⓴**, the former colonial capital of Guanacaste. Alternatively, Nicoya is an easy 27km (17-mile) drive west, from the Río Tempisque Bridge. The pride of Nicoya is its central park and the **Church of San Blas**, a classic, white, adobe colonial church, originally built in 1644, then restored after an 1831 earthquake. The church, is now a museum (irregular hours), with notable, folk-art stations of the cross carved in wood. Nicoya is a good place to stop and shop, eat at one of the town's many Chinese restaurants, and top up your gas tanks at one of its 24-hour service stations.

The adobe Church of San Blas in Nicoya town.

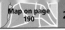

Playa Nosara

Nicoya is the gateway to the beaches of nearby Sámara and the more remote Nosara, both popular destinations for North American and European vacationers who prefer a calmer alternative to the high-octane tourist scene in northern Guanacaste. The road is paved south from Nicoya, until the turn-off for **Playa Nosara ㉑**. Then it's a very bumpy ride along an alternately dusty or muddy road for 18km (11 miles), depending on the season. During the worst of the rainy season, this road is sometimes impassable, so many visitors fly directly to Nosara from San José. The actual town of Nosara is a small, rather nondescript inland place. The star attractions here are idyllic **Playa Pelada** and **Playa Guiones**, two long white-sand beaches with excellent surfing waves and many kilometers of beach bordered by shade trees and tendrils of green sea grape edging the sand.

Despite the difficulty getting here by road, the Nosara area has experienced a major building boom. Happily, though, a development plan has restricted building heights and density, so most of the private villas, small hotels, and restaurants are screened behind trees and attractive landscaping. The international cast of characters who have settled in Nosara include a large contingent of nature-loving Swiss. Nosara is also a haven for New Agers; yoga, alternative therapies, and vegetarianism abound. The **Harmony Hotel** (tel: 2682 4114; http://harmonynosara.com) is a model of sustainable tourism, as well as a haven of luxury for well-heeled surfers and spa seekers. A large part of Nosara is still protected as a reserve, and as a result it is more forested and richer in wildlife than other parts of the region.

Coconut tree on Playa Sámara.

Nosara protected areas

At the far northern edge of Nosara, the **Nosara Biological Reserve** is a private nature reserve with hiking trails leading down to the mangrove-lined shores of the Nosara River. It's part of the Swiss-run **Lagarta Lodge** (tel: 2682 0035; www.lagarta.com), which occupies an eagle's aerie, high above the ocean. There are guided

The best surfing along the Nicoya Peninsula can be experienced between December and April.

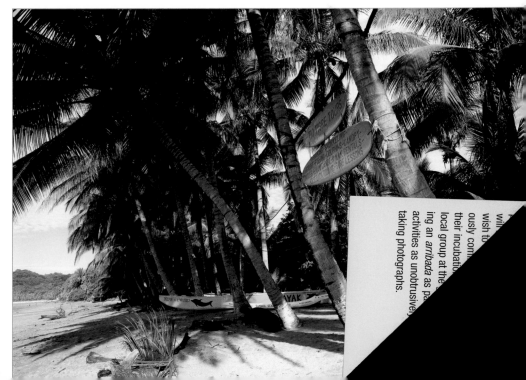

nature tours daily or you can take a self-guided tour of the reserve. About 7km (4.5 miles) north of Nosara, the **Refugio Nacional de Vida Silvestre Ostional** is an important turtle-nesting site for Olive Ridley turtles, which arrive by the thousands to nest on the beach. To witness an *arribada*, as it is called, you must join a guided tour organized by a village cooperative (tel: 2682 0428).

Sadly, in season, you can still buy the eggs of endangered turtle species, considered by many men to be an aphrodisiac. Some of the eggs have been excavated by adventurers, but most are part of a cache of eggs taken legally by local villagers who are given permits by the government to take the eggs during the first 36 hours of an *arribada*.

Playa Sámara and south

Playa Sámara ㉒ is just an hour south of Nicoya along a beautifully paved, scenic road. Or you can take a regular flight from San José to Sámara. This is a beautiful white sand beach, with a reef that's good for snorkeling, but

Glorious Playa Sámara.

more importantly, also protects the beach from direct waves. Swimming here is safe in crystalline, shallow waters with minimal surf. Off season, there is a feeling of dramatic isolation. During the high season, Playa Sámara is very popular with Costa Ricans, and many *Ticos* have summer homes here. Italians, too, have discovered this idyllic beach and settled here, opening restaurants that have raised the culinary standards considerably.

Diving, snorkeling, fishing, bicycle and horseback tours, and kayaking can be arranged by all the local hotels. The waves are small for surfing, but just right for beginners. To the north of the beach are some basic *cabinas*, small hotels, and some excellent restaurants. A block north of the beach, bougainvillea-draped **Hotel Giada** (**tel:** 2656 3232; www.hotelgiada.net) has a lot of Italian style, and excellent pizza. Walking west along the beach, you'll find **El Lagarto** (**tel:** 2656 0750; www.ellagartobbq.com)**,** a dinner-only hotspot right on the sand, famous for its delicious and huge portions of barbecued beef and

THE ARRIBADA

Created to protect the endangered Olive Ridley turtle, the Ostional National Wildlife Refuge is witness to the spectacular phenomenon known as the *arribada*, when tens of thousands of turtles come to the beach to lay their eggs. It is estimated that during these brief periods as many as 100,000 Olive Ridleys may come ashore to this isolated beach, and leave behind more than 10 million eggs. *Arribadas* generally occur at two- to four-week intervals between the third quarter and full moon from April to December, peaking during July through September.

Presently, there is a controversial program of egg collecting in operation at Ostional, which gives the people of the nearby village the legal right to gather as many of the turtle eggs as they can during the first 36 hours of every *arribada* in an attempt to prevent further poaching. One of the pro-collecting arguments is that the first eggs [wil]l be dug up by succeeding waves of nesting turtles anyway. If you [want to] see the amazing sight of thousands of these creatures labori[ng] [com]ing ashore to thump the sand with their flippers and dig [ope]n holes to lay their eggs, make a reservation with the [g]uard station on the beach. You can only visit dur[ing as pa]rt of a guided group. Remember to watch the [quietl]y as possible, and do not use a flash when seafood. Even the vegetables are barbecued here.

Another 7km (4 miles) south of Sámara is **Playa Carrillo** ㉓, a near-flawless, half-moon, white sand beach protected by an offshore reef and populated only by coconut palms. Beyond Carrillo are other extraordinary beaches: isolated, lonely places, sometimes with fresh water available, sometimes not. One of these is **Playa Caletas**, with its own gardens and plunge pools and every conceivable comfort, is the ultimate in sophistication.

Barra Honda National Park

About 21km (13 miles) east of the town of Nicoya is **Barra Honda National Park** ㉔ (tel: 2659 1551; daily 7.30am–4pm) a rocky outcropping containing a vast network of caves. Look for national park signs pointing the way on the Nicoya side of the Friendship Bridge that spans the Río Tempisque. On the flat ridgeline, 300 meters (1,000ft) above the caves, a *mirador* (lookout point) can be reached via marked paths. Standing on the ridge, you can drink in the view across the vast Nicoya Peninsula, accompanied by the sounds of an enormous waterfall, screeching tropical birds, scary-sounding howler monkeys, and iguanas scuffling in the trees.

You don't have to be a dedicated spelunker to enjoy Barra Honda, though some of the caves are quite deep and require steep vertical drops to enter. With names such as *La Trampa* (The Trap) and *Terciopelo* (Fer-de-Lance viper), they may not sound inviting, but the formations are dazzling, including one called The Organ, which produces melodic tones when gently touched.

Blind salamanders, vampire bats, and strange birds share the world of darkness in the Barra Honda caves, which have escaped vandalism and exploitation because they lack an easily accessible horizontal entrance. A community group has the exclusive right to lead cave tours, and provide basic lodging and good *campesina* food. In the dry season (Dec–Apr) it gets extremely hot, so be sure to bring a wide-brimmed hat and water.

A shady spot on Playa Carrillo.

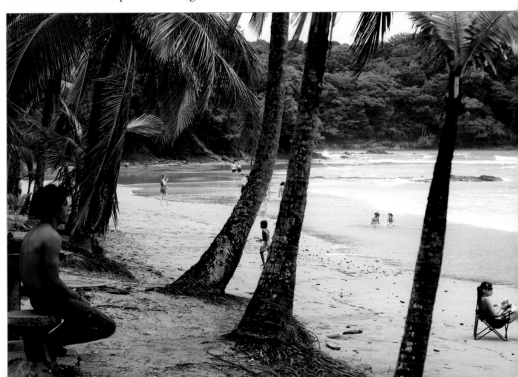

COSTA RICA'S WINGS OF WONDER

With more than 850 species of resident and migrant birds, Costa Rica is one of the world's foremost destinations for professional ornithologists and amateur birders.

Despite its small size, Costa Rica has almost the same number of bird species as the whole of North America, and significantly more than Europe or Australia. This tremendous diversity is explained, in part, by the country's tropical location, and partly by its position on one of the world's great bird migration routes, over the Central American land bridge linking North and South America.

For most birders Costa Rica's resident species – rather than its migrants – are the ones that hold the most interest. The most sought-after sightings are undoubtedly the resplendent quetzal, two species of toucans, and two endangered macaws, the scarlet and the green. Opportunities for birdwatching are everywhere in Costa Rica, with eco-lodges, reserves, and tours geared to it. A world-class cadre of resident birding guides also makes birdwatching here a pleasure, even for visitors who have never bothered to look at a bird before.

The fairy-like green violet-ear, one of the country's 50-plus species of hummingbirds, harvests nectar from a flower. Only 4.5ins (11.5cm) long, this hummer lives in the highlands.

Montezuma oropendolas inhabit colonies of hanging nests, built by females and patrolled by males. At sunset, you may spot flocks of oropendoloas flying back to their nests, making a gurgling sound.

Nectar Feeders

Costa Rica has 54 species of tiny but pugnacious hummingbirds, including the violet sabre-wing, the largest at 152mm (6ins); and the volcano hummingbird, one of the smallest at 76mm (3ins). Hummingbirds feed largely on a diet of sugary nectar and insects. They are often lured to artificial feeders filled with sugar water and placed around eco-lodge verandahs and in gardens. Station yourself and your camera nearby and you are in for an unbeatable spectacle of color and whirring wings.

The keel-billed toucan with its colorful, hollow bill is called Arco Iris in Spanish, which means "rainbow." His cousin, the chestnut-mandibled toucan, has an equally impressive brown and yellow bill.

A great green macaw.

ENDANGERED SPECIES

Despite Costa Rica's efforts to protect its forests, habitat destruction has had a serious effect on some of its birds. The quetzal is particularly vulnerable because it largely depends for survival on one special *aguacatillo* tree, found only in cloud forest. The three-wattled bellbird shares this habitat, and is equally threatened when forests are converted to pasture. Great green macaws are the most threatened species of macaw. Conservation efforts on the Caribbean coast, where they exclusively live, include honoring farmers who maintain the *dipteryx* trees upon which the macaws feed. There are only 30 active nests recorded in the protected breeding area straddling Costa Rica and Nicaragua. National parks and private reserves, such as Maquenque National Wildlife Refuge, are a lifeline to survival.

Even higher on the critical list is Costa Rica's biggest raptor, the American harpy eagle. This giant monkey-eating bird is known to breed in the forests of the Osa Peninsula, but sightings of it have become extremely rare. A handful of species, such as the cattle egret and roadside hawk, have actually benefited from man-made changes to the environment, because they need open ground on which to feed.

Thanks to conservation efforts, the scarlet macaw has been brought back from the brink of extinction. The most reliable location for spotting them in the wild is at the Osa Peninsula, near Carate.

From his perch on a tree snag in a river, this green heron is concentrating on catching fish for his supper. While herons are plentiful, the great green macaw is on the endangered list, owing to deforestation of his natural habitat.

Tabacón hot springs.

Cataratas del Río Fortuna waterfall.

San José

THE NORTHEAST

Volcán Arenal, a classically cone-shaped volcano, and its hot springs are the star attractions of the region, though the Sarapiquí River and nearby rustic eco-lodges and wild nature reserves are hotspots for more adventurous travelers.

The region to the northeast of San José corresponds roughly to the area known as the Northern Zone, where the landscape is lush and agricultural for the most part. The main attractions for visitors are the spectacular Arenal volcano with its surrounding hot springs and spas, and some remote rainforest reserves.

Around Ciudad Quesada (San Carlos)

At the foot of the Cordillera Central, **Ciudad Quesada ❶**, often called by its former name, San Carlos, is the gateway to the country's northern attractions, as well as the bustling agricultural and commercial heart of the region.

Some 7km (4.5 miles) east of San Carlos, **Termales del Bosque** (tel: 2460 4740; www.termalesdelbosque.com) is a low-key, family-run hotel with its own *termales*, thermal hot springs, in a forest setting alongside a fast-running river. You can soak in a series of pools at different temperatures, and then cool off in the river. There are also trails through primary and secondary forest, and ponds filled with tilapia, destined for the hotel restaurant. Horseback riding, guided nature tours, and natural spa treatments are also on offer.

The **Tilajari Hotel Resort** (tel: 2462 1212; www.tilajari.com) near Muelle,

around 22km (14 miles) north of Ciudad Quesada, is a luxurious spread, set on several hectares of gardens, overlooking the wide San Carlos River. It makes a good base for exploring this region, and offers tennis, swimming, horseback riding, and hiking in 400 hectares (1,000 acres) of rainforest, as well as spa and beauty treatments. Farther afield you can take fishing trips and jungle river tours to Caño Negro Wildlife Reserve.

The Tilajari is also the lift-off point for an enchanting hot-air balloon

Main Attractions
Arenal Volcano
Tabacón Grand Spa Thermal Resort
Caño Negro National Wildlife Reserve
Puerto Viejo de Sarapiquí
La Selva Biological Reserve

Riding near San Ramón.

TIP

Tabacón Springs is
pricey and often
crowded, especially on
weekends, so try to
choose an off-season
weekday to visit.

ride over the **San Carlos Valley** with Serendipity Adventures (tel: 2556 2222; www.serendipityadventures.com). Standing in a traditional wicker balloon basket under a multicolored balloon, you ascend just after dawn, over tree tops where howler monkeys and toucans are just waking up, then float over cattle pastures alternating with fields of sugar cane and pineapple. It's expensive – about $385 per person – but it really is a once-in-a-lifetime experience.

La Fortuna

From Muelle it's around 25km (16 miles) west to **La Fortuna** ❷ (also known as Fortuna de San Carlos). This busy, sun-baked village near the base of Arenal Volcano is the center for tours, accommodations and eateries.

Some 5km (3 miles) east of La Fortuna is the turnoff to the **Cataratas del Río Fortuna**. These falls are accessible in an hour's easy horseback ride from La Fortuna through pastures and fields of corn, bananas, and peppers. If you are going to drive, the trip requires a four-wheel-drive vehicle. Once at the falls, a muddy hike down a slippery slope to the swimming area at the base of the falls makes the clear, fresh water all the sweeter.

Tabacón hot springs

Closer to the volcano, between La Fortuna and Lake Arenal, **Tabacón Grand Spa Thermal Resort ❸** (tel: 2479-2099; www.tabacon.com) is one of Costa Rica's most popular tourist destinations. From here you can look directly up the volcano's lava-rock slopes. The volcano appears dangerously close – and it is. Volcanologists have predicted that if Arenal erupts, Tabacón Springs will likely be in the path of the lava flow. Meanwhile, the volcano has a benign effect, heating Tabacón's therapeutic waters to a perfect temperature. Tiled slides, waterfalls, and pools of varying temperatures are surrounded by tumbling warm-water creeks and exquisitely landscaped gardens.

Although the springs are often crowded with day-trippers, hotel guests can enjoy volcano views at night from quiet pools under a starry sky. And should you be there when the full moon waxes over Arenal, that single experience may be worth the expense of staying here.

Just west of La Fortuna, you can luxuriate in the warm mineral waters of the more affordable **Baldi Hot Springs** (tel: 2479 8811; www.arenalonline.com). For US$50 you get a day pass with dinner, and grown-ups can enjoy a warm soak in a plethora of pools with varying temperatures with a volcano view, while children can play on a variety of water slides.

Down the highway, past the Tabacón Hot Springs Resort, is a dirt road to the left leading 9km (5 miles) to **Arenal Observatory Lodge** (tel: 2290 7011; www.arenalobservatorylodge.com) formerly a volcano research facility for the Smithsonian Institution. It is the only lodge in the national park and the closest accommodations to the volcano, only 2.7km (1.7 miles) away. The lodge has comfortable rooms in bungalows, set in a huge estate with primary and secondary forest, waterfalls, and hiking and horseback trails. The birdwatching here is quite spectacular.

Arenal Volcano

Until early July 1968, Arenal was a heavily wooded low hill, similar to many others in the area, near the village of La Fortuna. One morning local people began feeling a few earth tremors.

Beautifully landscaped grounds of the Tabacón Hot Springs Resort.

Volcán Arenal rising from the plain is an unforgettable sight.

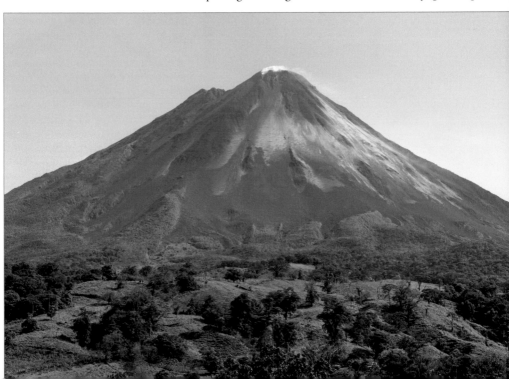

It is possible to take a boat across Lake Arenal to Monteverde.

Suddenly, the forest started smoking and steaming. Women washing their clothes marveled at the sudden warm water that flowed in the creeks. Then, on July 29, **Volcán Arenal** ❹ exploded. Rolling clouds of gas and fountains of red-hot boulders and molten lava hit the countryside. Official estimates put the death toll at 62, but local people claim that more than 80 people were killed. More than 5 sq km (2 sq miles) of land near the volcano was abruptly changed from pastoral farmland to a landscape out of Dante's *Inferno*. Since then, Arenal was continuously active, until October, 2010, when it just as suddenly stopped spewing and spitting out fiery rocks. In 2013 it awoke again to send a column of steam high into the air. The Arenal is officially still active, but in a 'resting phase,' and no one can predict when it may become a star performer again. Even without the pyrotechnics, Arenal is still everyone's preconception of a volcano: conical, rising abruptly out of flatland vegetation. But do not attempt to climb the upper reaches. Although it's in a resting phase, the volcano still occasionally belches dangerous gases.

Nuevo Arenal ❺ is a town reborn from the old village of Arenal, in the valley that was flooded in 1973 to create the lake and the huge hydroelectric project here. Along the road to Nuevo Arenal there are some very pleasant small hotels and bed-and-breakfasts. The scenic road winds around the edges of the lake, but drivers need to be aware that although it is paved, it is often washed out, especially during the rainy season.

Lake Arenal

Laguna de Arenal ❻ offers some of Costa Rica's most challenging freshwater fishing. Whether or not you choose to fish, do charter a boat and a guide to take you sightseeing on the lake. Better still, set off in a rented kayak. Go in the early morning, when, for much of the year, the lake's surface is like glass, and the volcano can be viewed as a crystalline reflection.

From December through April, usually in the afternoon, northeasterly winds blow almost daily, and the lake is anything but calm and glassy. Between 40 and 50 knots of sustained breeze whips the west end of the lake into a sea of whitecaps, making it a favorite destination for experienced windsurfers. **Tico Wind** (tel: 2692 2002; www.ticowind.com), 30km (18 miles) west of Nuevo Arenal, rents a full range of windsurfing equipment and offers lessons from December through April.

The **Lake Arenal Hotel & Brewery** (tel: 2695 5050; http://lakearenalhotel.com), within walking distance of the best windsurfing, is an arresting replica of the ancient Palace of Knossos on the island of Crete, 9km (5 miles) north of the town of Tilarán. This is a good place to spend the night, refreshingly cool in a hilltop-garden setting above the lake. And if you are a beer drinker, you can sample the hotel's microbrews, made on the premises.

To Arenal via San Ramón

An alternative route to Arenal from San José is via **San Ramón**, a bustling market town famous for its

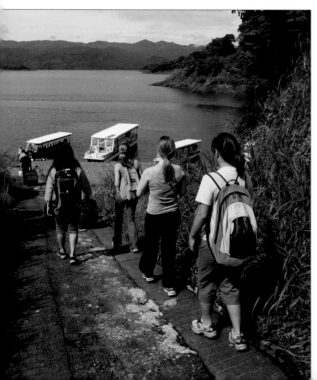

earthquake-proof concrete church and as the birthplace of Costa Rica's most famous poets – Lisimaco Chavarria Palma and Felix Ángel Salas Cabezas. In keeping with its cultural heritage, the **José Figueres Cultural Center** (http://centrojosefigueres.org), across from the north side of the church, offers art exhibits, concerts, and a small museum about 'Don Pepe' Figueres, the president who abolished Costa Rica's army. The cultural center occupies the house where he was born.

About 20km (12 miles) north of San Ramón, along a scenic, winding road, is **Villa Blanca** (tel: 2461 0300; www.villablanca-costarica.com), set in a cloud forest preserve. The hotel is like a village of small *casitas*. Each bungalow is luxuriously furnished, and equipped with a cozy fireplace. Some also have Jacuzzi bathtubs, making it a favorite with honeymooners and for weddings in a charming small chapel decorated with handpainted tiles. There are nature trails to explore, on your own or with resident naturalist guides, and there is a full-service spa and a small movie theater for those who prefer indoor experiences.

Heading north

If you want to get off the beaten track, head northeast from San Carlos toward Aguas Zarcas, then take the gravel road past Pital to reach **Laguna del Lagarto Lodge** (tel: 2289 8163; www.lagarto-lodge-costa-rica.com), a total of 135km (78 miles). This remote eco-lodge has rustic rooms and serves buffet-style meals. The main attraction is the setting, in 505 hectares (1,250 acres) of rainforest, home to almost 400 species of birds. As its name promises, there is also a reedy lagoon that shelters *lagartos* (caimans). There are 10km (6 miles) of hiking trails, plus horseback riding, canoeing, and opportunities for boat trips up the Río San Carlos to the Nicaraguan border.

Nearby **Maquenque Eco-Lodge** (tel: 2479-82-00; www.maquenqueecolodge.com) is a newer, more luxurious lodge, with high-roofed cabins, a swimming pool, and an excellent restaurant set around lakes in the 60,000-hectare (148,000-acre) **Maquenque National Wildlife Refuge**.

Both the above lodges are smack in the middle of the last remaining

FACT

Misty Lake Arenal has a resident monster, reputedly seen by local fishermen who described a hairy serpent with horns. The Monster of Lake Arenal is now firmly entrenched in local folklore.

Tranquil countryside around the town of La Tigra, near San Ramón.

TIP

Heavy clouds often obscure Arenal Volcano. If your heart is set on seeing Arenal in full profile, plan to stay at least two nights in the area to increase your chances of getting a clear view.

breeding grounds for great green macaws. You will need a four-wheel-drive vehicle, and be sure to bring stout rubber boots for walking the trails.

Caño Negro

West of San Carlos, north of Arenal toward the Nicaraguan border, lies another natural treasure, the magnificent and still uncrowded **Refugio Nacional de Vida Silvestre Caño Negro ❼** (Caño Negro National Wildlife Reserve; tel: 2460 0055; daily 8am–4pm), part of the Unesco Agua y Paz International Biosphere. It provides excellent birdwatching opportunities, mostly from quiet boats navigating a huge, shallow lake that covers around 800 hectares (2,000 acres). The lake is created during the wet season when the nearby Río Frío overflows, but dries up almost completely during the dry season. Residents include large flocks of water birds: anhingas, roseate spoonbills, white ibis, and Jabirú storks, the largest bird of the region and in great danger of extinction. Caño Negro is also home to caimans and crocodiles, although their numbers are threatened

Paddling along the Río Frío in Caño Negro National Wildlife Reserve.

by poachers, often from neighboring Nicaragua, who hunt the crocodilians for their valuable skins.

Access to Caño Negro is from La Fortuna, Los Chiles, or Upala, on good roads northwest of Cañas. Basic accommodations are available in Los Chiles, and the village of Caño Negro has two upscale hotels. Several tour agencies in La Fortuna, including **Sunset Tours** (tel: 2479 9800; www.sunsettour.net), offer day trips to Caño Negro.

The Sarapiquí region

The lush, tropical jungles of the **Río Sarapiquí** region, on the Caribbean side of the Cordillera Central, are less than 100km (60 miles) east of San José. La Selva Biological Station, Selva Verde Lodge, and Rara Avis, private reserves with lodging, are all accessible via the Braulio Carrillo Highway east of San José, through the spectacular Parque Nacional Braulio Carrillo. An even more scenic route, via Heredia and Varablanca, suffered heavy damage during the 2009 Poás earthquake, but the road has been reopened as far as San Miguel, and it is an eerie experience to

A CELESTIAL EXPERIENCE

One of the most enchanting, and least visited, national parks is **Tenorio Volcano National Park** (daily 8am–4pm), about 55km (38 miles) north of Cañas on the road to Upala. The most beautiful river runs through it: the Río Celeste, which lives up to its name with heavenly blue water. The color is actually a chemical reaction of sulphur and calcium carbonates, but it's magical, nonetheless.

You can hike through primary cloud forest to a waterfall and swim in the cool blue water. Along the river there are also pockets of hot springs and volcanic mud, which you can smear on your face for a natural facial. Butterflies, birds and wildlife abound, including snakes that enjoy sunning themselves on sunlit paths, so be sure to wear hiking boots and look where you are treading. The park office (daily 8am–4pm) has restrooms and fresh water.

You can stay overnight nearby at **Las Heliconias Lodge** (tel: 2466 8483; www.heliconiaslodge.com), an eco-lodge run by a local cooperative, near the village of Bijagua. Basic cabins and comfortable private bungalows overlook Lake Nicaragua in the distance, and there are miles of birding trails running through the adjoining forest. This is one place in the country where you have a chance of spotting the tiny and rare tody motmot *(Hylomanes momotula)*, the smallest of the motmot bird family.

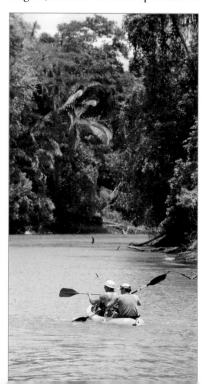

see the after-effects of the earthquake and the accompanying landslides. Beware of driving the Braulio Carrillo highway after sunset, since thick night fog blankets this steep, winding route.

Puerto Viejo de Sarapiquí and Rara Avis

Puerto Viejo de Sarapiquí ❽ is a small, colorful port town from which river boats used to depart for otherwise inaccessible settlements along these jungle waterways, before the coastal canal was built. Boats still depart from the dock, but most are loaded with tourists on a scenic river trip with a naturalist guide to point out the monkeys, birds, and other riverside animals along the way. You can also take a full-day trip up the Sarapiquí to the **Río San Juan**, on the Nicaraguan border; be sure to bring along your passport because the river crosses into Nicaraguan territory.

Oasis Nature Tours (tel: 2766 6108; www.oasisnaturetours.com) organizes both kinds of river trips. If you are looking for more hands-on, exciting action, there are stretches of the Río Sarapiquí with various classes of whitewater for

river rafting. **Hacienda Pozo Azul** (tel: 2438 2616; www.pozoazul.com) offers a range of whitewater rafting trips.

Rara Avis Rainforest Lodge (tel: 2764 1111; www.rara-avis.com) is a pristine, 600-hectare (1,500-acre) rainforest reserve adjacent to Braulio Carrillo National Park. Established in 1983, it was Costa Rica's first eco-lodge. The main office and departure point for the reserve is in Las Horquetas, a village 17km (11 miles) south of Puerto Viejo de Sarapiquí. Whether you are continuing by horseback or tractor-drawn cart, travel to Rara Avis can be grueling, especially in wet conditions, which are the norm. It can only be recommended for those who are both physically and mentally fit. The bumpy three-hour journey encounters ruts, bogs, and rivers. On the road, the transition from cattle ranches to deep jungle illustrates the devastating effects of deforestation more dramatically than any textbook or film could possibly do.

Deforested land ends at El Plástico, named for a former prison colony where inmates slept under plastic sheets. It's another 6km (4 miles) along a trail

The nectar of the hibiscus flower is highly prized by hummingbirds.

Caño Negro has a protected caiman colony.

No through road – even for a four-wheel-drive.

through a cool, cathedral-like forest to Waterfall Lodge, high in the forest. The lodge, just a five-minute walk from a spectacular waterfall, has eight rustic rooms, each with its own bathtub with hot water. There are also separate cabins, one along the river, and three cold-water cabins nearby. The main attractions here are birdwatching, forest hiking, swimming, and wildlife viewing. Because it is such a rarefied and isolated place, you must always book well in advance, and you should stay for at least two nights to make the journey worthwhile..

La Selva Biological Reserve

About 7km (4.5 miles) south of Puerto Viejo you will see the sign for 'OTS' (the Organization for Tropical Studies) and the gravel road to La Selva. The diversity and abundance of life in the lowland tropical forest of the Sarapiquí River region attracted tropical biologists here more than 40 years ago. They subsequently founded OTS and in 1968 established the **Estación Biólogica La Selva ❾** (La Selva Biological Reserve and Research Station; www.ots.ac.cr). In 1986 the Costa Rican government

A stream in the lowland rainforest.

also made a major commitment to rainforest conservation by extending the boundaries of Braulio Carrillo National Park to meet the outer reaches of the La Selva Reserve. As a result of this decision, a total of 21,000 hectares (52,000 acres) of virgin forest now preserves the migratory pathways and large territories required for the survival of several species of Costa Rica's rare and endangered birds and mammals.

La Selva has become one of the most important sites in the world for tropical rainforest research, and today virtually all of the world's tropical biologists have spent time at La Selva as students, teachers, or scientists – or at the very least they have been strongly influenced by the vast amount of scientific research that has been accomplished there over the past few decades. Many Sarapiquí residents who work at eco-tourist lodges were also trained as naturalist guides at La Selva.

The reserve is primarily a research and educational facility, but it offers excellent, naturalist-led, half-day or full-day tours of the trails (tel: 2766 6565 or 2524 0607; www.threepaths.co.cr; daily).

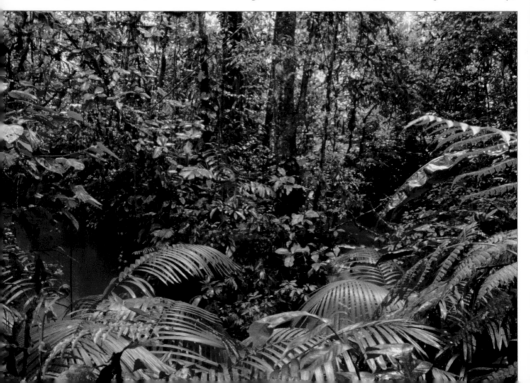

Fledgling bird-watchers can sign up for a day-long Birdwatching 101 course, and more experienced birders can set off on a two-hour guided bird walk at 5.45am. There are also two-hour night tours. The well-developed trail system includes trails with raised boardwalks in order to give access during the wet season. Comfortable new cabins for visitors have greatly improved the accommodations here, and overnight guests can enjoy the trails on their own. But visitors still share the cafeteria-style food with the students and researchers who live in dormitories.

Selva Verde

In 1986, Giovanna and Juan Holbrook, conservationists from Florida, bought **Selva Verde ⑩**, (tel: 2761 1800; www.selvaverde.com) 200 hectares (500 acres) of primary and secondary tropical lowland forest, along the banks of the Sarapiquí River, in order to save the land from deforestation.

They designed their beautiful river lodge to have minimal impact on the environment, perching it on posts above the forest floor. Guests stay in tropical hardwood rooms at the end of covered corridors, which radiate from a central conference room into the forest. The jungle and its denizens are never more than a few meters away. Selva Verde carries the Certification for Sustainable Tourism, a voluntary program that sets a standard for lodges in sustainability, including environmental and community impact.

Spectacular birds are commonplace at Selva Verde: keel-billed and chestnut-mandibled toucans feed on the fruit of the nutmeg trees near the front porch of the lodge. A stroll along the path to the main lodge building is likely to be rewarded with the iridescent colors of several species of hummingbirds. Nearby, Montezuma oropendolas utter gurgling mating calls, which harmonize with the songs of other birds and countless frogs and insects in a continual symphony. The lodge's other main wildlife attractions are incredibly slow-moving arboreal sloths. Selva Verde lodge is very popular with tour groups, so be sure to book in advance. If you are not staying here, you can also come just for lunch and a trail walk.

> **FACT**
>
> Sloths descend to the forest floor once a week to defecate. This unusual behavior may be an attempt to move their scent away from their home.

The attractive Heleconia latisphata, or Expanded Lobster Claw, grows wild in this region.

A WILDLIFE BONANZA

La Virgen de Sarapiquí is a hub of wildlife-viewing options. Bats and frogs are the focus of two separate night tours at the **Tirimbina Rainforest Center** (tel: 2761 0333; www.tirimbina.org), a 304-hectare (750-acre) primary forest reserve. The daily, guided birdwatching tour starts bright and early at 6am, to search the reserve's 8km (5 miles) of trails for lowland species.

Visitors who are keen to not only look but also shoot wildlife, will appreciate the neighboring **Sarapiquí Eco-Observatory** (tel: 2761 0801; www.eco-observatory.com; daily 7am–5pm) a nature reserve with a spacious covered deck – safe from ever-present downpours here – where you can set up tripods for camera gear, make Wi-fi connections for downloading photos, and re-charge batteries. Photo set-ups made up of tree branches and fruit attract birds for close-up shots.

If reptiles and amphibians are your preferred choice of wildlife, you can safely feast your eyes on more than 60 species, including pit vipers, boa constrictors, and pythons at the **Snake Garden** (tel: 2761 1059) next door. Father-son herpetologists Pompilio Campos Sr and Jr can also arrange a four-hour photo session at the Eco-Observatory, featuring your choice of eight creatures from the *serpentario*'s collection. Photographers can shoot away in safety, while Campos Sr and Jr pose the animals and share their 25-year store of reptilian lore.

MOUNTAINS OF FIRE

Vulcanologists are always busy in Costa Rica, which has five active volcanoes and some 112 dormant and extinct ones. Visitors can explore volcanic peaks and soak in thermal waters.

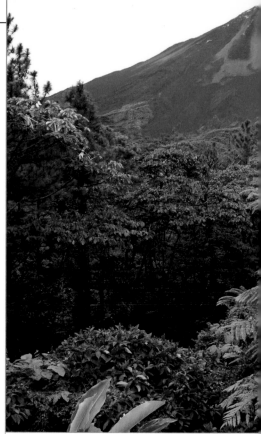

Costa Rica is a land of earthquakes and volcanoes, where hikers and mountaineering enthusiasts can climb the Central Valley's four active cones in just two days. Visitors should remember, though, that an active volcano demands respect; proper equipment is essential. Taking a guided tour will ensure the greatest safety. Local people are proud of their explosive geology, and have made Poás and Irazú volcanoes the country's most visited parks.

Follow the sign to see the old lava flow.

The most dynamic and majestic of Costa Rica's active volcanoes is Arenal, a nearly perfect cone. The 1,633-meter (4,950ft) -high volcano rises above farmlands, adjacent to its own lake, and offered a spectacular show of clouds of gas and steam spewing out of the top. Arenal is still considered active, but it is currently in a resting phase.

Tourists looking for active volcanoes won't be disappointed, however, as two other 'resting' volcanoes have suddenly come back to life – Volcán Rincón de la Vieja, to the northwest of Arenal; and Volcán Turrialba, east of the Central Valley. The latter has been spewing ashes, rocks, and gases since late 2014. Poás Volcano has also shown more activity lately and the popular national park surrounding it sometimes closes temporarily when the sulfurous gas levels get too high.

On its best daytime behavior, Arenal Volcano is picture-perfect with its cone-shaped profile etched against the sky. But the pointy tip often catches passing clouds, disappointing many a photographer.

When Arenal spewed out streams of red-hot rocks and lava at night, visitors were treated to spectacular pyrotechnic show.

A short hike along a forest trail leads visitors to the placid crater lake in Poás Volcano National Park. Along the way, watch out for volcano juncos, chubby sparrow-like birds, hopping along the path.

Hot springs, heated up by Arenal Volcano, create a water wonderland for visitors at upscale Tabacón and other nearby thermal resorts, including the lower-key Termales del Bosque, near San Carlos, where hot pools edge a cool, fast-running river.

BELOW THE VOLCANOES

To observe Arenal in true luxury, pamper yourself at the Spanish colonial-style Tabacón Grand Spa Thermal Resort, built on the site of a 1975 hot avalanche deposit that provides the source of heat for the thermal waters.

Although vulcanologists feel there is a risk of future hot avalanches, this hasn't stopped the Ticos and tourists who flock here to exclaim excitedly over the activity of the volcano and soak their aching muscles. A dip in the waters is also supposedly beneficial for anyone suffering from skin problems and arthritis.

Twelve pools of varying depths and temperatures (the warmest is a sizzling 38°C/102°F), a Jacuzzi, hot waterfall, slides, and an individual tub tucked deep in the beautifully landscaped tropical gardens mean fun for everyone from children to senior citizens.

A spa offers mud facials, and the resort has lockers, towel rental, and showers. The hotel here is elegant and expensive. Book well in advance.

If you are on a budget, try the Baldi Hot Springs just west of La Fortuna or the low-key but lush Termales del Bosque near San Carlos.

Poás Volcano has the world's largest active crater.

The vast craters of Volcán Irazú look deceptively peaceful, but since 1723 this very active volcano has erupted more than 20 times.

POÁS VOLCANO IS IN ACTIVITY
YOU ENTER UNDER YOUR OWN RISK
SPN – MIRENEM

Coco's Bar, Cahuita.

BAR

COCO'S
BAR
GRILL

SPECIALIZED
IN
TIPICAL
AND
AMERICAN
FOOD

TRY THE
BEST FOOD
IN TOWN
Welcome
to
cahuita

RED SNAPPER
FRESH LOBSTER
RICE AND BEANS
COCOS BAR AND GRILL

COCO'S BAR
CAHUITA

THE CARIBBEAN COAST

Beautiful warm water glowing blue and
turquoise, radiant sunshine, and coconut
palms rustling in the gentle breeze welcome
you to Costa Rica's Caribbean coastline.

The three-hour drive from San José to the Caribbean coast is on a paved, slow-moving highway winding past the canyons, mountains, waterfalls, and virgin forests of Parque Nacional Braulio Carrillo. Descending from the cool cloudiness of Braulio Carrillo into the tropical lowland forests of the Caribbean, the temperature rises and the air becomes heavy.

Puerto Limón

Puerto Limón ❶ (pop. 61,000) is pure Caribbean. With its rich, ripe jumble of sights and sounds and smells, it is a hot, steamy, laid-back place. Most middle-class *Ticos* who live in the Central Valley consider it something of a disgrace, crime-ridden and poor. But multimillion-dollar plans are afoot to give Limón a face-lift and make it more visitor-friendly. The main tourist focus here is the huge cruise-ship dock that disgorges thousands of visitors every year.

In the center of Limón you won't find the usual cathedral or soccer field facing a plaza such as you see in all the towns of the Central Valley. Instead **Parque Vargas**, named after a local governor, is filled with huge banyan trees with buttress roots that the townspeople use for seats while they wait for a bus.

There are few decent hotels in Limón. Most travelers stay at the **Hotel**

Coconut trees painted in Rasta colors, Manzanillo.

Park (tel: 2798 0555; http://parkhotel limon.com) or more upscale hotels north or south of the city center. Beware, however, that theft (particularly from cars) and muggings are a problem in the city and it is worth paying a little more for accommodations.

Coffee, bananas, and the railroad

Commerce began in Limón in the 17th century, when cacao plantations were worked by slaves. It wasn't until 1871, however, when the growth of the

Main Attractions
Parque Nacional Tortuguero
Puerto Viejo
Surfing the Salsa Brava
La Pecora Nera Restaurant
Snorkeling at Punta Uva
Manzanillo

Caribbean Coast

0   10 km

0   10 miles

coffee market demanded an Atlantic port, that 'El Limón,' a migrant black fishermen's village consisting of just five huts, was chosen.

That same year, the government contracted the construction of the Atlantic railroad from San José to the Caribbean Coast. Minor Keith, the North American responsible for building the railroad, had the bright idea of planting and cultivating bananas alongside the track in order to raise additional funds for the rising costs of construction of the Atlantic railroad.

Limón thus became a railroad and banana town, populated largely by Afro-Caribbean and Chinese immigrants who had come to Costa Rica looking for work. Since 1872, Limón and the banana industry have experienced great booms and busts: bumper banana crops; labor troubles and violent strikes; and hard times of high unemployment when the United Fruit Company abandoned the Caribbean Coast.

Throughout all those hardships, Limón was effectively ignored by the national government of Costa Rica. The black workers and their families had no rights of citizenship; they were not permitted to work in the Pacific Zone nor in the Central Valley. After the Civil War of 1948, living conditions improved somewhat for the black residents of the city. Today, they are at last full-fledged citizens of Costa Rica, and can travel and work anywhere they wish.

Carnaval

For many people, Puerto Limón's annual *Carnaval* (Carnival) is the best reason to visit the place. This week-long jubilant event is held every October (rather than in February, the usual carnival month elsewhere). It is not an ancient Puerto Limón tradition: Carnival first began here in 1949, under the leadership of a barber called Alfred Henry King, who timed the festivities to coincide with the anniversary of Christopher Columbus's landing near Limón on October 18, 1502. *El Día de la Raza*, 'The Day of the People', which falls during Carnival Week and traditionally includes the participation of the indigenous peoples who live in the region, has been renamed *Día de las Culturas* (Day of the Cultures) in recognition of the fact that not everyone remembers Columbus with equal affection. It is also a tribute to the contributions made to Costa Rica by people of various different cultures.

The highlight of Carnival Week is the parade, when local people joined by thousands of visitors take to the streets to revel in a glorious music and dance spectacle. The drums, the heat, the shining bodies of dancers and drummers in bright costumes, urge spectators to abandon their inhibitions and to surrender to the Caribbean beat. And so they do, *Limonenses* and tourists alike, filling the streets, shimmying, shaking, singing, and carousing, while the irresistible rhythms of steel drums fill the warm, humid air.

Tortuguero

Travel on the **Tortuguero canals**, up through the area north of Limón, has been likened to a trip on the *African Queen*, or to floating dreamily down the Amazon. It is certainly one of the most wonderfully lyrical trips to be taken anywhere in the world. As you drift lazily along, awash in the fragrance of white ginger blossoms, lavender water hyacinths, and the ylang ylang flower, the tranquility here soothes all your cares away.

With the help of an expert naturalist guide, you may catch glimpses of sloths, crocodiles, caimans, and basking freshwater turtles. High up in the exuberant vegetation, multi-colored parrots squawk noisily, while cranky howler monkeys shake the branches. Around 19,000 hectares (47,000 acres) of the coast and hinterland have been designated as the **Parque Nacional Tortuguero** ➋

(Tortuguero National Park; tel: 2709 8086; Mon–Fri 6am–4pm). There are many ways to navigate its maze of waterways, including renting a dugout canoe or kayak. The best way to tour the canals is on a boat with an electric motor, guided by an expert naturalist. Note that you cannot enter the land portion of the park without wearing rubber boots, which you can hire at the park office or in the village. Or take a package tour that includes a room at one of the jungle lodges that range from modest to luxurious, plus meals, naturalist guides, and the trip through the canals. All of the Tortuguero hotels offer guided river trips and transportation either by bus and boat or by small plane from San José. Launches going up to Tortuguero also depart from Moín, just a few kilometers north of Limón. NatureAir and SANSA have short, scheduled flights from San José to Tortuguero. It is also possible to explore the canals by hiring a boat in **Barra del Colorado**, famous for its remote fishing lodges north of Tortuguero, near the Nicaraguan border.

Kayaking through Tortuguero Park.

Taking a boat along Tortuguero's canals is the best way to spot wildlife.

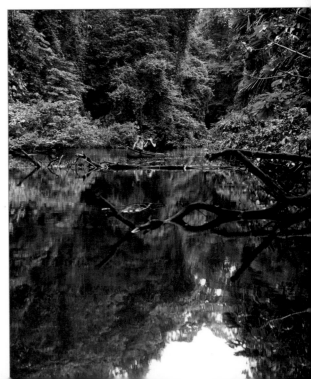

The green sea turtle

Tortuguero, from *tortuga*, which means turtle in Spanish, is the main nesting area in the Caribbean for green sea turtles, which have been listed as endangered since the 1950s. The **Caribbean Conservation Corporation** (CCC) was established at Tortuguero for the purpose of studying and protecting these vulnerable creatures.

The CCC runs a **Natural History Center** (www.cccturtle.org; opening times vary, check website for schedule) between the village and the more remote John H. Phipps Biological Field Station on the Tortuguero River. The center has a wildlife photo gallery and you can watch an informative video packed with information about the region's plant and animal life, including, of course, the green sea turtle. The area has been known for its turtle-hunting grounds since at least the mid-16th century, and turtles were exploited for their meat, shells, and eggs with impunity until as recently as 1970, when the area was established as a national park. Although poachers still exist, now

A baby iguana in Tortuguero National Park.

Green sea turtle in Tortuguero National Park.

at least the visiting green sea turtles and their leatherback cousins are afforded some degree of protection.

If possible, go to Tortuguero during the turtle-nesting season, in the company of a knowledgeable naturalist guide to help you understand the habits and sensitivities of these magnificent creatures. Official turtle-watching season is from February through November, and you must go with a certified guide. If you are lucky enough to spot a nesting leatherback turtle, it is an experience that affects even the most world-weary traveler.

Another exciting option for turtle-watching is the beach at **Parismina** halfway between Tortuguero and Puerto Limón. Accessible only by boat from Siquirres, this remote Caribbean village has opened a turtle hatchery for leatherback and green turtles. Tourists are warmly welcomed in this small community to help with the **Save the Turtles of Parismina Project** (www.parismina turtles.org), and there are a few *cabinas* and rooms to rent in the village.

Tortuguero village

Farther north, up the canals, the village of **Tortuguero** ❸ sits on a very narrow spit of land bordered by the Caribbean Sea and the Tortuguero River. The best thing about this village is that there are no cars, just narrow paths winding through exuberant greenery, with palm trees rustling overhead. Wooden houses sit on stilts, amid a growing number of restaurants, shops, and *cabinas* catering to tourists. Even so, village life seems to continue in a timeless way.

Canadian naturalist Daryl Loth (tel: 8833 0827; http://casamarbella.tripod.com) can answer most of your questions about Tortuguero. If you're hoping to sample Caribbean rice and beans cooked in coconut milk, you may have to wait until you get farther south on the coast. Sadly, authentically good Caribbean cuisine is harder to find these days.

Talamanca

Most travelers who come to the Caribbean are heading to the beach, following the coastal drive south, with glimpses of rivers off to the right, and the Caribbean Sea to the left.

Somewhere near Tuba Creek begins the **Talamanca** region of Costa Rica, extending from the Caribbean coast and reaching into the mountains that run from the Central Valley southeast into Panamá. This area was the refuge of many indigenous people who fled the Spanish conquerors.

Until the 1970s, the Talamanca region was populated mainly by the Bribrí and Cabécar who lived in the mountains, and by the descendants of English-speaking black immigrants from the Caribbean islands who settled along the coast. The black settlers were farmers and fishermen following the old ways brought from Jamaica, most affectionately described in their own words in Paula Palmer's fascinating folk history *What Happen*. They developed a local cuisine based on the foods they grew, and planted the coconut trees that still line the beaches. For the little money they needed, they sold coconut oil, hawksbill turtle shells, and cassava starch.

They spoke a creole English, played cricket, danced quadrilles, carved dugout canoes from local trees, and recited Shakespeare for amusement. Isolated by the sea and the mountains, no roads connected these people with the rest of Spanish-speaking Costa Rica, and their life continued quite peacefully and independently. All that has changed now, with the opening of a slick highway and other roads connecting the sleepy coastal towns of Talamanca with San José and the rest of the world.

Visiting the reserves

For the most part, the indigenous peoples of the region now speak Spanish in addition to their own native language (of which there are several), and take part in regional political and economic life, although many maintain ancient beliefs and customs. There are three indigenous

FACT

Veragua Rainforest Adventure Park (tel: 4000 0949; www. veraguarainforest.com), just west of Limón, combines hiking trails through pristine primary forest, accessed via an aerial tram, with wildlife exhibits and working research labs staffed by INBio biologists, plus a canopy tour.

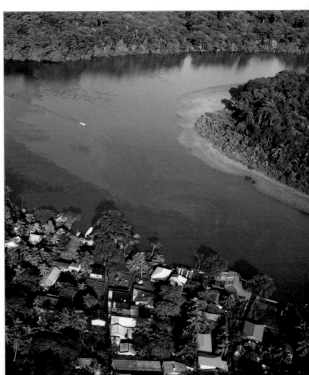

Aerial view of Tortuguero village.

Turtle tracks on the beach in Tortuguero Park.

A well-camouflaged green snake in Tortuguero Park – don't reach for a branch without looking first.

reserves in Talamanca: the large Talamanca-Bribri Reserve, the Talamanca-Cabécar Reserve, and the smaller Kèköldi Reserve. Access to the reserves by non-indigenous people is limited, and you usually need to obtain permission in advance. Tours in the **Kèköldi Wak Ka Koneke** reserve, run by residents, focus on history and culture, medicinal plants, crafts, and traditional foods, as well as birdlife and mountain hikes (tel: 2750 0191).

Cahuita

Local legend has it that in 1828 a turtle fisherman named William Smith (known as 'Old Smith') sailed north from his home in Panamá to fish for turtles. Finding a beautiful calm bay protected by a coral reef near Cahuita Point, he decided to settle there with his family. In those early days, green and hawksbill turtles were plentiful and, as they had not yet learned to fear man, made an easy catch. Old Smith is said to have been the first English-speaking Afro-Caribbean settler to the area, which at that time was populated

with Amerindians, and frequently visited by pirates.

Cahuita ❹ is a small scruffy town of faded but dignified-looking wooden houses, once painted bright colors that are now soft pastels, with a touch of Caribbean whimsy in the gingerbread details. Young travelers from Europe, Canada, and the US, oblivious to more modest local sensibilities, amble along the beaches and roadways in bright, scanty beachwear.

The main activities in Cahuita are snorkeling and eating. You can find both, side by side, at **The Snorkeling House** (tel: 8361 1924; www.snorkelinghouse.com), right next door to **Miss Edith's** restaurant, famous for its spicy Afro-Caribbean cuisine and Sunday-only *rondon*, a hearty stew based on fish and root vegetables. Sophisticated French dishes are also served at **Chez Fabien** (tel: 8301 6778), arguably the best gourmet restaurant in town. For tours and excursions farther afield, **Cahuita Tours** (tel: 2755 0101; www.cahuitatours.com) is an experienced, reliable tour operator in Cahuita.

Be aware that Cahuita has drug problems, and that petty crime against – and amongst – tourists is also rife, even though the authorities crack down every so often in an attempt to keep a lid on the situation.

Cahuita National Park

To the immediate south of Cahuita is **Parque Nacional Cahuita** ❺ (tel: 2755 0302; daily 8am–4pm), famous for its fine, sandy beach and coral reef. The reef extends 500 meters (1,500ft) out to sea from **Punta Cahuita** and offers great snorkeling, although the point of the reef was severely displaced during an earthquake. There are many species of tropical fish, crabs, lobsters, sea fans, anemones, sponges, seaweed, and innumerable other marine creatures to observe amidst the coral formations. You can admire it all and keep your feet dry aboard a glass-bottomed boat, or you can swim from the Puerto Vargas end of the beach. Diving equipment may be rented at **Reef Runner Divers** (tel: 2750 0480; www.reefrunnerdivers. com) in Puerto Viejo.

The main entrance to the park is at Puerto Vargas, 5km (3 miles) south of town. Lifeguards patrol the beach and there is good snorkeling at Punta Cahuita. Camping is permitted in the Puerto Vargas sector, which has toilets, showers, and picnic tables. Coatis and raccoons frequent the campgrounds looking for fruit and other edibles, and are not above overturning a tent to get them. From Puerto Vargas you can hike along a nature trail into the jungle.

North of Cahuita is a black-sand beach with gentle waters excellent for swimming. Accommodations, some with kitchens, are available throughout town and on the beach. Reservations are essential during Christmas and Easter periods and during Carnival, the second week in October. The best time to visit Cahuita is from February through April, and in October when the weather is driest.

Cahuita to Puerto Viejo

Heading south toward Puerto Viejo, along a partially paved road that runs parallel to the beach, you pass houses of every style and class, but there is something magical about the Caribbean air that gives even the humblest shack a picturesque quality when it is set amidst tall coconut trees. You won't find the spruced-up charm of any developed Caribbean island here. The settlements along this coast are mostly ramshackle and, quite frankly, shabby. But the total lack of pretension seems to sit easily with footloose young people from all over the world, as well as older Europeans in search of an idyllic and affordable beach life.

Just before the turnoff to Puerto Viejo is **Hone Creek**, named after a short palm with large roots. When the Jamaicans came to the Talamanca coast to work on the railroad in the 1890s, they began calling it 'Home Creek', and today there are road signs in the area announcing both 'Hone Creek' and 'Home Creek.' There is usually a checkpoint with a guard at

Canal signs help visitors put a name to the canal they're being guided along when taking a boat trip in Tortuguero Park.

Young Cahuita residents.

LANGUAGE DIFFERENCES

Most of the older black residents on the Caribbean coast still speak both English and Spanish, while more and more young people speak Spanish only. If you overhear older folks talking, listen carefully to pick up the local Caribbean patois form of English.

A few of the more common expressions: 'Wh'appen?' ('What's happening?') is the usual form of greeting, replacing the 'Adiós' of the Central Valley. 'How de morning?' is 'Good morning' and 'Go good' is 'Take care.' The polite form of address is to use someone's first name preceded by Mr or Miss.

With the influence of Jamaican reggae, accompanied by local people draped in dreadlocks, you will also hear a lot of 'irie,' meaning everything that is good, from nice to awesome.

Hone Creek, seeking to stem the flow of contraband goods north from Panamá. From here, the road to Puerto Viejo is often in various states of disrepair, and peopled with cyclists, so slow down.

Along the sides of the road, watch for cacao trees in the now-abandoned cacao plantations, destroyed by a country-wide fungus infestation. The fruit grows from the trunk of the tree and turns wonderful colors as it ripens: some becomes a soft turquoise color, others a brilliant coral. The seeds of the ripe fruit are slightly sweet and undeniably chocolatey, even in this raw state. To experience chocolate from bean to chocolate bar, you can choose between two chocolate tours: **Cacao Trails** (tel: 2756 8186; www.cacaotrails.com), 5km (3 miles) south of Cahuita, focuses on the history of cacao, as well as the processing of chocolate. The tour ends with a tasting and includes lunch. South of Puerto Viejo, **Chocoart** (tel: 2750 0075) is run by a Swiss owner, who knows how good chocolate should taste. The two-hour tour takes you through a healthy cacao plantation and ends with a tasting of the just-made, meltingly delicious product.

Traditional wooden architecture in Cahuita town.

The sandy beach in Cahuita National Park.

Puerto Viejo

Cahuita has a certain shabby dignity, but **Puerto Viejo de Talamanca ⑥** – to distinguish it from Puerto Viejo de Sarapiquí – is a tumbledown community. It is a hodgepodge of dilapidated wooden houses amidst tall grass. At the entrance to the town you pass a rusted-out barge anchored just off the black-sand beach.

It wasn't long ago that there were no roads to Puerto Viejo: no cars, no tourists, no money. But things have changed. Puerto Viejo's beautiful undeveloped beaches and easy-going ways have been discovered. New *cabinas*, hotels, and commercial developments throughout the area proclaim the arrival of tourism.

Puerto Viejo is famous in surfing circles for the Salsa Brava, a hot, fast, explosive wave that breaks over the reef from December through April and again in June and July. It attracts surfers from all over the world. At other times of the year the sea is quiet, particularly inside the reef, and good for snorkeling.

If you want to stay in town, where the action is, especially at night, try the **Casa Verde Lodge** (tel: 2750 0015; www.cabinascasaverde.com), a tidy, Swiss-run collection of colorfully decorated *cabinas* set in a lush garden. It's cheap and cheerful and in great demand, so make a reservation well in advance. To catch the reggae beat, head to **Johnny's Place** on a Friday or Monday night. For salsa and merengue, **The Lazy Mon at Stanford's**, practically on the beach, is the place to go on weekend nights. Or just wander through town at night, browse the souvenir stalls set up along the beach, and let your ears lead you to 'wha'happen.'

Vegetarian-friendly **Chile Rojo** (tel: 2750 0319) on Main Street serves spicy Thai and Middle Eastern food.

For casual breakfasts and baked goods, try **Café Rico**, at Avenida 69 (between Calle 217 and 219) with freshly-squeezed orange juice, excellent coffee, and tasty food served by amicable staff. Or treat yourself at the more upscale **Bread and Chocolate**, near the post office, which is famous for its oatmeal pancakes, muffins, French toast, and incredible brownies. This is notably one of the few restaurants in the entire country that serves excellent coffee made in individual French presses.

To the south of town there are *cabinas* and sophisticated hotels and restaurants lining the road across from beautiful stretches of white sand beach edged by palm and beach almond trees. Award-winning **Cariblue** (tel: 2750 0035; www.cariblue.com) at Playa Cocles is renowned for service, style, and gourmet Italian food. Another Italian import is **La Pecora Nera** (tel: 2750 0490), a romantic *rancho* where you can enjoy excellent Tuscan cuisine. Incongruously, this is perhaps the best restaurant in the whole country, hidden away off the main road south of Playa Cocles. Owner/chef Ilario Giannoni is always on hand to recite the day's specials – go for the tuna whenever it is offered.

If you haven't got a car, rent a bicycle and join the legions of cyclists meandering along the potholed road that is alternately muddy or dusty. Cycling is a great way to get around Puerto Viejo and to the nearby beaches.

If you would like to learn more about the Talamanca region, the non-profit **Talamanca Association for Ecotourism and Conservation** (ATEC; tel: 2750 0398; www.ateccr.org) provides environmentally and culturally oriented tours led by local guides who speak Spanish and English. Choices for outings include snorkeling, fishing, bird-watching, adventure treks, and visits to the Talamanca indigenous reserves and to the houses of local people for home-cooked meals.

Punta Uva and Manzanillo

To the south of Puerto Viejo is heavenly **Punta Uva** ❼, probably the

TIP

Animal-lovers shouldn't miss the Aviarios Sloth Sanctuary of Costa Rica (tel: 2750 0775; www.slothsanctuary.com) just north of Cahuita. The sanctuary conducts serious research, with the aim of returning orphaned and injured sloths to the wild. A visit here includes an informative video presentation, a visit with the resident sloths, and a canoe tour along canals to view birds and wildlife.

Puerto Viejo de Talamanca.

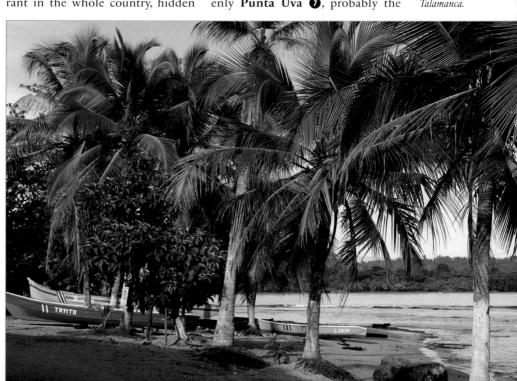

best, most easily accessible beach along Costa Rica's Caribbean coast. Crystalline, aquamarine water laps quietly on the palm-lined beach, and both the air and water temperatures seem fixed at a constant, perfect 27°C (80°F). This is the best snorkeling beach on the coast, with a healthy reef just meters offshore. It is also the only Caribbean beach where you can catch the sunset – it actually is sited in a westerly direction.

You can cycle here from Puerto Viejo and there are plenty of charming and affordable accommodations all the way down the road to Punta Uva. For people who like the idea of camping but don't want to rough it, there is **Almonds & Corals** (tel: 2271 3000; www.almondsandcorals.com), a tent lodge camp in the middle of a cool, shaded former cacao plantation. You will sleep in comfortable tents nested within larger tents set on platforms and complete with electricity, hot-water showers, and flush toilets.

Farther south, still on the beach, is **Manzanillo**, a tiny fishing village that can be reached by walking

along the sand for about two hours from Punta Uva, or 20 minutes from Puerto Viejo by car along the paved road that terminates here. Coral reefs offshore create a natural harbor. The water can be as calm as a lake for swimming in the early morning and late afternoon. Surfers enjoy it, too, for its fast beach break. Local people have decorated the beach with colorful painted concrete garden tables and benches, and a clean-up crew arrives every morning to remove litter and spruce up the beach. Local children play in the waves or bathe in the river, young men play a game of pick-up soccer on the beach, and elderly people sit around and talk quietly in the shade. Except for the bus loads of day-trippers from Limón who arrive on Sunday, not much else goes on around here. This is Costa Rica at its most relaxed.

You will see small fishing boats pulled up onto the sand all along the beach. The supply of fresh fish is put to good use at **Restaurant Maxi's** (tel: 2759 9073) a two-story wooden establishment, with a bar/disco downstairs

Playing in the surf at Manzanillo.

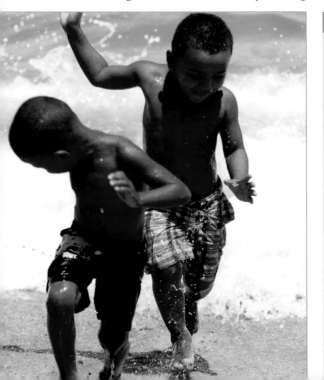

and a breezy multi-roomed restaurant upstairs overlooking the beach. Generous portions of fish, whole or filleted, are perfectly cooked here, or you can splurge on lobster. **Café Oh-la-la** brings a French touch to the town, serving breakfast and lunch.

There is a cluster of wooden houses back from the beach, a couple of *sodas* (neighborhood restaurants) serving hearty breakfasts and *comida tipica*, a grocery store, and very inexpensive *cabinas* at the entrance to the village.

A short walk along the beach, south of the village of Manzanillo, is the **Refugio Nacional de Vida Silvestre Gandoca-Manzanillo** ❽ (tel: 2759 9001; daily 8am–4pm), which protects swamplands, coral reefs, turtle nesting grounds, and the only mangrove forest on Costa Rica's Caribbean coast. The hiking trail along the coast crosses streams, clambers over rocks, and then climbs uphill into forest, where birds and wildlife are abundant. To get the most out of a hike, hire a local guide from the Association of Indigenous Naturalist Guides of Manzanillo (tel: 2759 9064). Bring your own supply of drinking water since there are no facilities available in the refuge.

Sixaola

Sixaola is a banana town on the Panamá border, 44km (26 miles) south of the turn-off to Puerto Viejo on the coastal highway. The road has been paved but potholes are not uncommon. There are no tourist attractions or services, save for the border crossing. Panamá and Costa Rica have signed an agreement to build a new border crossing here (for completion in 2017), but the shabby, one-way rickety railroad bridge lives on.

The area stretching from just outside the village of Bribrí to the border at Sixaola is 'Banana Land,' with banana-processing plants all along the road. It's interesting to stop for a break at one of the open-air plants to watch the workers handling the large bunches, called *racimos*, cutting bunches of bananas off the stalks, sorting, washing, and putting them in boxes bound for the waiting cargo ships in Limón.

TIP

Divers can rent equipment and sign up for dive trips at Aquamor Talamanca Adventures (tel: 2759 9012; www.greencoast.com) in Manzanillo, at the end of the paved road. They also offer scuba courses and operate snorkeling tours.

Playa Uvita at Punta Uva.

Sea Turtles

'Save the turtles' has become a conservationists' rallying cry, and Costa Rica is on the front line in the battle to do just that.

Sea turtles look more like their close but extinct relatives, the dinosaurs, than animals of today. Remarkable adaptations to life in the sea have enabled them to survive, largely unchanged, for more than 150 million years. They 'fly' like birds through the water using front flippers as wings. Yet they retain terrestrial traits and must surface to breathe air and crawl ashore to nest and lay their eggs.

Costa Rica is home to five species of sea turtles: green, hawksbill, Olive Ridley, leatherback, and loggerhead. They are more easily viewed here than anywhere else in the world. They nest at several well-known beaches on both Caribbean and Pacific shores. During the nesting season, if you happen to be in the right place at the right time, you may see one of the most amazing spectacles in the animal kingdom: *the arribada*, when 100,000 or more Olive

Olive Ridley (Lepidochelys olivacea) sea turtle returns to the sea after laying its eggs on the beach.

Ridley turtles come ashore to nest simultaneously (see page 204). Or, equally spectacular, is the sight of a 680kg (1,500lb) leatherback hauling her massive body out of the water and up the beach to bury her clutch of eggs in the sand.

Tortuguero Beach, a 35km (22-mile) stretch on Costa Rica's northern Caribbean coast, is the most important nesting area for green turtles in the Western Caribbean. Here, you can see green turtles, hawksbill turtles, and Ridleys.

Nesting season

Green turtles mate and nest several times from September through November. With the sharp hook on his front flippers, the male holds and mounts the female. If the sexually aggressive male can't locate a mate, he will eagerly clamber on top of anything that floats. Chunks of wood, other male turtles, even skin divers are not safe from a male's misguided passion.

An impregnated female waits offshore until dark before beginning her long struggle up the beach to the nesting site. During her crawl up the sand, disturbances such as noise and light will cause her to abort the nesting procedure, and to return to the safety of the sea. But once she has begun digging the nest, nothing will distract her. Using her rear flippers, she scoops out a vase-shaped hole, approximately 1 meter (3ft) deep. One hundred or more leathery, golf-ball-sized eggs covered with a mucus 'fungicide' drop into the nest one or two at a time until the entire clutch is deposited. She covers the nest, tamps down the sand and begins her long crawl back to the sea, leaving her progeny at the mercy of coatimundis, dogs, raccoons, and human scavengers (*hueveros*) who steal the eggs and sell them to local bars.

Race for the sea

In undisturbed nests, baby green turtles hatch in a couple of months. Using a temporary egg tooth, they tear open their shells. Soon the entire clutch is ready to rise to the surface. A critical mass of about 100 turtles all working together is needed to excavate the 1 meter (3ft) of sand that is covering them. Usually before dawn, they erupt onto the beach, look for the brightest part of the horizon over the sea, and scramble for the water running the gauntlet of ghost crabs and birds, perhaps then only to be met by sharks and predatory fish once they do reach the water. Hundreds of thousands race for the sea and probably less than 3 percent survive. Those that do make it go offshore to floating rafts of sargassum weed where they find shelter and food for their first and most difficult months at sea.

For several decades they live nomadic lives, migrating over vast distances of the open ocean to feed on turtle grass in the remote Miskito Keys off Nicaragua or at Cahuita on the Talamanca coast. Some navigate several thousand kilometers to the Windward Islands, using no apparent landmarks or visual cues. It is thought that crystals of magnetic iron located in the turtles' brains perhaps serve as internal compasses, guiding them across the seas. Or, more prosaically, they may just follow a certain smell or substance.

Although no one knows for certain, marine biologists estimate that it takes 15 to 30 years for these turtles to reach sexual maturity, at which point they reconvene on the beaches where they were born and proceed to mate, nest, and complete their incredible reproduction cycle.

To early explorers, fresh turtle meat was a welcome change from salt beef and sea biscuits, and, of course, this was before people became aware that species could be wiped out. People living in tropical regions still relish meat from the sea turtle. But sadly, the species is being endangered more from frivolous use than for subsistence purposes: six or seven species of sea turtle are on the brink of extinction. In bars from the Caribbean to Sri Lanka, sea turtle eggs are sucked from the shells in the mistaken belief that they act as aphrodisiacs. Tortoiseshell has a high value when carved, polished, and made into jewelry, combs, and spectacle frames. Turtle skin is even being used as a substitute for alligator skin in shoes and purses.

Turtles under threat

Sea turtles remain on the endangered species list, although worldwide conservation programs are under way. Importation of turtle products into the US and other countries is strictly prohibited and carries stiff penalties. But more and more adult turtles are caught in shrimp trawls and long-line fishing nets, and fishermen continue to hunt them, illegally.

Silt from unlawfully deforested land near Tortuguero washes onto the beaches, bringing weeds that take away valuable nesting space from the turtles. And floodlights from beach-side hotels and developments frighten off females who are ready to nest, and disorient hatchlings trying to reach the sea.

The future for many turtles is bleak. In 1991 the Las Baulas National Marine Park at Playa Grande on the Nicoya Peninsula. While the park authorities take a very strict line on poaching, business interests wishing to develop the beach still pose a threat. However, it is hoped that the efforts of the many volunteer programs and the commercial demands of ecotourism, will yet save the endangered turtles.

Baby sea turtle making its way to the sea.

Pacific Coast beach.

Giant buttress roots of a tree in Hacienda Barú.

THE SOUTH

Even by local standards, the south is a wild region. It includes the highest peak in Central America and the largest, most inaccessible national park with the most pristine tropical wet forest.

The Zona Sur, or Southern Zone, rises in the highlands around Cerro de la Muerte, the highest point in the country, then falls away into the agricultural lands of the Valle de El General and ends in the tropical lowlands at the Panamanian border. This is an unbeatable destination for hikers and nature-lovers with a sense of adventure, who like exploring off the beaten path.

Playa Dominical

A beautiful drive of 35km (22 miles) on a paved road from San Isidro de El General, west through misty mountains, brings you to the Pacific Ocean and **Playa Dominical ❶**. Dominical can also be reached by a faster route, using the toll road from San José to Caldera, then linking up with the paved **Costanera Sur** highway from Quepos, passing by beaches alternating with dense palm-oil plantations. Whichever way you choose, it's a scenic drive, with both ocean and forest vistas.

Just south of Dominical, stop off for the night at secluded **Pacific Edge** (tel: 2200 5428; www.pacificedge.info), a collection of comfortable wooden cabins perched high on a forested ridge with spectacular sea views. Or spend some time down at sea level at **Hacienda Barú** (tel: 2787 0003; www. haciendabaru.com), in the middle of a

private forest reserve, with kilometers of hiking trails through forest and along the beach, with excellent naturalist guides.

The beach at Dominical is a long stretch of brown sand offering excellent surfing waves, though beware of dangerous currents when swimming. Lifeguards, when they are on duty, mark off with flags the safer areas to swim. There are shady places on the sand for camping, but be sure to bring mosquito nets and repellent. The 'town' is a funky conglomeration of

Main Attractions
Parque Nacional Marino Ballena
Parque Nacional Corcovado
Golfo Dulce
Wilson Botanical Garden
San Gerardo de Dota
Parque Nacional Chirripó

Family fun on Dominical beach.

The South

0   15 km
0   15 miles

trendy restaurants and bars, simple *sodas*, surf and souvenir shops, and some comfortable hotels along with basic *cabinas* and hostels catering to young surfers. Playa Dominical's weather can be hot and humid but there are cool spots above the beach on the coastal ridge.

A two-hour horseback trip to **Nauyaca Falls**, also known as Santo Cristo and Barú Falls, will take you to two cascades a total of 65 meters (210ft) high, which tumble into a glorious warm-water swimming hole. **Don Lulo's Waterfall Tour** (tel: 2787 0541; http://cataratasnauyaca.com) arranges horseback trips to the falls.

Just south of Dominical is **Playa Dominicalito**, where there are good point-break waves for surfers. Swimming is best at low tide when beaches are exposed beyond coral rocks and there are beautiful views of the overlooking hills. This is also a great boogie-boarding spot and an ideal beach on which to stroll at sunset.

Up the hill from the community soccer field and across a shallow river, the Pozo Azul is a deep swimming hole at the base of a pretty waterfall, just a short hike in from the road. The local children have tied a Tarzan rope to a strong tree and you can swing out over the pool and plummet into it, making an impressive splash. There is no charge, but do tip the guard in the parking lot, if he's there, and don't leave any valuables in your car. If you are on foot, it's about a 20-minute walk up from Dominicalito beach.

Ballena Marine Park

Some 20km (12 miles) to the south of Dominical lies **Parque Nacional Marino Ballena ❷** (tel: 2786 5392; Tue–Sun 8am–4pm), easily accessible via four bumpy access roads off the smoothly paved Costanera Sur. Marino Ballena offers beautiful swimming beaches, camping on some beaches, a coral reef for snorkeling, and mangroves where you can spot caimans and wading birds. Along with the dolphins that play year-round in the bay, humpback whales and their young visit the park from December through April. The annual Whale and Dolphin Festival (www.festivaldeballenasydelfines.

TIP

For a bird's-eye view of Marino Ballena Park, climb the hill to Cristal Ballena (tel: 2786 5354; www.cristal-ballena.com), a luxury hotel with the best and biggest swimming pool on the coast, and a terrace restaurant with ocean view.

Playing in the surf, Dominical.

Ants in Your Plants

A hands-on guide to investigating the sometimes strange, but often mutually beneficial relationships between ants and their plant and tree hosts in the tropical forest.

Should someone point out a 'bull's horn acacia' to you, stop and have a close look at this thorny shrub. It measures between 1.5 and 3 meters (4–10ft) in height, and you will see along the branches pairs of reddish spines that look like miniature replicas of a Texas steer's horns. Hence its common name (its official name is *Acacia cornigera*).

Of the numerous symbiotic relationships that have evolved between tropical ants and plants, that of the bull's horn acacia and its stinging ants is one of the most curious. It is also one of the most dramatic examples of tropical co-evolution between species.

With some caution, shake the end of a branch. Ants burrow into the end of the spines (notice the tiny hole), excavate the inside of the branch, and

Leaf-cutting ant in Manuel Antonio National Park.

set up a colony where they rear their young and go about the day-to-day business of being ants. When the plant is disturbed, as in the case of your shaking the branch, the pugnacious ants charge aggressively from the spines, stingers armed and ready to defend their acacia host. It would only take one nasty sting to convince you that this unusual defense system works.

In addition to repelling would-be grazers, ranging in size from caterpillars to cattle, the ants manicure the ground around the acacia, keeping it clear of sprouts from other plants that might deprive their host of living space in a tropical forest containing 1,200 species of competing trees and countless other plants. And the acacia is appreciative. Not only does it shelter its guardians, it also feeds them. Tiny, sausage-shaped pores hang from the ends of the leaflets. Loaded with sugar and protein, these are harvested gratefully by the ants.

Leafcutters

On the forest floor you are almost sure to spot trails carved by leafcutter ants as they march through the jungle in search of tender leaves to attack. Their trails are veritable highways of activity. Imagine thousands of people walking home on the highway, each rushing along, carrying a 1.5 by 2.5 meter (4 by 8ft) sheet of green plywood overhead, and you have the basic concept of these ants.

Leafcutters are amazingly industrious insects, much to the distress of many a garden owner in Costa Rica. They can completely denude a full-grown mango tree overnight, carving circular slabs of leaf about 1cm (0.5in) in diameter, hoisting them overhead and marching down the tree trunk back to the hive, which may be a kilometer away or more.

Several highways lead to the ants' hive – often around the buttress roots of a large tree. Hives of more than 100 sq meters (120 sq yds), 2 meters (7ft) deep in the forest floor, are not uncommon. In these hives, millions, perhaps billions, of ants chew the leaf fragments, mixing them with nutrient-rich saliva, into a kind of gruel. From this gruel the ants grow and harvest mushrooms that provide their chief food source.

Large ant colonies can cut and process almost 45kg (100lbs) of leaves a day. During the decades-long lifespan of an ant colony, tons of vegetation decomposes and is worked back into the forest floor. Constant rain and heat rapidly degrade tropical soils, and so the vast storehouse of nutrients and compost from the ant mounds create a rich oasis in the soil.

com) is held at the park in September featuring whale-watching, concerts, activities for families, sand sculptures, and sport competitions.

Two sandy beaches within the park sweep to a meeting point at Punta Uvita, creating a sandbar at low tide that looks remarkably like a whale's tail.

In the village of **Bahía Ballena**, the main entry point to the park, there's a wide choice of cheap *cabinas* and *sodas* (neighborhood restaurants). **Dolphin Tours of Bahía Ballena** (tel: 2743 8013; www.dolphintourcostarica.com), on the road to the park entrance, can get you out onto the water for snorkeling, fishing, or whale- and dolphin-spotting. **Mystic Dive Center** (tel: 2786 5217; www.mysticdive.com), near Playa Ventanas south of the park, can get you under the water. And **Skyline Ultra Flight** (tel: 8318 9685; www.ultra lighttour.com), in Bahía Ballena, can take you above the water for a bird's-eye view from aboard an ultra-light plane.

Just south of the park, on the east side of the Costanera, is a sign for Ojochal, a French-Canadian enclave that is home to a French bakery and two wonderful restaurants that serve Mediterranean food with a tropical twist. The scenic Costanera Sur highway continues south, offering dramatic ocean and coastal mountain views with every twist and turn. **Playa Ventanas**, just south of Ballena National Park, has nearby rocky islands and a huge rock formation, popular with sea kayakers who paddle through a passage in the rock navigable at low tide.

One of the region's mysterious stone spheres.

The Osa Peninsula

Jutting out more than 50km (30 miles) into the Pacific, the Osa Peninsula shelters the **Golfo Dulce** from ocean swells and creates a magnificent natural harbor. It is sculpted with picturesque beaches and rocky headlands, and dissected by streams and rivers that cascade over volcanic cliffs on their way to the sea. The most majestic forests in all Costa Rica cover the hillsides and line the valleys of the Osa Peninsula and, in many cases, represent the last stronghold of nature and endangered animals and plants, endemic to the South Pacific. It is an imposing, impressive,

Tidal pools at Matapalo, on the Osa Peninsula.

and wild place. The most famous attraction is Corcovado National Park, the jewel in the crown of Costa Rica's national park system.

Drake Bay

On the northern coast of the Osa Peninsula, **Bahía Drake** ❸ is reputedly where Sir Francis Drake, the first English navigator to sail around the world, landed in 1579. Until recently, this outpost, surrounded by crystal-blue waters, pristine beaches, and jungle, was accessible only on foot, by water or by charter plane. Now there is a dirt road from Rincón, built by the national power company in order to bring electricity to the village. There are also direct flights from San José to the Drake airstrip, passing over Manuel Antonio Park and, on a clear day, providing aerial perspectives of the south Pacific coast en route to Corcovado. As you land on the grass airstrip, look out for scarlet macaws.

A trio of upscale lodges in Drake Bay tops the wide choice of accommodations. The most romantic is **La Paloma Lodge** (tel: 2293 7502; www.

A collared anteater in Corcovado.

lapalomalodge.com), built on a breezy bluff with sweeping views of the ocean; its elegant and comfortable *cabinas*, with thatched roofs and private decks, blend unobtrusively into the jungle environs. From the lodge you can arrange expeditions to fish or dive, kayak along a dreamy river, and visit Corcovado and Isla del Caño.

Just south of Drake Bay village, the **Coastal Footpath** begins. This easy-to-walk scenic trail cuts between dense jungle on the land side, and crashing surf on the Pacific side. There are also calmer sandy coves along the way. The path leads south all the way to **Punta Marenco Lodge** (tel: 2292 2775; www.lodgepuntamarenco.com), in the 500-hectare (1,200-acre) **Refugio Nacional de Vida Silvestre Río Claro** ❹. Guests stay in rustic but comfortable grass huts perched over the Pacific, with cool breezes, hammocks on private verandahs, and views of Caño Island.

Isla del Caño

The **Isla del Caño** ❺ biological reserve sits low on the horizon, about 19km (12 miles) seaward of the Corcovado coastline, a pleasant one-hour boat ride from either Marenco or Bahía Drake. According to archeologists, the island was both a cemetery for indigenous peoples and a refuge for pirates. Spotted dolphins ride the boat's bow wave, and flying fish sometimes escort boats to the island. Between December and April, 40-ton humpback whales come from their feeding grounds in Alaska. Males sing haunting songs to attract females, and often leap high in impressive breaches during their procreative sojourn in Costa Rican waters.

The island is ringed with turquoise water, tiny beaches, and acres of coral-covered rock reefs. Brilliantly colored tropical fish are easily seen by snorkelers and scuba divers within 15 meters (50ft) of the shore at the park headquarters. Steep, well-manicured trails lead through a rich forest drooping with epiphytes and enormous philodendrons to a clearing with ancient stone spheres.

Parque Nacional Corcovado

Covering 445 sq km (172 sq miles), **Parque Nacional Corcovado** ⑥ (tel: 2735 5036; Tue–Sun 7am–4pm) is Central America's largest lowland Pacific rainforest. It's the most important sanctuary of biological diversity and endangered wildlife in the country, and one of the most important in the world. Because Corcovado Park is inundated with nearly 6 meters (20ft) of rain a year, it is technically known as a 'tropical wet forest.' But the simplicity of that classification belies the ecological complexity of the park. Thirteen distinct habitats here are each characterized by unique assemblages of plants, animals, and topography. Five hundred species of trees – one quarter of all the species in Costa Rica – more than 6,000 kinds of insects, almost 375 species of birds, plus frogs, butterflies, and many of the world's most endangered and spectacular mammals, including tapirs and jaguars, live in this place.

Estimates of the number of jaguars in the whole country range from 300 on up, but the forests of Corcovado can support, at most, only 50 jaguars. An adult jaguar needs an enormous amount of land with abundant prey animals such as peccaries, deer, and agouti, to meet its food requirements. You are more likely to see jaguar tracks on many of the trails, however, than an actual jaguar. Poachers hunting peccaries have, unfortunately, cut seriously into the jaguar's food supply.

Although jaguars may be scarce, birds are everywhere. Scarlet macaws are perhaps the most spectacular birds in Corcovado. Also sought after are the red-breasted Baird's trogon and the melodious riverside wren, both of which are endemic to these forests.

Seeds or husks dropping through the canopy will often reveal the presence of troops of squirrel monkeys. White-faced monkeys also abound here, along with larger *monos colorados*, or reddish-brown spider monkeys, famous for their acrobatics as they swing from tree to tree. Other animals you are likely to see are long-snouted,

Corcovado National Park.

MYSTERY OF THE SPHERES

At the highest point on Isla del Caño, where the forest thickens and becomes silent, dried leaves crackle underfoot as you approach the pre-Columbian cemetery of the Boruca people. Two stone spheres sit among the trees. Green with moss and highlighted by shafts of sunlight from the forest canopy, the enigmatic spheres seem impossibly symmetrical in this forest of twisted plants. Thousands of spheres like this have been found in the south of Costa Rica, and a few also in northern Panamá. They pose one of the country's great riddles. Though their exact origin and significance have defied explanation, it is speculated that they were made in villages on the Osa Peninsula near Palmar Norte, brought to Caño in canoes, and then possibly rolled to the cemetery at the highest point of the island.

The smaller stone spheres were possibly toys, but the huge spheres, over 2 meters (6ft) in diameter, may have indicated the political or social standing of the deceased. Graves with spheres as headstones, oriented to the east, had secret chambers for precious ornaments and were covered with layers of sand, coral, and pebbles. The best place to see *las bolas*, as they're locally known, is the **Finca 6 Archeological Site** (tel: 2100 6000; Tue–Sun 8am–4pm), 6km (4 miles) south of Palmar Sur, where the stones can be seen in their natural surroundings. A small museum has displays exploring the history and significance of these

TIP

In Corcovado Park, you are largely on your own among such dangerous wildlife as coral snakes and fer-de-lance vipers. Although it is rare to come across these creatures, use common sense: wear sturdy boots, long floppy pants, and watch where you walk.

ring-tailed coatimundis. The males travel solo, but if you're lucky you may come across a group of females with youngsters – it's like a nursery-school playtime, with the babies scampering in the undergrowth and tumbling off lower branches. Agoutis, plump rodents that look like squirrels without tails, are also common, rooting for fallen seeds and fruits. To improve your chances of seeing these animals, hit the trail before dawn and walk very softly, and always stand very still when you see an animal.

Corcovado practicalities

One of Corcovado's blessings is its inaccessibility. It is a park only for those who are prepared to make a considerable commitment in time and energy. A continuing source of embarrassment to local conservationists is that despite its importance, La Sirena's lodging facilities are beyond rustic; in fact they are downright shabby. Camping with your own tent (make reservations well in advance) can be more comfortable than staying at the Sirena lodge. But there are other ways to

sample the beauties of Corcovado and the Osa Peninsula, from day trips by boat or charter flights, to accommodations at nearby luxury eco-lodges.

The ideal time to hike and camp in Corcovado is during the dry season, from December through April. A visit might include a night at each of the three park stations, with days spent hiking from one station to the next. (Stations are joined by trails, each of which requires from three to 10 hours of hiking time.) It is important to come well equipped: a tent, mosquito net, insect repellent, sunhat and sunscreen, good hiking shoes, and a couple of changes of socks are essential – plus your own food.

The park stations

Make arrangements for visiting the park at the administration office, next to the airport in Puerto Jiménez. Apart from the lodge at the main **La Sirena station**, other stations offer only camping facilities, by reservation, and you will need to walk to them or arrive by boat.

The **La Sirena station** has wonderful trails into the forest and along the beach, although the station itself, sadly, has been neglected. At the north end of the park is the **Los Patos Station**, an 11km (7-mile) hike from Sirena on a wide trail that runs parallel to the El Tigre River. The trail allows relatively easy wildlife viewing. Even though it passes through thick forest, you stand a reasonably good chance of seeing at least tracks of jaguar, ocelot, and tapir. Hikers used to be able to hike along the beach to the **San Pedrillo station**, midway between Drake Bay and Sirena, but that route is now closed because it was deemed too dangerous. You can still enter the park at the station if you arrive by boat. The **La Leona station** is the southernmost park station, and it's the easiest to hike to, along the beach from Carate. There is camping at all the stations.

A guide is a very good idea. Irish naturalist/zoologist Mike Boston of **Osa**

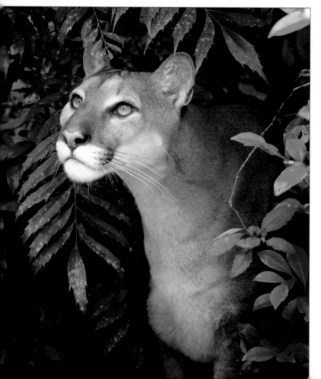

A young, watchful puma (cougar), one of the big cats in Corcovado.

Aventura (tel: 2735 5670/5758; www. osaaventura.com) specializes in multi-day hikes through the park; his website also has the most up-to-date information on hiking rules in the park.

Puerto Jiménez and Sierpe

Just outside Parque Nacional Corcovado to the east is **Puerto Jiménez ❼**, the biggest town of the Osa Peninsula and the main gateway to the park. It's a friendly, funky frontier town with a burgeoning tourist infrastructure. Inexpensive meals and lodging are available in the town, and there are some excellent new restaurants. A number of eco-lodges and ecotourism projects in all price ranges are to be found in the surrounding area. **Playa Platanares**, about 6km (4 miles) south of the airfield, has calm water for swimming, and a bird refuge bordering a sandy beach. Among the handful of beachfront lodges here, **Iguana Lodge** (tel: 8848 0752; http://iguana lodge.com) stands out for its lovely gardens, comfortable cabins, and knowledgeable, conservation-minded American owners.

Puerto Jiménez is accessible by car, bus, or small airplane. It's about a seven-hour road trip from San José on paved roads, and most lodges will arrange transportation for guests. Rugged four-wheel-drive vehicles can continue south from Puerto Jiménez to Carate, which is literally the end of a very bumpy road and a trip back through time. The drive can be harrowing, especially when rivers rise, but it is a memorable experience, driving along a road completely devoid of power lines.

A more adventurous way to access the remote Pacific coast of the Osa Peninsula is from the little inland town of **Sierpe**, where you board motorboats to cruise along the Sierpe River. The shores of the river are lined with mangroves whose branches and maze of roots support a healthy ecosystem of fish, crabs, iguanas, and water birds. Blue herons and snowy egrets may fly from the trees as the boat passes. Beware, however, that the water at the mouth (the *boca*) of the river, where it empties into the Pacific Ocean, is often very choppy. Check

TIP

Peccaries (wild pigs) have an exaggerated reputation as the forest's most ferocious animal. Nonetheless, if a group of them approaches, or worse, surrounds you, then you would do well to climb the nearest tree.

Squirrel monkey in Corcovado.

CORCOVADO WITHOUT A TENT

A pleasant alternative to sleeping in a tent in Corcovado National Park is to bed down at one of the nearby eco-lodges. At one end of the scale is **Lapa Ríos** (tel: 2735 5130; www.laparios.com), set in its own primary forest preserve, with super-comfortable thatched-roof bungalows perched on a hillside overlooking the ocean. It's as luxurious as it gets here, but like all lodges this far south, it's off the electrical grid – no TV, no air-conditioning and few cellular connections. Nearby **Bosque del Cabo** (tel: 2735 5206; www.bosquedelcabo.com) is just as luxurious, and a favorite hangout for monkeys and the odd puma. In Carate, within walking distance of the park entrance, cheery, laid-back **Lookout Inn** (www. lookout-inn.com) is right on the beach, with guaranteed sightings of scarlet macaws, while **Luna Lodge** (tel: 4070 0010; http://lunalodge.com), famous for its yoga retreats, contemplates Corcovado from a mountain perch. The closest you can stay to the park entrance, in some comfort, is at **La Leona Eco-Lodge** (tel: 2735 5705; www.laleonalodge.com), in a tent pitched on a platform, with a private bathroom attached. Guests at upscale **Casa Corcovado Jungle Lodge** (tel: 2256 3181; https://casacorcovado.com) can hike directly into the bordering park. Near the El Tigre park entrance, rustic **Bosque del Tigre Lodge** in Dos Brazos has some of the best birding and hiking in the Osa. Close to Los Patos, affordable **Danta Corcovado Lodge** (tel: 2735 1111; www.dantalodge.com) has

TIP

If you would like to learn more about the harsh conditions of the banana plantations, read the exuberant *Mamita Yunai*, written by pioneer labor organizer Carlos Luis Fallas and set in the 1930s and 1940s.

that your boat is equipped with life jackets and make sure yours is on when you near the *boca*.

Golfito

On the eastern shore of the Golfo Dulce, the port of **Golfito** ❽ has a perfect, sheltered harbor. In 1938, the United Fruit Company realized Golfito's potential, and built a major shipping port here. By 1955 more than 90 percent of the bananas shipped from Costa Rica departed on banana boats from Golfito. Boatloads of crewmen and 15,000 *Guanacasteco* immigrants came to work the plantations, and turned Golfito into a boomtown of brothels, smugglers, and drunks. Following crippling strikes and labor conflicts, United Fruit abandoned its Golfito operations in 1985 and economic depression set in.

The population today is about 11,000 and Golfito is making a slow comeback, based on tourism, sport fishing. It is also a base for the country's Coast Guard Academy and a port for US naval ships bent on intercepting drug traffic.

The old town, referred to as the **Pueblo Civil**, is regaining a touch of its boomtown atmosphere, with bars and restaurants overlooking the harbor and busy marinas. A duty-free shopping zone at the north end of town, known as *El Depósito*, sells consumer durables and liquor cheaper than in San José, and many Costa Ricans make weekend excursions to shop here. (Shoppers must stay in Golfito at least 24 hours in order to shop in the *depósito*.) The **American Zone** of Golfito was home to United Fruit Company executives, and many of the handsome wooden plantation-style homes on stilts, with screened porches and hipped roofs, have been restored. It's worth a drive or a wander, to see the lovely old houses shaded by stately old specimen trees that were imported from all over the world.

The main attractions here are sport fishing and boats to nearby eco-lodges that are only accessible by water. There is also a regular boat service between Golfito and Puerto Jiménez, across the Golfo Dulce; as well as boat taxis to

Local Ticos in Puerto Jiménez.

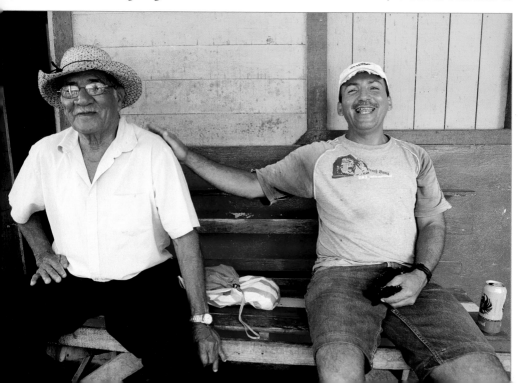

Playa Zancudo, to the south. **Parque Nacional Piedras Blancas** and the **Refugio Nacional de Vida Silvestre Golfito** (tel: 2783 5673; daily 8am–4pm), important wildlife corridors, lie just north of town. There are regular domestic flights to Golfito; for the more patient traveler, the very scenic seven-hour bus ride from San José to Golfito is a memorable experience.

North of Golfito

Facing the Golfo Dulce, accessible only by boat, are beautiful pebbled beaches, and dense jungle that starts almost at the water's edge. A 20-minute speedboat ride from Golfito brings you to lovely **Playa Nicuesa Rainforest Lodge** (tel: 2258 8250; www.nicuesalodge.com), which offers kayaking, snorkeling, fishing, and dolphin-watching out the front door of the lodge; and hiking, birdwatching, and waterfalls in the mountain forest just steps behind the back door. The main lodge is hand-crafted with more than eight kinds of tropical wood, and secluded cabins are scattered around a lush tropical garden.

Parque Nacional Piedras Blancas ❾ partly owes its existence to the generosity of Austrians who contributed the money to pay landowners, whose land was expropriated by a cash-strapped government, to create the park in 1991. Now incorporated into Parque Nacional Corcovado, this area has also been given the nickname 'Rainforest of the Austrians.' There's a biological station that houses students and scientists from around the world. More comfortable accommodation is available at **Esquinas Rainforest Lodge** (tel: 2741 8001; www.esquinaslodge.com). Hiring a local guide here is strongly recommended since the park trails are sometimes hard to follow.

Continuing north on the Interamericana Highway past Palmar Norte, the road heads east, following the Río Grand de Térraba. Just past Paso Real, watch for a steep, dirt road that leads to the village of **Térraba** ❿, a small village within the Boruca Indigenous Reserve. There is a small museum here showcasing Boruca culture, including exhibits of carved and painted

FACT

If you are lucky you may catch sight of the spectacular antics of the basilisk, a small, semi-aquatic lizard, which rears up onto its hind legs and appears to run across the surface of the water when it is alarmed. This trait has earned it the nickname of the Jesus Christ lizard.

The forest meets the sea at El Remanso Lodge, south of Puerto Jiménez on the Osa Peninsula.

A Heliconia rostrata, also known as 'lobster claw,' at Wilson Botanical Garden.

Butterflies are everywhere in Costa Rica and often found resting under leaves.

wooden masks and colorful woven cottons. Over New Year's, the annual *Fiesta de los Diablitos* (Festival of the Little Devils) attracts many visitors to watch a re-enactment dance/fight between the Spanish and indigenous population – only this time the Amerindians win.

South of Golfito

Between the mouth of the Río Coto Colorado (just south of Golfito) and Punta Banco, the last major point of land before the Panamanian border, lie some of Costa Rica's most inaccessible and remote beaches. From Golfito, head south to the turnoff at El Rodeo and cross the Río Coto Colorado on the new bridge that replaced an old cable ferry. In Pueblo Nuevo, turn right for **Playa Zancudo**, an 8km (5-mile) -long, sandy crescent with excellent swimming and surfing, and two castaway-style places to stay. Cabinas & Restaurant Sol y Mar (tel: 2776 0014; www.zancudo.com) has a friendly atmosphere and serves good food; nearby Cabinas Los Cocos (tel: 2776 0012; www.

loscocos.com) has beachfront, self-catering cottages and offers kayaking and river tours.

Or continue on the road parallel to the coast to **Pavones**, just before Río Claro. This rocky beach is not suitable for swimming, but it is a renowned surfing spot. Basic lodging is available, along with more comfortable rooms at La Ponderosa (tel: 2776 2076; http://laponderosapavones.com), which has a swimming pool set in a lush garden. Several *cabinas* and restaurants have been set up by surfers who have settled here, notably Café de la Suerte (tel: 2776 2388; www.cafedelasuerte.com), a delightful vegetarian restaurant with Wi-fi.

After the seemingly endless potholes, bogs, and washboard bumps in the road, continue on for another 30 minutes to **Punta Banco**. Wide intertidal flats of volcanic and sedimentary rock, riddled with tide pools full of marine life and battered by continual surf, characterize Punta Banco.

At the end of the point, a gate on the left marks the entrance to **Tiskita Jungle Lodge ⓫** (tel: 2296 8125; www.tiskita.com), a private rainforest reserve, experimental tropical fruit farm, and eco-lodge. The tortuous drive (a four-wheel-drive vehicle is essential) can be avoided by chartering a small airplane from Golfito that sets down on a grass airstrip near the lodge. Comfortably rustic cabins, some with ocean views, are sprinkled along trails, a short walk from the main lodge. Well-designed trails lead to waterfalls, idyllic swimming holes, and various points of natural history interest in Tiskita's 320-hectare (800-acre) primary and secondary forests. More than 100 species of fruit trees from around the tropical world are under cultivation here, attracting legions of monkeys and flocks of birds.

Wilson Botanical Garden

For the ultimate experience in tropical botany, visit the **Wilson Botanical Garden ⓬** (tel: 2524 0607; daily

8am–4pm), 6km (4 miles) south of San Vito in the Coto Brus region high above Golfito. The gardens are part of the Las Cruces Biological Station, operated by the Organization for Tropical Studies (OTS; www.esintro.co.cr). Trails wind through extensive, beautifully arranged collections of 'lobster claw' heliconias, bromeliads, tree ferns, orchids, and palms. Birds abound and there are early-morning birding walks, as well as garden tours. Overnight guests can also hike into Wilson's wild forest reserve, following the Río Java into primary forest full of birds and wildlife. Comfortable guest cabins have private verandahs, perfect for birdwatching. At family-style meals, you can talk with visiting scientists and researchers.

The nearby town of **San Vito** was founded by immigrants from post-war Italy, who were encouraged by the Costa Rican government to settle there. It's a clean, modern town of 15,000 inhabitants, high in a mountain valley, at a refreshingly cool 960 meters (3,150ft) above sea level. Nearby indigenous reserves are home to Guaymí, who work mostly in the surrounding coffee *fincas*. When the women come to town, they bring a splash of color with their intricately embroidered long dresses. You can get a good Italian meal here at popular **Pizzería Liliana**, in the center of town.

The winding, paved road north from **Ciudad Neilly** rises precipitously, offering spectacular views along the climb up to San Vito. The other approach to San Vito, traveling east from **Paso Real**, follows an equally scenic high ridge, with panoramic views of valleys on either side, and the vast Talamanca range rising in the distance.

Valle de El General

Since colonial times, people had attempted to find a pass through the Talamanca Mountains to join the Central Valley with the unknown lands on the other side of the Dota Mountains. But it was not until the end of the 1860s that Don Pedro Calderón found a way through. The opening of the road led to the colonization of the **Valle de El General**, and later, to the building of the Interamericana Highway, which connects San José and the Central Valley with the southern Pacific zone of Costa Rica. If you are traveling south to the Valle de El General, start early to avoid the fog and rain that often appear later in the day. From San José take the Interamericana Highway toward Cartago, veering right to take the road to San Isidro.

The route to the Valle de El General passes over the spectacular **Cerro de la Muerte** ⓭ (Death Mountain), which rises to 3,491 meters (11,520ft). Named for early travelers who died here from exposure while trying to cross on foot, the mountain is not as inhospitable as its name suggests. Rain, cold, and fog can make the first half of the drive miserable, but the road quickly rises above the clouds to cool, crisp sunshine, fields of flowers,

Handsome tropical plants grow along the roadside in some parts of Costa Rica.

DRINK

If you are traveling along La Ruta de Los Santos, call ahead to reserve a tour of the Coopedota Santa María coffee cooperative (tel: 2541 2828; http://coopedota. com), recently heralded as the first carbon-neutral coffee plantation in the world. For a taste of superlative Tarrazú coffee, stop in at the Cafe de Los Santos near the church in the town of Santa María de Dota.

and hillside farms. Blue hydrangeas and white cala lilies grow wild, and clouds swirl through the valleys and over peaks.

For almost-guaranteed quetzal sightings, visit the affordable **Paraíso Quetzal Lodge** (tel: 2200 0241; www. paraisoquetzal.com), just off the main highway at Km 70. Lodging here is in simple, wooden cottages with spectacular mountain views. Hot-water showers and hot-water bottles to warm beds help get you through the chilly nights. Many kilometers of trails are great for both hikers and birdwatchers. The lodge dining room, serving fresh trout, is kept cozy by a wood-burning stove.

Villages of the Valley

Down the road to the right from Empalme, at Km 51 on the Interamericana Highway, is **Santa María de Dota**, a traditional coffee town with a beautiful park and church. The paved road, which continues toward San Marcos de Tarrazú, San Pablo de Léon Cortes, and San Cristóbal Sur, is called **La Ruta de Los Santos** (The

Valle de El General.

Route of the Saints), since all the picturesque coffee towns here are named after saints. In **Copey**, a village in the mountains above Santa María, you can fish for trout at one of the many local trout farms, take a tour of an organic coffee farm, or lodge comfortably at **El Toucanet Lodge** (tel: 2541 3045; www.eltoucanet.com), a mountain lodge with verdant vistas and reliable quetzal sightings.

Continuing south on the Interamericana Highway, there is a sign at Km 80 for San Gerardo. This is the turnoff for **San Gerardo de Dota**, 9km (5 miles) down a phenomenally steep, partially paved road that runs parallel to the Río Savegre. In the midst of the valley, Don Efráin Chacón and his family offer comfortable *cabinas*, some with fireplaces and bathtubs, at the **Savegre Hotel, Natural Reserve & Spa** (tel: 2740 1028 www.savegre.com).

The area is renowned for its cloud forests and offers one of the best opportunities in the world to see the resplendent quetzal, which feeds on the fruit of the *aquacatillo* trees scattered along this mountain valley.

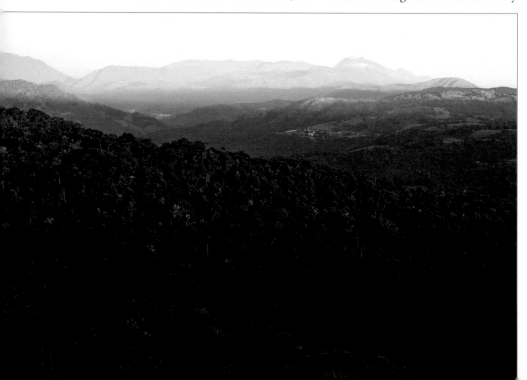

There are many kilometers of challenging trails here, including a hike to a magnificent waterfall. Resident bird guides can help you find some of the rarer highland species that live here, and you can gaze for hours at the hummingbirds buzzing around the hotel's gardens and bird feeders. Bring plenty of warm clothing as it becomes surprisingly chilly at night.

The winding drive down the mountain to **San Isidro de El General** is beautiful once the fog clears from Cerro de la Muerte. San Isidro, also known as Pérez Zeledón, is the commercial center for this agricultural area, a busy town with a large central park, crowded shopping streets, and lots of noisy traffic. The open-air market every Thursday is a visual and gustatory experience, laden with local produce and colorful photo opportunities.

Parque Nacional Chirripó

Parque Nacional Chirripó ❶ (tel: 2742 5083; www.parquenacionalchirripo. com; daily 5am–noon and 1–4.30pm), lying some 150km (94 miles) south of San José, covers 49,000 hectares (121,000 acres). Its main attraction, apart from the challenge of climbing the highest peak in southern Central America (at 3,819 meters/12,530ft), is its diversity of landscapes, including *páramos* – alpine moors – tall oak forests, fern groves, cloud forests, and crystal-clear glacial lakes.

Only really fit walkers willing to brave a long day of hiking, starting before dawn, in the cold, and quite possibly rain, make the ascent to the top of **Mount Chirripó**. A lodge and several trails, which are regularly maintained, make the ascent at least possible. Daytime temperatures reach 27°C (80°F) but at night they can drop to almost freezing. The best months to attempt Chirripó are February and March, the driest time of year, but during the rainy months the flora is splendid. Visits to Chirripó require reservations,

many months in advance during popular times.

If you arrive without reservations, you can try your luck at the ranger station in **San Gerardo de Rivas** (tel: 2742 5083). The best way to reserve is online at reservacioneschirripo@gmail. com. The hike to the top of Chirripó, including a day on the summit, takes at least four days. It costs $15 for each day you are there.

It's a good idea to arrive a couple of days in advance of your climb in order to acclimatize to the altitude. To get an early enough start, you should spend the night before your climb at one of the inexpensive hotels clustered in and around San Gerardo de Rivas. Before entering the park, check in at park headquarters in San Gerardo and pick up a park map. Good, large-scale topographical maps are available in San José. Rangers can put you in touch with guides and local people with horses who will be able to haul your pack to the hut ahead of you.

The area around San Gerardo is well worth visiting, even if you do

Accommodations that are close to nature but equipped with creature comforts.

See hummingbirds, quetzals, and woodpeckers at Paraíso del Quetzal Mountain Lodge.

not attempt to climb Chirripó. Bird-watching is excellent all along La Valle del General, and shorter hikes are very satisfying, with beautiful lush scenery, waterfalls, and natural hot springs where you can relax your sore muscles. At Chimirol, you can soak up the stunning scenery in total comfort at **Monte Azul Mountain Resort** (tel: 2742 5222; www.monteazulcr.com) a chic hotel that doubles as a contemporary artists' community, with studios and walking trails, set in a private nature reserve bordered by the rushing El General River.

A few kilometers beyond Chimirol, watch for a faded, wooden sign on the left advertising Queso Suizo/ Swiss Cheese. A local family, in the small community of Canaán, learned to make Swiss cheese from a visiting cheesemaker, and now they sell their excellent produce from their house.

Parque Internacional La Amistad

Adjacent to Chirripó, **Parque Internacional La Amistad** ⓫ (tel: 2795 4855; daily 8am–4pm) is part of the international Reserva de la Biosfera La Amistad, which straddles Costa Rica and Panamá. Most of the park's vast territory of more than 1,900 sq km (765 sq miles) is inaccessible. Unesco declared La Amistad (which means Friendship) a Biosphere Reserve and a World Patrimony site because of the diversity of its flora and fauna, and because of its great scientific value. More than half of La Amistad has yet to be explored. Hiking near **Reserva Forestal Las Tablas** is safe and rewarding, but only experienced tropical trekkers should venture into the interior.

There is a ranger station with camping facilities at the Altamira park entrance (tel: 2200 5355), and ASOPROLA (http://keytocostarica.com), a local rural tourism association, offers accommodations in a rustic lodge and arranges hiking tours. Day trips are possible from either San Isidro or San Vito, or you can stay at the eco-friendly, comfortable **Hacienda La Amistad Lodge** (tel: 2289 7667; www.haciendalaamistad.com), above San Vito, with the option of camping out in the forest.

Feeding hummingbirds at Paraíso del Quetzal Mountain Lodge.

Island of Wonders

Scientists value the remote, uninhabited island's biogeographic uniqueness, teeming with flora and fauna. But for Costa Ricans it is simply the country's No. 1 natural wonder.

Isla del Coco is the most remote part of Costa Rica, adrift in the Pacific Ocean nearly 600km (over 360 miles) southwest of the mainland, on the same latitude as Colombia. Because of this isolation it only counts its visitors in the hundreds, yet millions have seen it on film, in the opening moments of *Jurassic Park*. In all senses, this is a place of high drama.

At its crown is a thick coniferous forest full of springs and rivers. The cliffs around the entire island that tower more than 100 meters (300ft) are covered with incredibly thick tropical vegetation with magnificent waterfalls plummeting straight down to the sea. In all, there are 200 waterfalls on the island. Lionel Wafer, a pirate physician who visited over 300 years ago, wrote 'what most contributes to the loveliness of the place is the number of clear, freshwater springs that fill the entire lower part of the island.' And there are rocky crags and wondrously formed islets that have been shaped by the wind and water. No wonder then that it inspired Steven Spielberg, to whom it was the 'Isla Nebular.'

Island riches

With a coastline of about 23km (14 miles), roughly 12km by 5km (8 miles by 3 miles), Isla del Coco is the largest uninhabited island in the world. In 1978 it was designated a protected national park and is one of the richest in endemic species, with about 60, some of them endangered, that live only in or around this island.

As if these facts were not sufficiently alluring, the island's history is also full of pirate stories. Many insist that there is treasure hidden here still, although in the course of more than 500 expeditions none has ever been found.

Two bays, Wafer Bay and Chatham Bay, offer a way to tie up and gain entry to explore the island. Chatham Bay is small, with a rocky beach. Here, the ghosts of past explorers, and of pirates, are almost tangible. Today's visitors are mostly treasure hunters, divers and environmentalists.

Most visitors consider Wafer Bay to be the best access route to the island. From here, ancient natural paths follow steep cliffs all the way to the highest part of the humid forest. There are bromeliads, giant ferns, orchids, unnamed flowering plants, mosses, and ferns covering almost everything. And from a high peak there are views of an unbelievably blue sea above an impossibly green landscape, with white, angel-like doves moving gently, fluttering in the air.

Every natural path, every river, every waterfall, every beach has some rare treasure. The peace is astounding and deafening. And the views of the coral reef, the crisp clarity of the water, the lushness of the landscape, all somehow contribute to an atmosphere where the mysterious legends of the past come alive.

Camping is not permitted on the island: you have to sleep on your boat. There is drinkable water, however; and good opportunities for hiking, although the trails are not marked. Contact the National Parks Service for information and permission to enter.

A number of specialist tour companies operate out of Puntarenas, and offer the easiest way to visit the island, but be warned: the price of a trip is very high. For the majority of people, Isla del Coco remains just a dream – and perhaps that is no bad thing.

Scalloped hammerhead shark roaming the waters of Isla del Coco.

TRAVEL TIPS
COSTA RICA

Transportation

Getting There 260
   By Air.................................. 260
   By Bus................................ 260
   By Car 261
   By Sea................................ 261
Getting Around....................... 261
   To and From the Airport 261
   By Air.................................. 261
   By Bus................................ 261
   By Rail................................ 262
   By Ferry 262
   By Car 262
   Taxis 263
   Cycling 263

A – Z

Acccommodations.................. 264
Admission Charges 264
Addresses 264
Budgeting for your Trip 265
Children................................. 265
Climate.................................. 265
Conservation 266
Crime and Safety.................... 266
Customs Regulations 267
Disabled Travelers 267
Eating Out 267
Electricity 268
Embassies and Consulates ... 268
Emergencies........................... 268
Etiquette 268
Gay and Lesbian Travelers 268
Health and Medical Care 268
Internet 269

Left Luggage 269
Maps 269
Media 270
Money 270
Opening Hours....................... 270
Photography 270
Postal Services 271
Public Holidays 271
Religious Services 271
Shopping................................ 271
What to Buy 271
Student Travelers 272
Telecommunications.............. 272
Time Zone 272
Toilets.................................... 272
Tour Operators 272
Tourist Information 273
Visas and Passports.............. 273
Websites 273
Weights and Measures 273
Women Travelers.................... 273

Language

Survival Spanish..................... 274
   Numbers............................. 274
   Common Expressions........ 274
   Shopping and Eating.......... 274
   Getting Around 275
   Driving............................... 275
Speaking Tico:Tiquismos 275
Spanish Language Schools ... 275

Further Reading

Books 276
Other Insight Guides 276

TRANSPORTATION

GETTING THERE AND GETTING AROUND

GETTING THERE

By Air

Most international flights arrive in Costa Rica at Juan Santamaría Airport (www.fly2sanjose.com), about 16km (10 miles) from San José, the capital city.

At least 13 commercial airlines also fly to the Daniel Oduber International Airport in Liberia, the main terminal for North Pacific destinations: American Airlines, Air Berlin, Copa Airlines, Delta, Frontier Airlines, JetBlue, Sansa, United, Taca, US Airways, West Jet. Air Canada runs direct charter flights from Toronto.

From the US: Miami has the most direct flights, but you can also get to Costa Rica from the US in one hop from Atlanta, Charlotte, Chicago, Dallas, Denver, Fort Lauderdale, Houston, Los Angeles, Newark, Orlando, Phoenix, and Washington, DC. Air Canada offer direct flights from Toronto; Vancouver trips generally go through Houston or Dallas; flights from Montreal stop in eastern points of the US. Flights from Australia or New Zealand connect via Los Angeles and Dallas or Miami.

From Europe: Iberia is the only airline that offers scheduled, direct flights, from Madrid. Travelers from the UK may also connect in the US via Newark (the fastest route), New York, or Miami.

On departure: line-ups to check in can be horrendous, especially for a cluster of early-morning flights, so observe the recommended two-hours-before-departure arrival at the airport on your way home. Confirm flights the day before in case there are changes, but most airlines do not require it.

Baggage allowance: weight limits per checked bag are usually 23kg (50lbs), with only one bag free, maximum two bags. If necessary, determine how the airline is equipped to handle surfboards, bicycles, etc. Have your luggage well tagged and identified. Be prepared in case your luggage is lost.

Limited amounts of liquids and gels are allowed in carry-on baggage (containers 100ml or less, all items must fit in a quart-size zip lock bag). However, to get the most up-to-date policies, see www.catsa.gc.ca (Canada), www.tsa.gov (US), or www.baa.co.uk (UK).

Tax: there is a departure tax for foreign visitors of around US$29, payable in US dollars or colones, or by credit card (Visa, MasterCard, or American Express).

Airlines

Air Canada, tel: 888-247 2262 (US and Canada), 0871 220 1111 (UK), 0800 052 1988 (Costa Rica); www.aircanada.ca.
American, tel: 800-433 7300 (US and Canada), 0844 499 7300 (UK); 2248 2010 (Costa Rica); www.aa.com.
Avianca, tel: 800 284 2622 (US), 800 722 8222 (Canada); 2299 8222 (Costa Rica); www.avianca.com.
Condor Airlines, tel: 866-960 7915 (US and Canada), +49 (0) 180 570 7202 (Europe), 2243 1818 (Costa Rica); www.condor.com.
Delta, tel: 800-241 4141 (US and Canada), 0845 600 0950 (UK), 0800-056 2002/2257 4141 (Costa Rica); www.delta.com.

Airports

Juan Santamaría (international flights), tel: 2437 2400/2626
Daniel Oduber Quiros, Liberia (international flights; www.liberiacostaricaairport.net), tel: 2668 1010
Tobias Bolaños, Pavas (domestic flights), tel: 2232 2820

Iberia, tel: 800-772 4642 (Canada and the US), 02 036 843 774 (UK) 2431 5633 (Costa Rica); www.iberia.com.
JetBlue, tel: 800-538 2583 (US and Canada), 0800 012 1666 (Costa Rica); www.jetblue.com.
Spirit Airlines, tel: 800-772 7117 (US and Canada), 2441 6851, (Costa Rica); www.spiritair.com.
United Airlines, tel: 800 538 2929 (international reservations), 0800 044 0005 (Costa Rica); www.united.com.
US Airways, tel: 800-428 4322 (US), 888-240 4770 (Canada), 0845 600 3300 (UK), 0800-011 0793 (Costa Rica); www.usairways.com.

By Bus

There are bus services to Costa Rica from Mexico, El Salvador, Guatemala, Panama, or Nicaragua.
Tica Bus, Paseo Colón, 200 meters N/100 meters W. of Torre Mercedes, tel: 2296 9788; www.ticabus.com, provides a comfortable, reliable service throughout Central America. Daily buses to and from Nicaragua and Panamá.
Trans Nica, Calle 22, Avenida 3, tel: 2223 4242; www.transnica.com. Nicaragua, tel: 505-2277 2104; Honduras, tel: 504-2239-7933.

By Car

The most common car route from the US to Costa Rica runs along the Pacific coast of Mexico, Guatemala, El Salvador, Honduras, and Nicaragua. Along the Nicaraguan border, the two vehicle crossings are at Peñas Blancas, on the Pacific side, and at Tablillas (Alajuela) over the San Juan river. From the south, the main overland vehicle crossing is also on the Pacific side, at Paso Canoas, although a small post at Sixaola on the Caribbean side allows vehicles to pass over a very narrow bridge that joins the countries. There is also a crossing at Río Sereno.

Driving license: Drivers will have to show their license, an original copy of certified ownership (or a notarized authorization from the owner if the car is someone else's), and a *hoja de salida* (exit permit) from either Nicaragua or Panamá (whichever country you are arriving from).

Customs will mark in your passport that you have entered with a car, and the car is given a three-month permit. You can exit the country once to renew the permit; after six months the vehicle is subject to heavy import taxes. Rental car companies do not allow their cars to be taken across the border.

There are two recommended books with reliable information to help you navigate the roads and border crossings: *Americas Overland – The Driving Handbook*, by Donald Greene (www.lulu.com, US, 2008), and *99 Days to Panamá*, by John and Harriet Halkyard (Brindle Press, US, 2005). The website www.drivemeloco.com is also helpful.

It is advisable to confirm border information before travel because it can change without notice.

Car insurance: Costa Rica requires motorists to pay for insurance upon entry, which varies according to the value of the vehicle and the year, but starts around $18. The car is also fumigated (approximately $5).

Sanborn's Insurance (tel: 800-222 0158; www.sanbornsinsurance.com) in McAllen, Texas, is an excellent resource for insurance in Mexico and information you'll need for the trip, including travel tips and an itinerary.

By Sea

Cruise ships come into Puerto Limón on the Caribbean coast and Puerto Caldera and Puntarenas on the Pacific. Check with a travel agent about which companies currently sail to Costa Rica. Private yachts are also popular. The main point of entry is Playas del Coco, although immigration and customs services are also available at Caldera and Golfito, all on the Pacific side. It is possible to go through these procedures on the Caribbean side at Limón, but impractical, as there are no yacht facilities. You will need the original and one copy each of crew members' and passengers' passports, the crew list, the boat's documents, and the departure document from the last port you visited. All other international shipping protocols apply (quarantine flag, etc). Wait until you are boarded and cleared by both immigration and customs before going ashore.

GETTING AROUND

To and From the Airport

From the airport: It is a 20-minute ride (about US$30 by taxi) between downtown San José and the airport. Taxi Unidos (www.taxiaeropuerto.com) is the official airport taxi company and has a fleet of orange vehicles. There are also unlicensed taxis at the airports but fares can be significantly higher. Buses into town, operated by TUASA, leave from a stop close to the terminal exit between 4.30am and 11pm and costs less than US$1. Most buses from Guanacaste and Puntarenas beaches to the capital also stop at the airport.

By Air

Domestic flights *(vuelos locales)* are reasonably priced and are a comfortable alternative to many hours on bad roads. Nature Air allows one checked bag, up to 18kg (40lbs), per passenger, depending on the fare class purchased; fees for excess baggage vary from $7 to $60. On SANSA, any bag weighing more than 14kg (30lbs) is charged $1 for each additional 450 grams (1lb). Passengers are weighed as well, so if the plane is too heavy, your luggage may have to follow you on a later flight. Pack as light as you can.

If you're crisscrossing the country and are short on time, consider an air pass that covers travel to the commercial destinations of the country's main domestic airlines.

Nature Air, the world's first carbon-free airline, thanks to ambitious carbon-offset, sustainability and conservation programs, offers a 15-day pass for $599 and a seven-day pass for $349.

Aerotaxi Alfa Romeo
Tel: 8632-8150
www.alfaromeoair.com
Air taxi from Puerto Jiménez into Sirena Ranger Station in Corcovado National Park. Also offers charter services to 40 Costa Rican destinations, including San José, Carate, and La Fortuna, among others.

Nature Air
Tel: 2299 6000, 800-235 9272 (US and Canada)
www.natureair.com
Flies to Arenal, Liberia, Tamarindo, Nosara, Tambor, Quepos, Palmar Sur, Puerto Jiménez, Drake Bay, Punta Islita, Tortuguero, Bocas del Toro, Panamá, and Granada and Managua, Nicaragua, with additional destinations available for chartered flights. Surfboards accepted if there is space available, with an extra charge. Also offers a number of inter-destination flights.

SANSA
Tel: 2290 4100
From US: 1-877-767-2672
www.crc.flysansa.comServices to Golfito, Puerto Jiménez, Palmar Sur, Nosara, Sámara, Tamarindo, Puerto Jiménez, Manuel Antonio, Punta Islita, Quepos, Tambor, Liberia, and Drake Bay, with additional destinations available for chartered flights.

By Bus

You can go virtually anywhere by bus in Costa Rica, just as most Ticos do.

Around San José: the Sabana Cementerio bus cuts across town in both directions, just north and south of the center; ask for the stop closest to you (*¿Dónde está la parada para el Sabana Cementerio?*). All other buses leave for the suburbs from their respective quadrants; for example, those heading west (Rohrmoser, Escazú, Santa Ana) leave from the Coca-Cola area; ones heading east (Los Yoses, San Pedro, Curridabat) leave from near the east end of the pedestrian walkway.

Farther afield: San José has no central terminal for long-distance buses, each bus hub handles travel to a certain region. Major ones include the 'Coca-Cola,' near a former bottling plant at Calle 16, Avenida

1–3, the departure point for the Central Pacific; the Caribbean bus terminal, Calle Central, Avenida 11 (just east of the Children's Museum); and MUSOC, Calle Central, Avenida 30, to San Isidro (the hub for buses to the Southern Zone); www.visitcostarica.com.

Buy tickets a day in advance for popular routes and several days in advance for Easter week travel. Companies often only sell one way at a time; buy your return ticket upon arrival to ensure a seat. Watch your belongings closely.

Gray Line and Interbus provide reasonably priced (between $35 and $60) shuttle transportation in air-conditioned, comfortable vans. Hotel-to-hotel service makes this a good option. There are money-saving passes sold for unlimited travel for various time periods.

Gray Line
Tel: 2220 2126
www.graylinecostarica.com.
Interbus
Tel: 4100 0888
www.interbusonline.com.
The Costa Rican Tourist Institute (ICT) office in a new office on Central across from Lehman Brothers bookstore, 100 meters/yds north of the Plaza de la Cultura, has a list of bus company names and phone numbers, tel: 2299 5876; www.visitcostarica.com. Open weekdays 9am–5pm; closed for lunch 1–2 pm.

By Rail

San José's train service across town takes you within a hair's breadth of some buildings, but isn't particularly convenient. The central station is near the Clínica Bíblica on the south side of town, with a commuter-oriented schedule sending trains west from Estación Pacífico to Pavas. For a detailed schedule see www.trenurbano.co.cr.

A train service between San José and Heredia departs from San José's Atlantic Station, in the northeast corner of Parque Nacional, every half hour from 5.30–8am and 3.30–7.30pm; from Heredia, near the Central Market, on roughly the same schedule, 6am–8.30pm and 4–8pm. There are also train services to Belen and Cartago.

By Ferry

Most travelers to the southern Nicoya coast will arrive via the Puntarenas–Paquera ferry route (approximately 90 minutes), served by two companies. There is not much difference between the two services; the Tambor option is owned by the Hotel Barceló and is slightly snazzier, but at certain times can be packed with hotel guests. Avoid Friday and Sunday afternoons and evenings; you could be stuck waiting for hours.

Most travelers won't need to use the Puntarenas–Naranjo ferry, but it is an option if you are heading further north on the peninsula. Generally though, those sites are better served by bus or car via the Tempisque bridge. Drivers must leave the car to purchase tickets; any vehicle passengers must purchase tickets separately, and embark and disembark on foot.

Naviera Tambor
Tel: 2661 2084
www.navieratambor.com
Paquera to Puntarenas
Tel: 2661 2084
Departs 5.30am, 9am, 11am, 2pm, 5pm, and 8pm.
Puntarenas to Paquera
Departs 5am, 9am, 11am, 2pm, 5pm, and 8.30pm.
Peninsula de Nicoya
Coonatramar R.L.
Tel: 2661 1069
www.coonatramar.com.
Puntarenas to Playa Naranjo
Departs Mon–Thu 6am, 10am, and 4pm. Fri–Sun 6am, 10am, 2.30pm, and 6.30pm.
Playa Naranjo to Puntarenas
Departs Mon–Thu 8am, 12.30pm, and 6pm. Fri–Sun 8am, 12.30pm, 4.30pm, and 8pm.

By Car

Pothole-filled, unlit roads, careless (to put it mildly) drivers, and poor signage and road markings conspire to make driving in Costa Rica a definite challenge. But it can be done – extremely defensively.

Seat belts are compulsory, and drunk-driving laws are enforced. Drunk driving is defined as blood-alcohol levels of. 0.075 percent or higher, at which point, the driver is fined and loses his or her license and the car is confiscated. However, blood-alcohol levels between 0.049 percent and 0.075 percent qualify as 'pre-drunk' and earn a fine. Current monetary penalties are very high under a new traffic law, approximately $400 for driving without a seat belt, $600 for driving tipsy. Talking on a cell phone while driving may also cost you a hefty fine.

Car Rental

Renting a car makes sense for off-the-beaten-path trips outside San José. Reserve a car well in advance and get written confirmation. Prepayment is advised, especially during high season. Rates generally start around US$70 per day, including full insurance in high season; cheaper rates negotiable off-season. Four-wheel-drive vehicles start around US$80 per day. The majority of rental cars are manual transmission; automatics cost considerably more. Most insurance is deductible for the first US$750–1,000, although for an extra fee many companies offer a non-deductible policy. The following agencies all accept American Express, MasterCard, and Visa. Most agencies insist that the driver is over 21 years of age, holds a valid passport and driver's license, and has a valid credit card for a deposit (not cash).

Alamo, 13 locations including both international airports, tel: 2242 7733; US toll-free: 877-222 9075; www.alamocostarica.com.
Avis, seven locations including both airports, tel: 2293 2222; www.avis.co.cr.
Budget, nine locations including both airports, tel: 2436 2000; www.budget.co.cr.
Economy, 12 locations including both airports, tel: 2299 2000, toll-free 877-326 7368 (US); www.economyrentacar.com.
Hertz, Six locations, including both airports, tel: 2221 1818 (Costa Rica); www.hertzcostarica.com.
National, La Uruca, shares a building with Alamo head office, tel: 2242 7878, reservations: 877-8NATCAR; www.natcar.com.

Private Tour Drivers
An alternative is to hire a knowledgeable bilingual driver, experienced with Costa Rican roads. Ask at your hotel or consult classified ads in the *Tico Times*.

Driving: A Survival Guide

Four wheel drive *(doble tracción)* is recommended for many areas as the roads outside the Central Valley, especially during the rainy season, are muddy and rutted. Chains work well in the mud; try letting some air out of your tires to increase traction if the car is stuck.
Licenses: operating a motor vehicle without a license is a serious violation and invalidates any insurance. A valid driver's license

from another country can be used for three months. Always carry your passport (photocopies, including that of your entry stamp, usually suffice).

Import: foreign vehicles brought into Costa Rica for a period over six months must pay a large import tax. If you enter with a vehicle, you will have to leave with it or show papers proving you have sold it.

Driving habits: drivers weave all over the road to avoid the many ruts and holes. Two headlight blinks usually indicate the other driver is giving you the right of way (especially when you are making a left turn); on the highway two headlight blinks may mean that the police are ahead. Radar is often used.

Accidents: Costa Rica has a high accident and death rate. Always drive defensively. The law requires motorists to carry a set of reflecting triangles, a reflective vest, a fire extinguisher, and a first aid kit. If you are in an accident, do not move your car – not even to the side of the road – until the police and INS, the government insurance agency, arrive. Give no statements, but take witnesses' names. Do not leave your car at any time; locals have been known to re-position cars to make an accident look like your fault.

Parking: be careful not to park illegally. A yellow curb means no stopping. Even if you are in the car, police may prevent you from leaving and call a tow truck (grúa). You can ride in the car to the yard, where you will have to pay towing charges. Better to park in inexpensive parking lots (parqueos). This will reduce the chance of theft. Do not leave any valuables in cars. Thieves are known to have master keys to rentals and even 'watchimen,' people who offer to watch your car for a few coins, can work against you.

Flat tires or mechanical problems: If you are experiencing car trouble, drive to a well-lit area or gas station if possible. If not, keep an eye on your belongings and decline help from passersby. There have been incidents where thieves pop your tire, distract you as they help fix it, as another person takes off with your belongings.

Corruption: unfortunately, there are corrupt police who target foreign drivers. You may be stopped for no apparent reason. Have all necessary automobile documents

in the car and be polite. It is illegal for the police to demand payment on the spot. If you are badly treated, or if the policeman solicits a bribe or asks that you pay the fine immediately, ask for the ticket (Deme el parte), then ask for the officer's identification. Write it down, and report to the Dirección de Tránsito as soon as possible.

Taxis

Taxis are by far the easiest way of getting around San José; they are widely used and relatively inexpensive. You'll rarely have to wait long, although it is sometimes difficult to catch a cab in a rainy rush hour. All taxis should have operational meters (marías); be sure the drivers use them. If not, negotiate before getting in. If you are greatly overcharged, write down the driver's name and license number, and call the taxi company number marked on the outside of the cab.

Arrangements can be made to take trips by taxi to places outside San José. Beware – taxi drivers who are parked in front of major hotels will always charge more, and most will charge fixed rates. Taxis are red and have a 'Taxi' sign on the roof of the car. If they are not red and have no numbered yellow triangle on the door, then they are pirate taxis, or piratas, and are unlicensed.

Taxi Companies

Alfaro, tel: 2221 8466; http://taxi alfaro.com
Coopeguaria, tel: 2226 1366
Coopeirazu, tel: 2254 3211; www.taxi sirazu.com
Coopetaxi, tel: 2235 9966
Coopetico, tel: 2224 7979
Taxis Unidos, tel: 2221 6865; www.taxiaeropuerto.com

Cycling

Mountain bikers can see Costa Rica's back country, especially on the lightly traveled dirt roads crisscrossing rural areas. But cycling is very dangerous on paved roads since they have no shoulders.

While it is possible to go on your own, armed with decent Spanish skills and maps, your best bet is to book with a good biking company that knows the safest routes and can take care of logistics. Favorite routes include the trails around Lake Arenal in the Northern Zone, the rolling hills of Orosí or, for the hard-core, a Caribbean-to-Pacific trek. Most companies specializing in cycling tours provide excellent equipment, but you are welcome to bring your own (check with airlines on their bicycle policy). Consider installing kevlar inner tube protectors and bring a good lock.

For Sunday-style riders, most towns and many hotels have bike rentals, although the equipment quality tends to be a bit more wobbly.

Vintage Toyota Landcruiser in the town of San Marcos de Tarrazú.

A – Z

A HANDY SUMMARY
OF PRACTICAL INFORMATION

A

Acccommodations

The most popular places to stay in San José are in *el puro centro*, right downtown near the Plaza de la Cultura and in historic Barrio Amón, which has some boutique hotels with character. Other parts of downtown San José can be very noisy and polluted, so you may prefer to stay outside the center, in Escazú, Santa Ana, Alajuela, Heredia, and other Central Valley towns, which also give a good taste of Costa Rican life.

Note that high season in Costa Rica is from November 1 to April 30, and low season is from May 1 to October 31, excluding July and August, when greater demand means higher prices. During the low season, room prices may be discounted by as much as 40 percent. The price categories on the following pages indicate high-season rates.

Reservations made, but not paid for, may not be held, especially during high season, near the beaches and in Monteverde. Discounts may be given for stays of more than one night. Ask at your hotel about green (wet) season discounts.

Note that rates for remote lodges in areas such as Tortuguero or the Osa Peninsula may appear high but they usually include meals, and often transport and a tour or two.

The Instituto Costarricense de Turismo (see page 273) has a system of classifications for lodging based on size and facility; however, there is a wide range of popular names used unofficially:

Apartotel Apartments with cooking facilities and living area in a hotel-style complex. Weekly and monthly rates.
Cabina Usually a one-room cabin with a shower and bath, often close to the beach in coastal resorts. *Cabinas* vary widely in quality and price.
Bed & Breakfast Price and quality vary widely, from a modest room in someone's own house to elegant guesthouses all to yourself with pools and tennis courts.
Lodge Popular in more remote areas, usually near parks or natural attractions. Price usually includes meals. Stays at lodges are almost always linked with some outdoor activity: birdwatching, guided hikes, or horseback tours.
Villa or Chalet Often indistinguishable from a hotel.
Inn Often a Bed & Breakfast, but with more extensive amenities.
Resort Usually a luxurious, self-contained hotel complex.
Hotel Anything with more than 10 rooms.
Hostel There is a small youth hostel system. Prices vary.
Albergue/Pensión Modest, small hotels.

Homestays

To get a better understanding of the people and culture of Costa Rica, try a homestay. Visitors stay in the guest room of a host family and participate in as much of the family activities as they wish. Your options for finding a good homestay are best through one of the many language schools, which can help make homestay arrangements. Local families sometimes rent rooms at a price that includes meals and laundry. Check around the university and the bulletin board at the Costa Rican/North American Cultural Center, or see *The Tico Times* and local newspapers.

Admission Charges

As in many developing countries, attractions in Costa Rica sometimes charge two prices: one for tourists, and a lower one for Costa Ricans. Many of the smaller museums are free; the rest range from less than $1 to $15 (for the Jade Museum), usually with student and child rates. Most art galleries don't charge admission. National park admission fees vary, but are usually around $10.

Addresses

San José uses a grid system for its streets. North–south-running streets are *calles*, east–west-running streets are *avenidas*. Avenida Central (Av. Ctl) divides the city north and south; it becomes Paseo Colón west of Hospital San Juan de Díos. Calle Central (Ca. Ctl) divides San José east and west. The southern avenues and western streets are numbered evenly. The northern avenues and eastern streets have odd numbers.

Avenida Central passes through the downtown core as a wide pedestrian walkway, passing by many of the major attractions and shopping, making walking a viable way of getting around. A pleasant pedestrian way on downtown Avenida 4, between Calle 12 and Calle 7, is dotted with sculptures, including a life-size John Lennon sitting on a bench. On most other streets, you'll often have to squeeze through the narrow patches of sidewalk left by *chinamos* (streetside stands), and even with the streetlight in your favor, crossing can be a challenge. Taking common sense safety precautions, a walking tour of San José can be a pleasant way of seeing the sights.

Abbreviations used for addresses: Av. = avenida, Ca. = Calle, Ctl = central, Apto or Apdo = apartado (post office box, for mailing addresses). When an address is given using the street and avenues, the first part is the street or avenue on which the building is located, and the second part of the address indicates the streets or avenues the building is between. For example: the Metropolitan Cathedral location is Ca. Ctl, Av. 2–4. That is, the Cathedral is on Calle Central between Avenidas 2 and 4.

For the most part, there are no addresses or street names in Costa Rica. Although downtown San José has numbered avenues and streets, Costa Ricans do not refer to them. Homes and buildings are not numbered. Usually an address is given as the distance in meters *(metros)* north, east, south, or west from a known landmark. When it comes to walking, remember that cars have the right of way, not pedestrians, so always look twice before crossing the street.

B

Budgeting for your Trip

Many visitors find Costa Rica more expensive than they expected. It still can be an economic destination, and much of Costa Rica can be enjoyed independently, allowing you to keep costs down – although an itinerary organized by a tour operator may be worth the extra cost in efficient time savings. Costs for guided tours may be high for independent travelers, too (from $35 to $80, generally), but it is worth splurging on at least one or two such tours – particularly if you want to get the most out of a nature hike.

Shoestring travelers can get away with $50 or less a day, for just sun, sea, and self-guided hikes. An extensive public bus system gets you almost anywhere in the country from San José for less than $6 a time. Cheap cabins (usually cold or shared showers and less privacy) for under $25 per night (double

occupancy) abound, especially at the beach – but they fill up fast in the high season and on weekends. If you stick to the local *sodas* (small eateries), full plates of rice, meat, and beans that stick to your ribs are rarely more than $5. And you should still have enough for a few sunset beers (about $2).

To upgrade the comfort level, expect to pay $70 to $90 a night (double occupancy) for moderate lodging (private baths, hot water, some views, parking, extra amenities). Air-conditioned, minivan door-to-door hotel transport to the beach costs between $30 and $55 per person one way from San José. A dinner for two with a glass of wine can be easily had for $25.

No matter what your budget, you'll take cabs somewhere along the line. Taxis charge $1for the first kilometer and $0.02 cents every four seconds afterwards, but outside of San José taxi drivers tend to use their own flat rates, although it is illegal. Try to settle on a price before you set off.

C

Children

Costa Ricans adore children and they are welcome everywhere. To get the most out of Costa Rica's wildlife and natural attractions, though, children need to be old enough to be quiet and attentive. They also should be walking and not crawling on ground that may be home to biting or stinging insects and snakes. Dealing with diapers and baby gear is challenging in any country, but particularly so here, in remote areas where water and electricity may be scarce or non-existent. Keeping these conditions in mind, parents might want to wait till their children are five years and up, before bringing them on a tropical-nature adventure.

The San José area has any number of child-focused activities, but two of the best are the interactive exhibits at the **Museo de los Niños** (see page 132), housed in a castle-like former prison; and at **INBioParque** in Heredia (see page 143), with snakes, butterflies, and bullet-ant colonies.

Children usually enjoy **La Paz Waterfall Gardens** (see page 142) in Varablanca, about an hour north of San José, with its chain of impressive waterfalls, snake exhibit, and butterfly

gardens. It's not hard to convince anyone to spend a day immersed in a world of chocolate. On the Caribbean coast, try the **Chocoart** chocolate tour (see page 232), near Puerto Viejo. In the **Southern Zone**, near Puerto Jiménez, Finca Köbö (tel: 8398 7604; www.fincakobo.com) gives tours of its organic chocolate process.

For beach fun, **Tamarindo** on the North Pacific is a good beginner's beach for fledgling surfers. **Punta Uva** on the southern Caribbean coast and sheltered **Playa Manuel Antonio** on the central Pacific coast provide child-friendly snorkeling and swimming.

Night insect tours with **The Bug Lady** (tel: 8867 6134; www.thenighttour.com) add a touch of eerie fun. Older children may want to stay up for the mystical, nocturnal spectacle of giant sea turtles laying eggs at **Tamarindo**, **Tortuguero**, or **Ostional**.

Climate

Costa Rica has two seasons; the rainy or green season, which Costa Ricans call winter *(invierno)*, and the dry season or summer *(verano)*. In the Central Valley, the rainy season lasts from May through November and the dry season from December through April. Even during the rainy season, most mornings are bright and sunny.

During the rainy season there are fewer tourists and you can take advantage of green-season discounts in hotels.

Rain can fall at any time on the Caribbean coast but October is usually the driest month. Be prepared for higher humidity on the Caribbean coast.

The average temperature in San José is 24°C (75°F). In the highlands, temperatures drop approximately

CLIMATE CHART
Costa Rica

0.6°C for each 100 meters (500ft) of elevation. The temperature on the coasts varies from the mid-20s°C (70s°F) to the 30s°C (low 90s°F).

What to Wear

Clothing and footwear: pack to dress in layers. Sweaters and jackets are needed for the mountains and cool evenings, particularly in the Central Valley in December. Shorts are worn for athletic activities or at the beaches, not normally in the cities. Bring weatherproof gear and boots if you plan to do much hiking. Have a comfortable pair of walking shoes that are already broken in. Sidewalks are non-existent in many areas, and uneven at best. Costa Rican women are always well groomed and men like to wear cologne, lots of it. Bring dressy clothes for up-market San José restaurants and nightlife.

Conservation

Costa Rica is heralded worldwide for its progressive conservationist policies and biodiversity, making it a hotspot for ecotourism, a term that started out closely linked to conservation, but now is used to describe just about any activity or lodging in a nature setting.

Costa Rica tries very hard to do a great deal with few resources. The following are some of the more popular environmental organizations that are actively involved in saving and protecting Costa Rica's natural resources.

APREFLOFAS (Association for the Preservation of Wild Flora and Fauna) is a private, non-profit, non-governmental organization for nature conservation. Tel: 2240 6087; www.apreflofas.or.cr.

Sea Turtle Conservancy runs the green turtle tagging project at Tortuguero Beach on the Caribbean coast. Tel: 352 373 6441 (Florida); www.conserveturtles.org.

CEDARENA (Environmental and Natural Resource Legal Center): educates the public and government officials on the use of the law to protect the environment. Tel: 2283 7080; www.cedarena.org.

Corcovado Foundation: Created by concerned neighbors of Corcovado National Park to protect the wild heritage and future of the area through education and fundraising. Tel: 2297 3013; www.corcovadofoundation.org.

Find English-language reading material at bookstores and newsstands.

Friends of the Osa: Dedicated to preserving the Osa Peninsula's globally significant biodiversity through habitat conservation, science and research, and education. Tel: 2735 5756; www.osaconservation.org.

Fundación Neotrópica (Neotropic Foundation): works to foster 'sustainable development' in communities near wildlife preserves, parks, forest reserves, and other protected areas. Tel: 2253 2130; www.neotropica.org.

INBio (National Biodiversity Institute): this private non-profit research organization is amassing a catalogue of the country's flora and fauna and runs the 5.5-hectare (14-acre) INBioParkin Heredia. Tel: 2507 8107; www.inbio.ac.cr.

Kids Saving The Rainforest: based in Manuel Antonio, runs child-oriented conservation projects including an adopt-a-tree program ($20 to sponsor a planting), and Titi monkey bridges. Tel: 2777 2592; www.kidssavingtherainforest.org.

Rainforest Alliance: promotes sustainability by transforming land-use practices, business practices, and consumer behavior. Tel: 212-677 1900 (US); www.rainforest-alliance.org.

Rainforest Concern: buys and protects virgin forest, and helps locals develop responsible ecotourism. Partnering with The Endangered Wildlife Trust, the organization runs a turtle research and protection program just north of Limón. Tel: 01225 481 151 (UK); www.rainforestconcern.org.

The Nature Conservancy: US-based organization committed to land protection, focusing on two tracts of land in the Osa Peninsula and the Talamanca region. Tel: 2220 2552, (US) 703-841 5300; www.nature.org.

World Society for the Protection of Animals: Provides local mobilization and support for international campaigns, including whale conservation and Farm Watch. Tel: 617-896 9214 (US), 2562 1200 (Costa Rica); www.wspa-international.org.

Crime and Safety

Theft is a growing problem in Costa Rica. Pickpocketing, chain and watch snatching, backpack grabbing, and other thefts are becoming more common, especially in downtown San José and popular beach towns. It is, for the most part, non-violent, snatch-and-run thievery. Do not be paranoid and frightened, but do be vigilant.

Do not take valuables with you when you walk on the streets of San José. Carry only as much cash as you will need. Leave your backpack, passport, and jewelry in the hotel, preferably in a locked office. Keep an eye on wallets and shoulder bags. If you buy valuable items, make your return trip by taxi.

While walking on the street, be aware of who is around you and act confidently.

When driving through the city by car, keep your windows rolled up high enough so no one can reach inside.

Avoid deserted streets at night and walking in isolated areas.

Be especially watchful in these areas: the pedestrian walkway near the Coca-Cola bus terminal; the Plaza de la Cultura; Parque Central; Avenida 4 and Avenida Central; and Ca. 12 from Avenida 10 to Avenida 5.

Thefts from rental cars are common everywhere in the country. Do not leave anything unattended in your car, especially when you are unloading in a hotel parking lot. Do not assume items in a locked trunk are safe: they are not. Whenever possible, park in a guarded area.

Do not leave anything unattended on the beach, including towels, clothing, tents, and camping gear.

Most importantly, if you are mugged, don't resist.

Ask for the Fuerza Pública if you need a street police officer. For emergencies, call 911. English-speaking officers are few and far between but a new contingent of Tourism Police patrol high-tourist areas, usually on bicycles, and are specially trained to help tourists; they also man a post at the arrivals hall of the main airport, to offer safety advice. Report theft immediately to the Judicial Investigative Police (OIJ, pronounced oh-ee-ho-ta) if your passport is stolen or you require a police report for insurance purposes. Otherwise, this is a time-consuming process that will likely result in no more than a file collecting dust.

Customs Regulations

Personal effects may be taken into the country and up to six rolls of film, 500g (18oz) of tobacco, 2kg (4lbs) of candy, and 5 liters (170 fl oz) of wine or liquor (if over 21). Carry prescription drugs in original containers. Anyone caught with illegal drugs can face 8 to 20 years in jail and no bail.

D

Disabled Travelers

Much of Costa Rica's claim to fame is based around rugged nature, and the country's buckled and potholed roads and sidewalks (where they exist) can be difficult to navigate at the best of times. By no means, however, should people with mobility difficulties write off the idea of a rainforest vacation. Tourism establishments have made efforts to open up the country's treasures, although definitions of 'accessible' vary widely – call ahead with specific questions to avoid disappointment.

A variety of attractions, including the Poás and Irazú volcanoes, and Carara National Park, are set up to facilitate travelers in wheelchairs, and a handful of local companies organize excursions or arrange transport.

Accessible Journeys
Tel: 800-846 4537 or 610-521 0339 (US); www.disabilitytravel.com. Organizes tours September through May.

RoadMap
Tel: 2203 3038; www.moniquechabot. com.
Personalized itineraries for accessible vacations.

Team CRT
Tel: 2508 5000; www.costarica4u.com Arranges tours and transport for people with disabilities. An established Tico travel agency experienced in helping disabled tourists.

E

Eating Out

What and Where to Eat

Thanks to a continuing influx of international tourists and restaurateurs, Costa Rica's culinary offerings are very cosmopolitan, along with traditional local fare, comida típica.

The most sophisticated dining can be found in San José, downtown, and in the eastern suburbs of Barrio Escalante, San Pedro, and Curridibat. The upscale, western suburbs of, Escazú and Santa Ana have seen an explosion of trendy restaurants, many of which disappear almost as quickly as they pop up.

Beyond the Central Valley, there are concentrations of fine cuisine in popular tourist areas on the Pacific coast. One fine-dining enclave of note is Ojochal, a tiny French-Canadian village south of Uvita, which boasts a French bakery, and two excellent French restaurants. On the Caribbean coast, Cahuita and the Puerto Viejo area have a cluster of very tasty options, ranging from classic, spicy Afro-Caribbean fare to an amazing array of Italian restaurants, including two of the best in the country.

Reservations are a good idea at upscale eateries, but usually not necessary elsewhere. By law, menus must show prices with tax and tip included (totaling a

whopping 23 percent). However, many restaurant menus, especially those denominated in US dollars in high-volume tourist areas, disingenuously do not. Before you order, ask if service and tax are included. Unless the service is truly excellent, a tip is not necessary, since the mandatory 10 percent service charge goes to the waiters (in theory if not in practice).

Vegetarians will not go hungry. There are more and more vegetarian options available and even in the simplest local eatery, there is always rice and beans and salad as a last resort. Beware, however – sin carne means 'without meat,' but is often understood as 'without beef.' Specify sólo vegetales if you want to be sure.

Covered markets have permanent sodas, food counters where shoppers can fill up cheaply on local fare. At the Puntarenas Fish Market, you can watch shrimp-shellers work at a furious pace, while perched on a stool at a market soda.

Weekly street markets are also a bonanza of seasonal tropical fruits and vegetables at farm prices. Vendors are happy to taste the mystery produce and cut you off a slice to taste. Markets are also good for quick breakfasts, as vendors of gallo pinto, cheese-filled tortillas, Salvadoran pupusas, and fresh juices set up around the action. Many areas have a market on Saturday or Sunday morning; try the Zapote market by the old bullring, southeast of San José (Sunday); the Coronado market near the Gothic church (Sunday); and Heredia's Saturday market, which stretches a kilometer (0.6 miles) along the old railroad tracks.

Drinking Notes

Local beers, good but not exceptional, include Imperial, Pilsen, Rock Ice, and Bavaria. Microbreweries are improving the beer scene at some of the trendier restaurants and bars. Wine is not common with meals, but there are some good-value South American wines increasingly available.

You must be 18 years of age to drink alcohol in Costa Rica. Some bars require you to show identification.

Guaro, the local sugar cane-based firewater, is cheap and can strip paint. Fruit-based cocktails are more popular these days, with some very unusual local variations on martinis and margaritas.

Useful Numbers

Local collect calls: 110
Information: 1113
International information: 124
Airport information: /2442 2960
/ 2442 2139
Tourist information: 1192 or
2299 5800
Rate of exchange: 2243 4143
Time: 1112
Fire, police, ambulance: 911
National Parks: 2522 6500

Opening Times

Monday to Saturday, most bar/
restaurants open any time from
8.30am to 11am, and stay open until
around midnight or 2am in cities.
On Sunday, some may close earlier,
others do not bother to open at all.
Out in the campo, away from tourist
areas, you will have to eat early or go
hungry. Even in many tourist areas,
restaurants close early. Friday and
Saturday nights are busy, but earlier
in the week you may find happy hours
and other offers.

Electricity

110 volts, 60-cycle current. Two- and
three-prong flat plugs. Australian and
European appliances need a two-
prong adapter. Most accommodations
have equipment to convert power.

Embassies and Consulates

Embassies Abroad

Australia: General Consulate, PO Box
205, Spit Junction, Sydney, tel: 006-
129 969 4050.
Canada: 350 Sparks St. Suite 701
(Office Tower), tel: 1-613-562 2855;
http://costaricaembassy.com.
South Africa: Honorary Consulate,
Brynston 2021, Johannesburg, tel:
0027 11 705 3434.
UK: 14 Lancaster Gate, London W2
3LH, tel: 020-7706 8844; www.
costaricanembassy.co.uk.
US: 2112-S. Street, NW, Washington,
DC 20008, tel: 202-499 2991; www.
costarica-embassy.org.

Consulates in San José

The Canadian Consulate has an
agreement to assist **Australian**
nationals.
Canada
Oficentro La Sábana, Building 5,
tel: 2242 4400; http://costarica.gc.ca.
South Africa
(Consulate), 150 meters/yds west
of entrance to Pacific Rail Terminal,

Downtown, tel: 222 1470 or 223
8223.
UK
Edificio Centro Colón, 11th Floor,
tel: 2258 2025, https://www.gov.uk/
government/world/costa-rica.
US
Ca. 120, Avenida 0, Pavas, tel: 2519
2000; http://costarica.usembassy.gov.

Emergencies

Dial **911** anywhere in Costa Rica for
emergency assistance.
Car Accidents: tel: 800-8726 7486
(Transit Police in San José) and
800-800 8001 (National Insurance
Institute in San José).
Reporting a crime: tel: 2295 3272 or
911 (OIJ in San José, 24 hours).
24-hour Pharmacy: Farmacia Clínica
Bíblica (tel: 2522 1000, downtown
San José), Farmacia CIMA (tel: 2208
1000, Escazú).
Stolen Visa Card: tel: 0-800-011
0030.
Stolen MasterCard: tel: 0-800 011
0184.

Etiquette

Ticos are infinitely hospitable – so
always accept a bite to eat and a drink
if invited to a private home.
　Preceding any request with *Me
puede hacer el favor de...* (Could
you do me the favor of...) will go
a long way to ensuring the best
service. While you'll see Costa Ricans
snapping their fingers at wait staff and
calling out *muchacha* or *muchacho*
(girl or boy), foreigners should stick to
the more respectful *Disculpe, señor/a*
(Excuse me sir/ma'am).
Greeting: people shake hands when
first introduced. Women usually
greet each other with a kiss on the
cheek and say goodbye in the same
fashion; this also applies when a
friendly relationship exists, and men
and women often greet in the same
way. Children are very affectionate
and usually greet their elders with
a kiss. However, among adults,
excessive displays of affection in
public are not well received, as
attested to by the occasional *No se
permite escenas amorosas* (No public
displays of affection) sign in some
establishments. Having said that,
such displays are quite common.
　Elderly Costa Ricans are commonly
addressed as Don (men) or Doña
(women) followed by their first name,
an honorific considered an archaism
in most Spanish-speaking countries.
Nude bathing: there are no nudist
beaches in Costa Rica and topless

bathing is not acceptable; nor is
wearing bathing suits on the streets.
Prostitution: the sex trade is legal in
Costa Rica, but pimping is not. With
no official medical records kept for
prostitutes, however, the health risks
are high. Some beautiful 'women' are in
fact transvestites. Aids is a formidable
reality in Costa Rica, so practice safe
sex. Sex with a minor is illegal and
punishable by imprisonment. The
government has talked a lot about
cracking down on pedophiles, but so
far with little success.

G

Gay and Lesbian Travelers

Relatively free of active oppression
and intolerance, Costa Rica has
become a favorite spot for gay and
lesbian travelers from around the
region. It now even has its own
Gay Pride Parade (in June). The
atmosphere is distinctly 'don't ask,
don't tell,' and the general public
tends to be uncomfortable with same-
sex displays of affection.
　San José and Manuel Antonio both
have clusters of gay-only and gay-
friendly hotels, restaurants, and bars.
　Gay-Costa Rica (tel: 860-246
7777 US or 877-987 8482; www.gay-
costarica.com) offers three package
tours at different prices to hotels that
are gay-owned or very gay-friendly.
　The free bimonthly magazine
Playita Circuit (Manuel Antonio) can
be picked up at gay-friendly outlets.

H

Health and Medical Care

Costa Rica ranks near the United
States, Canada, and other Western
nations in health-care standards.
Inoculations: no inoculations are
required for visiting Costa Rica.
Water: in San José and the Central
Valley, water is treated. It is, with
some exceptions, potable throughout
the country. If you have persistent
intestinal problems, take a stool
sample to the Clínica Bíblica (tel:
2522 1000, results in minutes) to be
analyzed (about US$20).
Illness: malaria is not generally a
problem in Costa Rica, except in the
remote regions of Talamanca. Cholera
is not usually a problem, either, due
to Costa Rica's strong public health
efforts. There has been a marked
increase in the incidence of dengue
fever, however. Dengue symptoms

include the sudden onset of fever, headache, severe joint and muscle pains followed in most cases by a rash, which starts on the trunk and spreads to the limbs and face. The fever subsides in a few days but a bout can last three weeks or more, from start to finish. Dengue is spread by the *Aedes aegypti* mosquito, which bites principally at dusk. There is presently no prophylactic treatment available for dengue, but medical attention can significantly reduce the effects. Prevention is the best medicine: use repellent and wear long-sleeved shirts and long pants. **Snake bites**: although rare, it is worth wearing closed high-top shoes or boots and floppy long pants and walking with a stick. If you are bitten, apply a compress (not a tourniquet). Try to remember what the snake looked like so the doctor can locate the correct antivenin. Then get to the nearest clinic or hospital.

Medical Services

Costa Rica has an excellent health-care system, much less expensive than in the US. Many doctors are trained in the US or Europe and speak English, especially those at private clinics. In some remote communities, you can get help through the public clinic system, called **EBAIS**.

It is essential to have comprehensive insurance when traveling to Costa Rica. Some bank cards and credit cards may include insurance, but this may not be adequate. You need enough coverage for both medical expenses and repatriation.

Public Medical Centers
Hospital Dr Calderón Guardia
San José
Tel: 2212 1000
Hospital de los Niños
San José
Tel: 2523 3600 (for children).
Hospital México
San José
Tel: 2242 6700
Hospital San Juan de Díos
San José
Tel: 2547 8000

Private Medical Centers
Clínica Bíblica
Central San José
Tel: 2522 1000
www.clinicabiblica.com
Clínica Católica
Guadalupe
Tel: 2246 3000
www.hospitallacatolica.com

Hospital Cristiano Jerusalem
Guadalupe
Tel: 2216 9191
www.hospitaljerusalem.com
Hospital San José CIMA
Escazú
Tel: 2208 1000
www.hospitalsanjose.net

Dentists

Costa Rican dentists provide competent and affordable cosmetic as well as general dentistry.

The Tico Times contains ads placed by English-speaking dentists, who can also be found on the US Embassy website (http://costarica.usembassy.gov).

I

Internet

Internet cafés with high-speed connections abound in San José, making it easy and cheap (less than $1 per hour) to stay dialed in. With the latest in internet technology, the quality of computer-based calls has improved dramatically and internet cafés have essentially replaced public international call centers.

Once you leave the capital, you will be able to find public internet access and Wi-fi spots in just about any town of any size, but service becomes slower and more expensive – up to $5 per hour in beach towns. If you really need to keep in touch in the most remote places, expect to pay

astronomical amounts for satellite internet.

Most upscale hotels offer a computer with internet service, Wi-fi, or both. Eateries such as Bagelmen's outlets in San José and Denny's at the Hotel Irazú are popular wireless hotspots, but be extra careful when taking advantage of the service; reports of laptop theft near these centers have increased.

L

Left Luggage

Neither international airport has an area for left luggage. However, most hotels and some tour companies will allow you to store extra gear and luggage for a few days for free or for a small charge.

M

Maps

The ICT tourist information centers at the airport and on Avenida Central in downtown San José hand out decent, free road maps, but often run out of copies.

Check Maptak (www.maptak.com) for detailed topographic and political maps of Costa Rica's provinces, national parks, and more. For simple maps, directions, and driving distances, www.costaricamap-online.com is a good pre-trip reference.

Looking for an attraction, accommodation, bike hire, or internet?

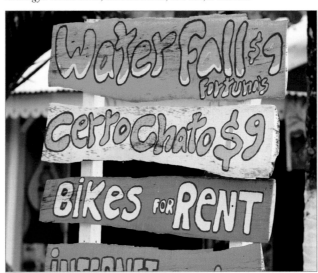

Media

Radio

Radio stations in English include 107.5 FM, which plays classic rock and has news and other information in English, and Radio Dos (99.5 FM), a Spanish-language station that plays pop and rock classics, has a morning show in English, and news in English, every other hour.

Television

There are more than 70 cable TV channels listed in the local TV guide; more are available. Programming includes approximately 30 channels in English, one in German, one in French, and one in Chinese.

Newspapers and Magazines

Available in English, Spanish, and other languages, at bookstores, supermarkets, newsstands, and hotel outlets. Weekly English-language publications include:

The Tico Times (www.ticotimes.net), published weekly on Friday. Widely available at most newsstands in central San José, Cartago, Heredia, and Alajuela. Gives the week's news in Costa Rica, up-to-date listings of what's happening, and where. Also provides online daily news and publishes a Restaurant Guide.

Costa Rica Outdoors (tel: 2231 0306, www.costaricaoutdoors.com). Bimonthly magazine featuring fishing, birding, and *Tico* culture. Daily Spanish-language newspapers include: *La Nación*, *La Prensa Libre*, *La República*, and *Al Día*.

Money

The currency unit is the colón. The current rate of exchange can be found in the English-language *Tico Times* business pages; the daily *La Nación* publishes a daily list of the rates offered at each bank. The Central Bank posts a page with the daily rates of the country's institutions at www.bccr.fi.cr .

State Banks: the main ones are Banco Nacional (tel: 2212 2000) and Banco de Costa Rica (tel: 2287 9000), with offices throughout the country. If you need an early bank stop, the latter has a branch that opens at 7.30am on the east side of town in Curridabat.

Private banks: the main ones are Davivienda (tel: 2287 1111) and BAC San José (tel: 2295 9797). Other private banks include Scotiabank, Banco Promerica, and Banco CMB.

Many of these have branches that are open until 7pm. BAC San José's Rápido Bancos in most Central Valley malls are even open Sunday for basic transactions, including exchange.

Traveler's checks: while the tourism industry has become more familiar with traveler's checks, high fraud rates have led some businesses to ax this method of payment. For safety, it's a good idea to bring some money in this form, which can always be changed in banks, but check with stores or hotels before trying to pay this way. You must have your original passport with you to cash traveler's checks or to get cash advances on credit cards.

Cash: you may not be able to break 10,000 or 20,000 colón notes when paying for taxis and such. US dollars in small denominations are often accepted in taxis and shops, particularly in towns and cities. Counterfeiting has made many businesses highly suspicious of US$100 bills and it is better to bring smaller denominations.

Credit cards: American Express, Visa, and MasterCard are widely accepted in the Central Valley area. Their telephone calls are handled by local credit card firm Credomatic (tel: 2295 9000).

Access numbers for international credit card calls are:

AT&T: 0-8000-114 114
British Telecom: 0-800-044 1044
Canada Direct: 0-8000-151 161
MCI: 0-8000-122 222
Sprint: 0-8000-130 123

Bank Machines: ATMs are widely available. For locations, check banks' websites. Some banks accept either Visa or MasterCard but not both; check www.mastercard.com/global/atmlocations; or http://lac.visa.com/home.jsp, to see where you can get cash advances in machines. Look for machines during the day, especially ones with nearby guards.

Changing money: exchange rates vary slightly between banks, and day-to-day rates go up and down. The fluctuation is generally no more than a cent per dollar, and most banks are within a cent of each other in rates. Private banks (particularly BAC San José) are the best places to exchange money if you want to avoid long line-ups. Your hotel may also change money for you. Some banks now handle euros as well as dollars.

Money can be exchanged at the airport (BAC San José) from 5am to 10pm – if you have colones, it's best to change them to euros or dollars before you get on the plane. Avoid the Casa de Cambio Global Exchange,

which offers a relatively poor rate of exchange.

Taxes and Tipping: restaurants add 13 percent tax to the bill plus a 10 percent service charge. Hotels add 13 percent tax and service. Bellboys should be tipped. In restaurants tipping is not expected, unless service is outstanding. Do tip barmen and taxi drivers who are helpful.

O

Opening Hours

Business opening hours are generally 8am–5pm, often with a lunch break from noon–1pm. Retail stores are usually open Mon–Sat from 9am until 6–7pm. State banks usually open from 8.30am–3.30pm Mon–Fri and some also open on Saturday morning.

P

Photography

Whatever your travel plans in Costa Rica, you won't regret packing a telephoto lens to capture wildlife sightings. Water damage and theft are two very real threats to your photo equipment. Consider a dry bag, or at the least a waterproof case or plastic bag, and, depending on the value of your camera, you may want to insure it separately.

It is possible to upload and burn photos from your camera onto a CD or hard-drive key in many internet cafés; some even have a universal cable lying around if you forget yours.

Tours catering to the multiplying masses of traveling photographers are directed at beginners, amateurs, and semi-professionals and often provide a stress-free way to find the best images.

Costa Rica Birding Journeys
Tel: 8417 9015
www.costaricabirdingjourneys.org
Small groups of four to six led by expert bird photographer Randall Ortega.
Costa Rica Gateway
Tel: 2433-8278; 888 246 8513 (US)
www.costaricagateway.com
Custom photography tours, specializing in birds and wildlife.
Foto Verde Tours
Tel: 8396 0363
www.fotoverdetours.com.
Based in the birding hotspot of Sarapiqui, professional wildlife photographer Greg Basco gives one-day seminars and multiday excursions to many locations in the country.

Postal Services

Airmail between the US or Europe and Costa Rica should take about five days, but a wait of two or more weeks is not uncommon. The central post office is at Ca. 2, Avenida 1–3, tel: 2223 9766. Mail can be received there in the general delivery section (Lista de Correos). Outgoing mail should be posted at either a hotel desk or a post office. It is usually difficult, time-consuming, and expensive to receive packages in the mail. Outrageous duties are sometimes applied and you can spend days trying to deal with numerous officials. A receipt showing a low value may help if it is included with the package. There are agents (agencias de aduana) listed in the phone book who will handle the customs clearances for a fee.

Couriers: there are many international courier services. The most popular are: FedEx and DHL. Consult the Yellow Pages for numbers.

Public Holidays

Costa Rica moves certain public holidays to the following Monday if a date falls on a weekend. When holidays fall within the week, government offices and some businesses will push the holiday to the following Monday, while other businesses will close on the day itself.
January 1 New Year's Day
March/April Good Thursday
March/April Good Friday
April 11 Juan Santamaría Day
May 1 Labor Day
July 25 Annexation Day
August 2 Virgin of Los Angeles Day
August 15 Mother's Day
September 15 Independence Day
October 12 Meeting of the Cultures Day
December 25 Christmas Day

R

Religious Services

Costa Rica's official religion is visibly Catholic, but there is full freedom of religion. Visitors are welcome to sit in on Spanish-speaking services in the cathedrals, of course showing common-sense courtesy and dressing appropriately.

The Central Valley has active Anglican, Baha'i, Jewish, Baptist, Jehovah's Witness, and Quaker communities and many evangelical Protestant churches, among others, and approximately 25 houses of worship offer services in English. Check The Tico Times weekly newspaper's calendar section for an extensive list.

S

Shopping

What to Buy

Costa Rica's selection of souvenirs has been increasing slowly but steadily over the past few years. The traditional classics – miniature ox-carts, wood products, indigenous masks, and coffee – are now sold alongside locally produced CDs that rival any world-music offering. The 'Symbiosis' DVD features an original score set to riveting video of the rainforest and its inhabitants. It's also worth checking out conservation organizations, such as ANAI, which raise money by selling beautiful CDs, DVDs, and other souvenirs. Bartering is low-key, but you can usually get a discount off the ticket price for paying cash.

The following products can be found just about everywhere.
Ceramics
Be skeptical of many of the 'indigenous' ceramics you see for sale. The best are made in the northern Pacific area – Guaitil and Santa Cruz – where artisans still use pre-Columbian pottery techniques.
Coffee
Costa Rican coffee is excellent and relatively inexpensive. Café Britt stands out for its wide variety of top-quality coffee in flashy packages – great for gifts, and available in grocery stores and gift shops. Top-quality Coopedota coffee from the Tarrazú region is available in some supermarkets. If it is just what's inside that counts, rather than the packaging, Café Rey, Café Volio, Toscafe and Café 1827 are good, less expensive alternatives.
Woodwork
Wooden items, including bowls, plates, cutting boards, and boxes, are widely available in most gift shops. The mountain town of Sarchí is known for its intricately painted woodwork. The finest quality wooden boxes and bowls are made by Barry Biesanz of Biesanz Woodworks. He welcomes visitors to his beautiful, light-filled studio in Bello Horizonte, near Escazú: www.biesanz.com.
Leatherwork
Leather bags, wallets, and briefcases are good quality and available in many stores throughout the Central Valley. While they are a bit bulkier, fold-up leather rocking chairs, packed for shipping, are a great deal.
Woven Bags
Look for interesting woven-cotton bags and hats colored with natural dyes by indigenous artisans, available at many locations.

The Maria Inmaculada religion revolves around children.

Jewelry

Inexpensive handmade earrings and jewelry are sold everywhere, including street artisans' stalls in San José.

Music

Papaya Music releases are available at Universal, Lehman's, and many other stores, featuring local legends and traditional tunes. The great sounds, funky art, and English liner notes for tourists make the CDs a great souvenir.

Paper

Beautiful handmade papers, made from recycled plant materials – bananas, coffee, mangoes – and using natural dyes, are sold in many gift stores.

Student Travelers

An international student ID card will get discounts on some attractions, airfares to Costa Rica, and most museums. It never hurts to ask if a discount is available. But it's the proliferation of cheap *cabinas*, dirt-cheap transport, and affordable plates of rice and beans that make Costa Rica a student-friendly destination.

Many conservation organizations charge low rates to take on student volunteers for a true immersion experience. The Association of Volunteers Working in Protected Areas (ASVO; tel: 2258 4430; www. asvocr.org) is a good bet for short-term volunteering stints maintaining trails, monitoring marine turtle conservation, or teaching English, requiring only basic Spanish.

T

Telecommunications

The international code for Costa Rica is 506. To make a call from a public phone, you will need a phone card (*tarjeta telefónica*), available at most shops and pharmacies. Phones accepting coins are very rare these days. Operators including Kölbi, TuYo Movil, Movistar, and Claro offer cell phone service using GSM technology (1800 MHz and 850 MHz). It is also possible to buy a prepaid SIM card with a local number in order to avoid expensive roaming fees. You will need to show a valid passport and it is essential to re-charge the card at least once in three months to keep it active.

International Calls

Dial 124 for country codes. International phone cards are available at various locations. If you do not have access to a phone, international calls can be made from any internet café.

Time Zone

Costa Rica is on North America's Central Standard Time which means it is six hours behind GMT. It does not observe Daylight Savings, so this time difference increases one hour during the northern summer months. Since Costa Rica is close to the equator, the number of daylight hours does not vary much from season to season; the sun sets year-round more or less around 6pm.

Toilets

There are very few public restrooms in towns, but in the capital it is easy to slip into a fast-food restaurant; outside of the Central Valley many restaurants and road stops allow you to use the facilities, sometimes for a 100-colón fee. Always carry a small supply of toilet tissue.

Tour Operators

Thanks to high levels of English spoken in a well-established tourism circuit, and extensive, inexpensive transport, visitors to Costa Rica will find the country fairly easy to navigate as independent travelers.

However, booking with a local tour company can save transport time – and hair-raising driving experiences – and most are valuable resources if a wrench is thrown into your plans. In some remote areas, such as Tortuguero, options are largely, but not completely, restricted to a two- or three-day package, including meals, tours, and often transport.

Drive-yourself tours, such as those offered by Costa Rican Trails (www.costaricantrails.com), balance well-planned itineraries and in-country support with independence. Agro-tourism tours are among the best ways to immerse yourself in Costa Rica and its culture

Specialist Tour Operators

Coast to Coast Adventures
Tel: 2280 8054
www.coasttocoastadventures.com.
Adventure tourism and races; cycling tours.
Costa Rica Expeditions
Tel: 2521 6099
www.costaricaexpeditions.com.
The original whitewater rafting and nature tour company. Offers nature tours to Tortuguero, Corcovado, and Monteverde, with knowledgeable bilingual guides.
Costa Rican Trails
Tel: 2280 6705
From US: 888-803 3344
From Canada: 866-865 7013
www.costaricantrails.com.
Friendly company that offers a variety of nature, family, and adventure tours including motorcycling.
Costa Rica Sun Tours
Tel: 2296 7757/ 866 271 6263
(US, Canada)
www.crsuntours.com.
Off-the-beaten-track tours with a naturalist focus; family tours a specialty. Volcanoes, national parks, cloud forests, rainforests, beaches. Turtle-watching tours. Whitewater rafting, hiking, biking, and horseback riding tours.
Discovery Costa Rica
Tel: 2289 4747/ 866 839 2158

(US, Canada)
www.discoverycostarica.com.
Design your own package from a large range of tours.
Sirenas Diving Costa Rica
Playas del Coco/Playa Hermosa
Tel: 8387 4710
www.sirenasdivingcostarica.com.
Long-established dive and adventure operator.
Horizontes
Tel: 2222 2022
www.horizontes.com.
Customized nature tours of all types throughout Costa Rica, including tours for families, photographers, birdwatchers. Day trips in the Central Valley.
Ríos Tropicales
Tel: 2233 6455/866 722 8273 (toll free US)
www.riostropicales.com.
Leading tour company for rafting and kayaking.
Serendipity Adventures
Tel: 507 1358
From US: 888 226 5050
www.serendipityadventures.com.
Specialists in hot-air ballooning.
Swiss Travel
Tel: 2282 4898
www.swisstravelcr.com.
Organizes upscale ecotourism and adventure vacations.

while directly benefitting local communities.

Regardless of how independent you would like to be, hiring a good guide is essential for spotting wildlife. The National Apprentice Institute has an excellent program that trains and licenses naturalist guides. Another good yardstick is a recommendation from your hotel or established tour agency.

The **National Chamber of Tourism** (**CANATUR**) lists tourism agencies on its website (www.canatur.org).

Ecotourism

Ecotourism is still the buzz word in Costa Rica and hotels can provide or recommend excellent guides.

A fledgling organized rural tourism network is the latest way of guaranteeing a vacation that minimizes impact on the environment and maximizes benefits to those working in tourism. The bilingual (English/Spanish) Rural Community Tourism Guide put out by COOPRENA (www.turismoruralcr.com), a national ecotourism network, lists several of these rural tourism projects.

These two associations are the most reliable sources for community-based tourism:
Rural Tourism Association (ACTUAR), tel: 2290 7514, www.actuarcostarica.com
Well-established community tourism with extensive network of rural lodges.
Simbiosis Tours, tel: 2290 8646, www.turismoruralcr.com
The tourism branch of COOPRENA, a comprehensive national ecotourism network that organizes tours to member lodges.

Tourist Information

The Costa Rican Tourism Institute's (ICT; www.visitcostarica.com) most useful office is on Avenida Central, just steps from the Plaza de La Cultura, but private agencies around the country provide just about everything you need to know. The following offices are particularly good:
ICT Avenida Central, pedestrian walkway office, tel: 2222 1090, Mon–Fri 9am–5pm, closed noon to 1pm. Good information and maps.
ICT Central Office, East Side of Juan Pablo II Bridge, over the highway General Cañas, tel: 2299 5800, 866 267 8274 (from the US), 8am–4pm. Staffed by bilingual operators.
National Parks Information, tel: 2283 8004 or 192, www.costarica-nationalparks.com. Official government

site for extensive information on all national parks.
Talamanca Ecotourism and Conservation Association (**ATEC**), tel: 2750 0398, www.ateccr.org. A good option for community and tourism information around Puerto Viejo.

V

Visas and Passports

Citizens of the US, Canada, UK, Ireland, Australia, New Zealand, and South Africa need only a passport valid for at least six months beyond the date of entry to Costa Rica. Travelers may remain for 90 days. If you leave the country for 72 hours, when you return you will be allowed another 90 days. But immigration is cracking down on 'perpetual tourists' so multiple exits and entries are not advisable.

Travelers from other nations should contact the nearest Costa Rican consulate or embassy or the Costa Rican Foreign Relations Ministry (www.rree.go.cr).

More and more often, airlines are requiring that *before* they board their flight to Costa Rica travelers present a ticket showing they are leaving within 90 days.

Leave your passport in a safe place in your hotel, but always carry a photocopy including the page that contains your entry stamp in case of immigration authorities' spot checks. Report lost ID to the police immediately.

W

Websites

AM Costa Rica: daily online tabloid, www.amcostarica.com.
Chamber of Tourism (CANATUR): www.canatur.org.
Costa Rican Foreign Relations Ministry: information on consulates and embassies; official translators, www.rree.go.cr.
CostaRica.com: blogs, Costa Rican recipes, culture, real estate information, www.costarica.com.
Costa Rican Tourist Board (ICT): comprehensive tourism information and news, www.visitcostarica.com.
Inside Costa Rica: daily summary of news in English, www.insidecostarica.com.
Costa Rica Guide: excellent general guide with plenty of practical

What's On

The *Tico Times* newspaper (in English) publishes a calendar of activities and shows in its weekly edition (Friday), as well as a daily brief with selected events on its Daily News Page. The Spanish-language daily *La Nación* publishes an extensive events calendar in its Friday 'Tiempo Libre' section, as well as daily theater and music ads.
AM Costa Rica (www.amcostarica.com/calendar.htm) has fairly comprehensive online listings.

There is no major central ticket agency in Costa Rica; points of sale, usually stores, vary according to sponsors; *La Nación* ads generally list the ticket outlets. Tickets for local theater and musical presentations can be purchased by phone at major theaters, in person at the box office, or, in the case of the Teatro Nacional, online.

information from Ray and Sue who have more than two decades' experience of traveling in Costa Rica, http://costa-rica-guide.com.
La Nación Newspaper: summarizes news of the week in English on Friday, www.nacion.com.
Sustainable Tourism Certification: overview of program and detailed list of certified establishments, www.turismo-sostenible.co.cr.
The Tico Times: weekly and daily news and general information, www.ticotimes.net.

Weights and Measures

Costa Rica uses the metric system. When asking for directions, remember that 100 meters usually means one block, regardless of how long the block is. While most real estate information speaks of square meters and hectares, the *manzana* (7,000 sq meters, or about 1.75 acres) is still widely used as a unit of measurement.

Women Travelers

Costa Rica is considered to be a very safe destination for women, and rarely will women face persistent or physical harassment, but it is best to take precautions. Travelers of both sexes are advised to walk in pairs or groups, and take cabs at night. Always sit in the back seat, and make a note of the driver's ID.

LANGUAGE

UNDERSTANDING THE LANGUAGE

SURVIVAL SPANISH

Spanish is Costa Rica's principal language, so learn some phrases before you arrive, if only the simple courtesies: 'Good morning.' 'How are you?' 'I'm well, thanks.' These seemingly inconsequential phrases are an important part of daily life in Costa Rica. English is spoken by many people in San José and in the larger hotels, and one can always get by without Spanish; but if your idea of a good trip includes some contact with local people, then speaking a bit of Spanish is important.

If you are going on an extended trip, consider spending the first week enrolled in one of the many language schools, which offer tailored programs and schedules of all kinds, many with excursions and cultural programs.

Numbers

1 *uno*
2 *dos*
3 *tres*
4 *cuatro*
5 *cinco*
6 *seis*
7 *siete*
8 *ocho*
9 *nueve*
10 *diez*
11 *once*
12 *doce*
13 *trece*
14 *catorce*
15 *quince*
16 *dieciseis*
17 *diecisiete*
18 *dieciocho*
19 *diecinueve*

20 *veinte*
21 *veinte y uno*
30 *treinta*
40 *cuarenta*
50 *cincuenta*
60 *sesenta*
70 *setenta*
80 *ochenta*
90 *noventa*
100 *cien*
101 *ciento uno*
200 *doscientos*
300 *trescientos*
400 *cuatrocientos*
500 *quinientos*
600 *seiscientos*
700 *setecientos*
800 *ochocientos*
900 *novecientos*
1,000 *mil*
2,000 *dos mil*
10,000 *diez mil*
100,000 *cien mil*
1,000,000 *un millón*

Common Expressions

Good morning *Buenos días*
Good afternoon *Buenas tardes*
Good evening *Buenas noches*
Goodbye *Hasta luego/Adiós*
How are you? *¿Cómo está Usted?*
I'm well, thanks *Muy bien, gracias*
And you? *¿Y Usted?*
Please *Por favor*
Thank you *Gracias*
No, thank you *No, gracias*
You're welcome *Con mucho gusto*
How kind of you *Usted es muy amable*
I am sorry *Lo siento*
Excuse me *Disculpe* (when apologizing). *Con permiso* (when leaving the table or passing in front of someone)
Yes *Sí*
No *No*

Do you speak English? *¿Habla Usted inglés?*
Do you understand me? *¿Me entiende?*
Does anyone here speak English? *¿Hay alguien aquí que hable inglés?*
Just a moment, please *Un momentito, por favor*
This is good *Está bueno*
This is bad *Está malo*

Shopping and Eating

What is the price? *¿Cuánto cuesta?* or *¿Cuánto es?*
It's too expensive *Es muy caro*
Can you give me a discount? *¿Puede darme un descuento?*
Do you have ...? *¿Tiene Usted ...?*
I will buy this *Voy a comprar esto*
Please show me another *Muéstreme otro, por favor*
Please bring me ... *Tráigame por favor ...*
coffee with milk *café con leche*
black coffee *café negro*
tea *té*
a beer *una cerveza*
cold water *agua fría*
a soft drink *una gaseosa*
the menu *el menú*
the daily special *el plato del día*
May I have another beer? *Puede darme una cerveza más, por favor*
May I have the bill? *La cuenta, por favor*
[To get the attention of the waiter/waitress] *Disculpe Señor/ Señora/ Señorita*
Where is the dining room? *¿Dónde está el comedor?*
the pharmacy *la farmacia*
the gas station *la bomba* (the pump)
key *la llave*
manager *el gerente* (male)/*la gerente* (female)

owner, proprietor **el dueño** (male)/**la dueña** (female)
Can you cash a travelers' check?
¿Se puede cambiar un cheque de viajero?
money **dinero** or **plata**
credit card **tarjeta de crédito**
tax **impuesto**
letter **carta**
postcard **tarjeta postal**
envelope **sobre**
stamp **estampilla/sello**

Getting Around

Please call a taxi for me **Pídame un taxi, por favor**
How many kilometers is … from here?
¿Cuántos kilómetros hay de aquí a …?
How long does it take to go there?
¿Cuánto se tarda en llegar?
What will you charge to take me to …? **¿Cuánto cobra para llevarme a …?**
How much is a ticket to …? **¿Cuánto cuesta un billete a …?**
I want a ticket to … **Quiero un billete a …, por favor**
Where does this bus go? **¿Adónde va este bus?**
Stop (on a bus) **¡Parada!**
Please stop here **Pare aquí, por favor**
Please go straight ahead **Vaya recto, por favor**
right **a la derecha**
left **a la izquierda**
What is this place called? **¿Cómo se llama este lugar?**
I'm going to … **Me voy a …**
bus stop **parada del bus**
reserved seat **asiento reservado**
reservation **reservación**
airplane **avión**
train **tren**
bus **bus**
Where is there an inexpensive hotel? **¿Dónde hay un hotel económico?**
Do you have a room with… **¿Hay un cuarto con …?**
bath **baño**
fan **abanico/ventilador**
air-conditioning **aire-climatización**
Where is …? **¿Dónde está …?**
the exit **la salida**
the entrance **la entrada**
the airport **el aeropuerto**
a taxi **un taxi**
the police station **la delegación de policía**
the embassy **la embajada**
the post office **la oficina de correos**
a public telephone **un teléfono público**
a bank **un banco**
a hotel **un hotel**

a restaurant **un restaurante**
a restroom **un servicio**
a private bathroom **el baño**
the ticket office **la oficina de billetes**
a department store **una tienda**
the market **el mercado**

Driving

Fill it up, please **Lleno, por favor**
Please check the oil **Vea el aceite, por favor**
Please fill the radiator **Favor de llenar el radiador**
the battery **la batería**
I need … **Necesito …**
a jack **un gato**
a tow truck **una grúa**
a mechanic **un mecánico**
a tire **una llanta**
Help me, please **Ayúdeme, por favor**
Call a doctor quickly! **¡Llame a un médico de prisa!**

SPEAKING TICO: TIQUISMOS

If you already speak some Spanish, learn a few **Tiquismos**, uniquely Costa Rican expressions. **Tico** (Costa Rican) Spanish is rich with them.

The familiar '**tú**' (you) is not used in Costa Rica, even with children. They often use an archaic form, '**vos**.' The rules regarding the use of '**vos**' are tricky and elude even advanced students of Spanish: best to stick with '**Usted**,' which is always correct.

When walking in areas outside of San José, people passing on the street greet one another with '**Adiós**,' or ' '**dios**.' '**Hasta luego**' is used to say 'goodbye.'

Costa Ricans love to use **sobrenombres**, nicknames. More often than not, the nicknames have to do with a person's physical appearance: **Macho/Macha** if he or she is ever-so-slightly fair-skinned or fair-haired (not to be confused with **machismo**, an attribute of Latin males, used in Mexico); **China** if she has a slight slant to the eyes, or is actually Asian; **Negro** if his skin is dark; **Gordito** for someone even slightly overweight; **Moreno** if the person is slightly dark-complexioned, and so on.

If someone asks, '**¿Cómo está Usted?**' it's always correct to reply, '**Muy bien, gracias a Dios**' ('Very well, thanks to God') or '**Muy bien, por dicho**' (Very well, fortunately') but you might want to try something

a little more zippy and informal, such as: '**Pura vida**' ('Great') or '**Con toda la pata**' ('Terrific' – literally, 'with all the paw') or '**Tranquilo**' ('Relaxed,' or 'cool').

SPANISH LANGUAGE SCHOOLS

Whatever a student's language needs, whether merely conversational, for business, or to master the structure of Spanish, an appropriate language school exists in Costa Rica. Listed below are some of the better-known schools. Consult the **Tico Times** for others.
COSI
Tel: 2234 1001
www.cosi.co.cr
Intensive classes for groups and individuals offered by the Costa Rica Spanish Institute. Programs from 1 to 16 weeks. Classes start every Monday in San José and Manuel Antonio. Arranges homestays.
CPI
Tel: 2265 6306
www.cpi-edu.com
Classes, group, and private, offered by the Centro Panamericano de Idiomas, in Heredia, Monteverde, and Flamingo. Academic credit offered, as well as specialized medical courses that include work in local hospitals. Arranges homestays.
ILISA
San José
Tel: 2280 0700
Toll-free from US: 1-800 ILISA-4-U (454 7248)
www.ilisa.com
Courses with a maximum of four students. Also one-to-one programs. Spanish for professionals available. ILISA uses a communicative approach rather than a method. Arranges homestays and hotels. Free email and computer access.
Intensa
Barrio Escalante, San José
Tel: 2281 1818/ 866 277 1352 US, Canada
www.intensa.com
Language school with 30 years' experience and five locations, including Alajuela and Playa Jacó.
Mesoamerica Language Institute
San Pedro
Tel: 2225 0508
www.icads.org. A department of the Institute for Central American Studies, dedicated to peace, justice, and the wellbeing of the people and land of Central America. Offers one and four-week programs.

FURTHER READING

BOOKS

Because reference books are often unavailable or expensive in Costa Rica, buy books before leaving home. The ones listed below give a good insight into Costa Rican life.

A Bird Finding Guide to Costa Rica, by Barrett Lawson. Highlighting 53 of the best birding destinations with itineraries and techniques for spotting birds in rainforest canopies.

The Birds of Costa Rica: A Field Guide, by Richard Garrigues, ill. by Robert Dean. Extraordinary, up-to-date reference; 116 color plates.

Butterfly in the City: A Good Life in Costa Rica, by Jo Stuart. Musings by long-term resident.

Costa Rica: National Parks, by Mario Boza. Lavish bilingual coffee-table book by one of the founders of the national park system.

The Costa Rican Indigenous People, by Rodrigo Salazar. Bilingual overview of the country's indigenous history.

Costa Rica: A Traveler's Literary Companion, Barbara Ras (ed.). English translation of 26 short stories by Costa Rican writers.

Costa Rica: Wildlife of the National Parks and Reserves, by Michael and Patricia Fogden. Gorgeous coffee-table book with fascinating text.

Gallito Pinto: Traditional Recipes from Costa Rica, by Andrea Corrales. Recipes from Costa Rican homes with illustrations and cultural notes.

The Green Republic: A Conservation History of Costa Rica, by Sterling Evans. History of conservation ethics in Costa Rica.

A Guide to Amphibians and Reptiles of Costa Rica, by Twan Leenders.

A Guide to the Birds of Costa Rica, by Gary F. Stiles and A.F. Skutch. The bible for birders in Costa Rica.

A Guide to Tropical Plants of Costa Rica, by Willow Zuchowski. Highly recommended guide by a botanist.

Happier than a Billionaire by Nadine Hays Pisani. An interesting and highly entertaining account of an American couple's search for a better life in Costa Rica.

The History of Costa Rica, by Iván Molina and Steven Palmer. Complete overview of the country's history.

Hostile Acts: US Policy in Costa Rica in the 1980s, by Martha Honey. An insider's look at how Costa Rica's official neutrality was compromised during the era of Iran-Contra and the civil war in Nicaragua.

INBio Pocket Guides, Various easy-to-carry and complete guides

Send Us Your Thoughts

We do our best to ensure that information in our books is as accurate and up-to-date as possible. The books are updated on a regular basis using local contacts, who painstakingly add, amend and correct as required. However, some details (such as telephone numbers and opening times) are liable to change, and we are ultimately reliant on our readers to put us in the picture.

We welcome your feedback, especially your experience of using the book "on the road". Maybe we recommended a hotel that you liked (or another that you didn't), or you came across a great bar or new attraction we missed.

We will acknowledge all contributions, and we'll offer an Insight Guide to the best letters received.

Please write to us at:
Insight Guides
PO Box 7910
London SE1 1WE
Or email us at:
hello@insightguides.com

on plants, mammals, insects, butterflies, and fungi. INBio (www. inbio.ac.cr).

Monkeys are Made of Chocolate, by Jack Ewing. A collection of stories from a long-time conservationist on the southern Pacific coast of Costa Rica.

The New Key to Costa Rica, by Beatrice Blake and Anne Becher. Detailed information on off-the-beaten-track nature-focused tourism.

Osa: Where the Rainforest Meets the Sea, by Roy Toft. The Osa Peninsula seen through the eyes of a BBC photographer. Beautiful rainforest images.

The Painted Oxcart, by Michael Sims. A gorgeous, illustrated history of the Costa Rican oxcart.

Potholes to Paradise, by Tessa Borner. Personal account and advice about moving to Costa Rica.

The Surfer's Guide to Costa Rica, by Mike Parise. Low-budget but comprehensive surfing guide.

The Ticos: Culture and Social Change in Costa Rica, by M. Biesanz, R. Biesanz, and K. Biesanz. Socio-anthroplogical analysis of Costa Rican society and culture.

The Tico Times Restaurant Guide to Costa Rica, by Eliot Greenspan. Comprehensive bilingual guide to the country's culinary hotspots.

What Happen, by Paula Palmer. A history of the Talamanca Coast.

OTHER INSIGHT GUIDES

Insight Guides cover nearly 200 destinations, providing information on culture and all the top sights, as well as superb photography. Other guides on Central America and the Caribbean include Insight Guides *Belize*; *Caribbean*; *Cuba*; *Guatemala, Belize and the Yucatán*; *Mexico*; and *Puerto Rico*.

CREDITS

Insight Guide Credits

Distribution
UK
Dorling Kindersley Ltd
A Penguin Group company
80 Strand, London, WC2R 0RL
sales@uk.dk.com

United States
Ingram Publisher Services
1 Ingram Boulevard, PO Box 3006,
La Vergne, TN 37086-1986
ips@ingramcontent.com

Australia and New Zealand
Woodslane
10 Apollo St, Warriewood,
NSW 2102, Australia
info@woodslane.com.au

Worldwide
Apa Publications (Singapore) Pte
7030 Ang Mo Kio Avenue 5
08-65 Northstar @ AMK
Singapore 569880
apasin@singnet.com.sg

Printing
CTPS-China

All Rights Reserved
© 2016 Apa Digital (CH) AG and
Apa Publications (UK) Ltd

First Edition 1995
Sixth Edition 2016

www.insightguides.com

Editor: Rachel Lawrence
Author: Dorothy MacKinnon
Head of Production: Rebeka Davies
Update Production: AM Services
Picture Editor: Tom Smyth
Cartography: original cartography Colourmap Scanning Ltd, updated by Carte

Contributors

This new edition was commissioned and edited by **Rachel Lawrence**. It was updated by **Maciej Zglinicki** who has traveled extensively in Central America. It builds on the work of earlier editions produced by **David Burnie**, **Henry Genthe**, **Donna Haber**, **Harvey Haber**, **Cindy Hilbrink**, **Dorothy MacKinnon**, and **Paul Murphy**. Many of the stunning photographs in this edition were taken by experienced travel photographer Corrie Wingate.

About Insight Guides

Insight Guides have more than 40 years' experience of publishing high-quality, visual travel guides. We produce 400 full-colour titles, in both print and digital form, covering more than 200 destinations across the globe, in a variety of formats to meet your different needs.

Insight Guides are written by local authors who use their on-the-ground experience to provide the very latest information; their local expertise is evident in the extensive historical and cultural background features. All the reviews in **Insight Guides** are independent; we strive to maintain an impartial view. Our reviews are carefully selected to guide you to the best places to eat, go out and shop, so you can be confident that when we say a place is special, we really mean it.

Legend

City maps

	Freeway/Highway/Motorway
	Divided Highway
	Main Roads
	Minor Roads
	Pedestrian Roads
	Steps
	Footpath
	Railway
	Funicular Railway
	Cable Car
	Tunnel
	City Wall
	Important Building
	Built Up Area
	Other Land
	Transport Hub
	Park
	Pedestrian Area
	Bus Station
	Tourist Information
	Main Post Office
	Cathedral/Church
	Mosque
	Synagogue
	Statue/Monument
	Beach
	Airport

Regional maps

	Freeway/Highway/Motorway (with junction)
	Freeway/Highway/Motorway (under construction)
	Divided Highway
	Main Road
	Secondary Road
	Minor Road
	Track
	Footpath
	International Boundary
	State/Province Boundary
	National Park/Reserve
	Marine Park
	Ferry Route
	Marshland/Swamp
	Glacier
	Salt Lake
	Airport/Airfield
	Ancient Site
	Border Control
	Cable Car
	Castle/Castle Ruins
	Cave
	Chateau/Stately Home
	Church/Church Ruins
	Crater
	Lighthouse
	Mountain Peak
	Place of Interest
	Viewpoint

INDEX

Main references are in bold type

A

accommodations **264**. *See also* lodges
all-inclusive resorts 196
eco-hotels 169
homestays 264
activities 89. *See also* sports and activities, activities by name
admission charges 264
adventure sports 98
agriculture **19**, 151. *See also* coffee
bananas 226, 234, 235
cacao 74, 232
palm oil 241
tobacco 74
air travel
domestic flights 261
international 260
sightseeing flights 99, 245
Alajuela 46, 142
Museo Histórico Cultural Juan Santamaría 142
Amerindians. *See* people
ancient sites 33
Guyabo 151
Isla del Caño 34, 247
animal parks. *See* zoos and animal parks
aquariums. *See* zoos and animal parks
architecture 75
Arenal, Volcán 20, **213**, 212
Arias, Oscar 59
arribada 236, 204. *See also* wildlife – sea turtles
art and crafts 157
Amerindian legacy 33
CASEM cooperative 185
pottery 202
shopping for 271
wood crafts 149, 154
art galleries. *See* museums and galleries
arts and entertainment. *See also* theaters and concert venues
listings sources 273
Atlantic railroad 65, 226
ATMs 270

B

Bahía Ballena 193, 245
Bahía Drake 158, 246
Coastal Footpath 246
Bahía Salinas 93
Baldi Hot Springs 213, 221
Barra del Colorado 227
Barva de Heredia 145
Basílica de Barva 145
Virgen de Lourdes grotto 145
Barva, Volcán 145
beaches 8, 22. *See also* Playa place names

Bandera Azul (blue flag) beaches 69, 190
Caribbean Coast 228, 229
Central Pacific **165**, 119
Nicoya Peninsula 189, 194
Northwest Mainland 183
Papagayo Peninsula 196
South 241, 243, 251
birds 21, **83**, 149, 175. *See also* national parks, nature reserves
birdwatching course 219
birdwatching tours 219, 255
hummingbirds 206, 219
macaws 165, 216, 246, 247
parrots 227
quetzals 146, 184, **187**, 254
raptors 207
toucans 206, 219
wading birds 166
water birds 216
boat travel
ferries 262
to Costa Rica 261
boat trips
Caribbean Coast 227, 230
Nicoya Peninsula 190, 192
Northeast 217
Papagayo Peninsula 197
South 249
whale- and dolphin-watching 245
Boza, Mario 80
Brasilito 198
Braulio Carrillo Highway 216
business hours. *See* opening hours
bus travel
international 260
within Costa Rica 261

C

Cabezas, Felix Ángel Salas 215
Cachí Hydroelectric Dam 148
Café Britt 111, 145
Cahuita 230
Caldera 97
Caldera Highway 167
Calderón Fournier, Rafael Angel 59
Calderón Gurdia, Rafael Angel 54
camping
Caribbean Coast 231, 234
South 241, 243, 248, 256
Carazo, Rodrigo 81
Caribbean Coast **19**, 119
Caribbean Conservation Corporation (CCC) 228, 266
car rental 262
Carrillo, Braulio 45, 47
Cartago 44, 46, 146
Basílica de Nuestra Señora de los Angeles 147
Las Ruinas 147
Casa del Soñador 149
Cataratas del Río Fortuna 212

cathedrals. *See* churches and cathedrals
Central Pacific 163
Central range 20, 89
Central Valley 19, 119, **139**
Centro Agronómico Tropical de Investigación y Enseñanza (CATIE) 151
Cerro de la Muerte **253**
Chang, Franklin 68
children 132, 265
Chinchilla, Laura 59
churches and cathedrals
Agonía (Liberia) 177
Basílica de Barva (Barva de Heredia) 145
Basílica de Nuestra Señora de los Angeles (Cartago) 147
Catedral Metropolitano (San José) 131
Inmaculada Concepción (Heredia) 144
Nuestra Señora de la Limpia (Ujarrás) 148
San Blas (Nicoya) 202
Cinchona 143
Ciudad Neilly 253
Ciudad Quesada 211
climate 20, 141, 265
climbing 220
clothing 266
cloud forest. *See* rainforest and cloud forest
coffee 48, 53, 143, 226
Aventura de Café (Cafe Britt) 111, 145
impact on the economy 110
plantation tours 254
shopping for 271
Columbus, Christopher 31, 37
commerce and industry 72, 76
conservation. *See* environmental issues
Copey 254
coral reefs 22, 230, 234, 243, 246
Corobicí River 175
Corrohore, Chief 43
Costanera Sur 241
courier services 271
cowboys 176
crime and safety 59, 73, 151, **266**
Caribbean Coast 230
Central Pacific 165, 166
human trafficking 57, 59
in San José 128, 132
Puerto Limón 225
customs and entry regulations 267
cycling and mountain biking 169, 204, 263

D

de Balboa, Vasco Nuñez 39
de Castillo, Florencio 46
de Cavallón, Juan 42, 46

de Coronado, Juan Vásquez 42, 149
de las Casas, Bartolomé 41
de Nicuesa, Diego 39
de Ribera, Perafán 43
Diriagen, Chief 40
disabled travelers 267
diving and snorkeling 235
 Caribbean Coast 230, 232, 234
 Nicoya Peninsula 192, 197, 204
 Northwest Mainland 178
 South 245, 246
Drake Bay. See Bah'a Drake
driving. See also car rental
 to Costa Rica 261
 within Costa Rica 262

E

earthquakes 220
 of 2009 143, 216
eating out 102, 267
Echandi, Alberto 54
economy 53, 58
 US-Central American Free Trade
  Agreement 59
ecosystems 20
ecotourism 57, **82**, 233, 273. See
 also lodges
education 71
El Bosque Eterno de los Niños 186
electricity 268
embassies and consulates 268
emergencies 268
environmental issues 151
 air pollution 77, 128
 awareness 69
 carbon neutrality 59
 conservation 81, 218, 266
 deforestation 22, 81, 217
 habitat destruction 207
 water pollution 81
 wildlife poaching 181, 204, 216,
  237, 247
Escazú 154
 Bello Horizonte 154
 Biesanz Woodworks 154
 San Rafael de Escazú 155
etiquette 130, 268

F

Fallas, Carlos Luis 54, 250
festivals and events
 Baroque Music Festival (Santa
  Ana) 155
 Carnaval (Puerto Limón) 68, 226
 Día de los Boyeros (San Antonio
  de Escazú) 154
 Fiesta de los Diablitos (Térraba)
  252
 folklore festival (Santa Cruz) 202
 international music festival
  (Monteverde) 186
 Meeting of the Cultures Day 35
Figueres, José (Don Pepe) 55, 215,
 253
Figueres, José Maria 58
filibusteros 49
Fischer, Karen Mogensen 80

fishing **94**, 167
 licenses 96
 Nicoya Peninsula 192, 197, 204
 Northeast 214
 sea angling 96
 South 245, 250, 254
flora and fauna. See plantlife,
 wildlife
Flores, Alfredo González 53
food and drink 102. See
 also coffee, eating out
 artisan beers 214, 267
 artisan cheese 256
 chocolate 232
 coconuts 105, 234
 fruits 106
 gallo pinto 102, 175
 maté 191
 Monteverde cheese 68, 184
 pejibaye 150
Fortuna de San Carlos. See La
 Fortuna
Fournier, Rafael Calderón 58
further reading 276

G

Gallegas, José Rafael 47
gardens. See parks and gardens
gay and lesbian travelers 268
geography and geology 19
gold 31, 34, 39, 247
golf **93**, 193, 196, 201
Golfito 250
 American Zone 250
 Pueblo Civil 250
Golfo Dulce 97, 119, 245
González, Gil 40
Grecia 156
 World of Snakes 156
Guaitil 158, 202
Guanacaste province 92, 119,
 173, 189
 cultural traditions 175
Guanacaste range 20

H

health and medical care 268
 medical tourism 71
 standards of 71
Heredia 45, 128, **143**
 InbioPark 143, 266
 Inmaculada Concepción church
  144
 National University 144
hiking 9, 220
 Caribbean Coast 229, 235
 Central Valley 145, 146, 149
 Northwest Mainland 178, 179,
  181, 183
 South 248, 249, 254, 255, 256
history 31
 civil war 55, **57**
 colonial era 44
 independence 46
 Indian Resettlement Policies 45
 modern times 53
 Second Republic 57
 Spanish Conquest 37

Hone Creek 231
horseback riding
 Central Pacific 169
 Central Valley 144, 156
 Nicoya Peninsula 193, 204
 South 243
hot-air ballooning 211
hot springs and geysers
 Baldi 213, 221
 Las Pailas 178
 Tabacón Springs 213, 212
 Termales del Bosque 211, 221

I

insurance 269
Interamericana Highway 174, 253
internet 269
Irazú, Volcán 20, 46, 119, 152, 146
Isla del Caño 246
Isla del Coco 20, 257
Isla de Pájaros 175
Isla San Lucas 192
Isla Tortuga 192

J

jade 35
Janzen, Dan 180, 181
Jiménez, Jorge Volio 53
Jiménez, Ricardo 54

K

kayaking 150, 169, 204, 214, 245
Keith, Minor C. 64, 65
Keköldi Wak Ka Koneke reserve
 230
kite-surfing 180

L

La Cangreja Waterfall 178
La Catarata Manantial de Agua
 Viva Waterfall 165
La Fortuna 212
La Garita 143
Laguna Barva 146
Laguna de Arenal 22, 93, 97, 214
 monster legend 215
Lake Nicaragua 94, 179
language 72, 231
 language schools 275
Lankester, Charles 147
Lankester Jardín Botánico 147
La Paz Waterfall Gardens 142
Las Pailas 178
Las Pumas wildlife refuge 174
left luggage 269
Le Lacheur, William 48
Liberia **176**
 Agonía Church 177
Llanos de Cortés 176
lodges 119. See
 also accommodations
 Arenal Observatory (Northeast) 213
 Casa Verde (Puerto Viejo de
  Talamanca) 232
 Certification for Sustainable
  Tourism 219

Corcovado National Park (South) 249
El Toucanet (Copey) 254
Esquinas Rainforest (South) 251
Guacamaya (Nicoya Peninsula) 201
Hacienda Barú (South) 99, 241
Hacienda Guachipélin (Northwest Mainland) 179
Hacienda La Amistad (South) 256
Iguana (Playa Platanares) 249
Lagarta (Nicoya Peninsula) 203
Laguna del Lagarto (Northeast) 215
La Paloma (Bahía Drake) 246
Las Heliconias (Northeast) 216
Maquenque Eco-Lodge (Northeast) 215
Playa Nicuesa Rainforest (South) 251
Poás Volcano (Central Valley) 142
Punta Marenco (Bahía Drake) 246
Rara Avis Rainforest (Northeast) 217
Rincón de la Vieja (Northwest Mainland) 179
Selva Verde (Northeast) 219
Tiskita Jungle (South) 252
Volcán Turrialba (Central Valley) 152

M

Malpaís 196
mangrove swamps 22, 164, 180, 201, 203, 235, 243, 249
Manzanillo 234
maps 269
markets 267. *See also* shopping
fish market (Puntarenas) 189
Mercado Central (San José) 131
Mercado Nacional de Artesanías (San José) 134
San Isidro de El General 255
media 270
medical. *See* health and medical care
Miskitos 45
money 270
budgeting for your trip 265
Monte de la Cruz 144
Monteverde 68, 119, 183, 184
Bat Jungle 185
CASEM 185
El Jardín de las Mariposas 185
Frog Pond 185
international music festival 186
Jardín de Orquídeas 186
La Fábrica de Queso 184
Reserva Santa Elena 186
Reserva Sendero Tranquilo 185
Selvatura 186
Serpentarium 185
Sky Trek zip-line 98, 185
Sky Walk 185
Montezuma 194
Monumento Nacional Guyabo 151
Mora Fernández, Juan 47
Mora, Juan Rafael 49
Mora, Manuel 54, 55

Morazán, Francisco 48
mountain biking. *See* cycling and mountain biking
mountaineering. *See* climbing
Mount Chirripó 20, 255
museums and galleries
Church of San Blas (Nicoya) 202
Galería Nacional (San José) 132
Museo de Arte Costarricense (San José) 132
Museo de Arte Religioso (Orosí) 149
Museo de Arte y Diseño Contemporáneo (San José) 133
Museo de Cultura Popular (Santa Lucía de Barva) 145
Museo del Jade (San José) 35
Museo del Oro Precolombino (San José) 34, 42, 131
Museo de los Niños (San José) 132
Museo de Numismática (San José) 131
Museo Filatélico (San José) 131
Museo Histórico Cultural Juan Santamaría (Alajuela) 142
Museo Nacional del Jade (San José) 133
Museo Nacional (San José) 133

N

national parks 8, **80**. *See also* Unesco
Area de Conservación Guanacaste 180
Barra Honda 205
Braulio Carrillo 153
Cahuita 230
Carara 163
Chirripó 255
Corcovado 247
Isla del Coco 257
La Amistad 256
Manuel Antonio 119, 167
Marino Ballena 243
Marino Las Baulas 200, 237
Palo Verde 22, 90, 175
Piedras Blancas 251
Rincón de la Vieja 177
Santa Rosa 80, 180
Tapantí 149
Tenorio Volcano 216
Tortuguero 227
Volcán Irazú 152
Volcán Poás 141
National Symphony Orchestra 129
nature reserves. *See also* lodges, national parks
Bosque Nuboso de Monteverde 183
Cabo Blanco Absolute Wildlife Reserve 80, 195
Caño Negro 22, 216
Curú 193
El Bosque Eterno de los Niños 186
Estación Biólogica La Selva 218
Gandoca-Manzanillo 235

Golfito 251
Isla del Caño 246
Maquenque National Wildlife Refuge 207, 215
Nosara Biological Reserve 203
Ostional 204
Rainmaker 167
Rancho Humo 176
Río Claro 246
Santa Elena (Monteverde) 186
Sarapiquí Eco-Observatory 219
Sendero Tranquilo (Monteverde) 185
Tirimbina Rainforest Center 219
Nauyaca Falls 243
Negrita, La 147
Nicaragua, border with 217
Nicoya 158, 202
Church of San Blas 202
Nicoya Peninsula 20, 93, 119, **189**, **192**
nightlife 198
Northeast 211
Northwest Mainland 173
Nosara. *See* Playa Nosara
Nuevo Arenal 214

O

Ojochal 245
opening hours 270
Orosí 149
Museo de Arte Religioso 149
Orosí Valley 149
Osa Peninsula 20, 82, 119, 245
ox carts, decorated 156, 156

P

Pacheco, Abel 58
Pacific coast 19
Palma, Lisimaco Chavarria 215
Palmares 157
Panama, border with 235
Papagayo, Gulf of 96
Papagayo Peninsula 196
Paquera 192
parasailing 99
Parismina 228
Save the Turtles of Parismina Project 228
parks and gardens
El Jardín de las Mariposas (Monteverde) 185
InbioPark (Heredia) 143, 266
Jardín de Orquídeas (Monteverde) 186
Lankester Jardín Botánico 147
La Paz Waterfall Gardens 142
Parque Central (San José) 131
Parque España (San José) 128
Parque Francisco Alvarado (Zarcero) 157
Parque La Sabana (San José) 134
Parque Morazán (San José) 128
Parque Nacional (San José) 133
Parque Vargas (Puerto Limón) 225
Veragua Rainforest Adventure Park (Puerto Limón) 229
Wilson Botanical Garden 252

parque nacional. *See* national
parks
Parrita 167
Paso Real 253
Pavas 154
Pavones 93, 252
Pedrarias, governor 40
people 63
Amerindians 32, 31, **63**, 40, 63
black Costa Ricans 63, **64**
Boruca 158
gringos 68
Guanacastecos 63, 173
illegal immigrants 73
indigenous reserves 35, **64**, 229,
251, 253
Italians 68
of Talamanca region 229
other Latin Americans 70, 73
Quakers 68, 184
Sino-Costa Ricans 63, **66**
photography 219, 270
tours 270
Picado, Teodoro 56
pirates 45
plantlife 21, 244. *See also* parks
and gardens, rainforest and cloud
forest
Guanacaste tree 175
statistics 81
Playa Avellanas 93, 201
Playa Bonita 93
Playa Brasilito 198
Playa Caletas 205
Playa Carrillo 205
Playa Conchal 198
Playa Copal 180
Playa Dominical 92, 241
Playa Dominicalito 243
Pozo Azul 243
Playa Doña Ana 191
Playa Espadilla 168
Playa Esterillos 165
Playa Flamingo 199
Playa Grande 200
Playa Hermosa 92, 166
Playa Herradura 165
Playa Jacó 91, 163, 165
Playa Junquillal 201
Playa Langosta 201
Playa Nancite 183
Playa Naranjo 92, 183
Playa Negra 93, 201
Playa Nosara 203
Playa Guiones 203
Playa Pelada 203
Playa Ocotal 197
Playa Panamá 92, 196
Playa Pan de Azúcar 199
Playa Platanares 249
Playa Pochote 193
Playa Potrero 198, 199
Playa Sámara 204
Playas del Coco 197
Playa Tamarindo 198, 199
nightlife 198
Playa Tambor 193
Playa Ventanas 245
Playa Zancudo 252
Poás, Volcán 20, 119

politics and government 53
Constitution 46, 53
corruption 59
postal services 271
public holidays 271
Puerto Caldera 189
Puerto Jiménez 249
Puerto Limón 31, 225
Carnaval 68, 226
Parque Vargas 225
Veragua Rainforest Adventure
Park 229
Puerto Soley 179
Puerto Viejo de Sarapiquí 217
boat trips 217
Puerto Viejo de Talamanca 93,
232
nightlife 232
Punta Banco 252
Punta Cahuita 230
Puntarenas 97, 189
boat trips 190
fish market 189
Paseo de Turistas 191
Puntarenas Marine Park 190
Puntarenas province 189
Punta Uva 233

Q

Quepos 167
Quesada, Macedonio 149
Quitao, Chief 42

R

rafting 89, 90, 150, 169, 175, 217
safety issues 91
Rainforest Aerial Tram 153
rainforest and cloud forest 19, 21,
21
Central Pacific 167
Central Valley 145, 146, 149,
153
Northeast 218
Northwest Mainland 183, 186
South 247, 251, 252, 254
Ramírez, Gregorio José 47
Rancho Humo 176
rapelling 99
refugio nacional. *See* nature
reserves
religion 35
religious services 271
restaurants. *See* eating out
restrooms 272
Reventazón Gorge 89
Rincón de la Vieja, Volcán 20
Río Colorado 94
Río Corobicí 90
Río Frío 95
Río Pacuare 90
Río Reventazón 90
Río San Juan 95, 217
Río Sarapiquí 90, 216
Río Savegre 97
Río Sixaola 94
Río Tárcoles bridge 163
rivers. *See* R'o
rodeo 176

Rodríguez, Miguel Angel 58
Rohrmoser 154
Ruta de Los Santos 254

S

sailing 169
Sanabria, Victor 55
San Carlos. *See* Ciudad Quesada
San Carlos Valley 212
Sánchez, Oscar Arias 58, 59
San Gerardo de Dota 254
San Gerardo de Rivas 255
San Isidro de El General 255
San José 45, 119, **127**
accommodations 264
Barrio Amón 75, 77, 134
Barrio Mexico 77
Casa Amarilla 132
Catedral Metropolitana 131
Correos 131
Edificio Metálico 132
Fábrica Nacional de Licores 133
Galería Nacional 132
Gran Hotel Costa Rica 131
history **74**, 127
INS Building 132
Mercado Central 131
Mercado Nacional de Artesanías
134
Museo de Arte Costarricense 134
Museo de Arte y Diseño
Contemporáneo 133
Museo del Jade 35
Museo del Oro Precolombino 34,
42, 131
Museo de los Niños 132
Museo de Numismática 131
Museo Filatélico 131
Museo Nacional 133
Museo Nacional del Jade 133
orientation 128
Parque Central 131
Parque España 128
Parque La Sabana 134
Parque Morazán 128
Parque Nacional 133
Parque Zoológico Simón Bolívar
132
Plaza de la Cultura 129
Pueblo Antiguo 134
Spirogyra Jardín de Mariposas
133
Teatro Nacional 75, 128, **129**
tourist information 131
transportation 128, 130, 261,
262
San Pedro 152
San Rafael de Heredia 144
San Ramón 214
José Figueres Cultural Center
215
Santa Ana 155
University for Peace 156
Santa Cruz 202
folklore festival 202
Santa Lucía de Barva 145
Museo de Cultura Popular 145
Santa María de Dota 254
Santamaría, Juan 49, 142

Santa Teresa 196
San Vito 68, 253
Sarchí 158, 156
scenic drives 9
shopping 271. *See also* markets
    duty-free 250
Sierpe 249
Sixaola 235
slave trade 45, 49
snorkeling. *See* diving and
    snorkeling
soccer 89
society 70
    family values 71
    US influence 72
Solís, Ottón 59
Somoza, Anastasio 57, 181
South 241
sports and activities 89, 98. *See
    also* activities by name
student travelers 272
surfing 91, 166, 183
    Caribbean Coast 232, 234
    Nicoya Peninsula 191, 196, 198,
        200, 201, 203
    South 241, 252
swimming 241, 243. *See
    also* beaches
    riptide hazards 192

T

Tabacón Grand Spa Thermal
    Resort 213
Talamanca Association for
    Ecotourism and Conservation
    233
Talamanca range 20, 89
Talamanca region 45, 229
Tambor 194
taxis 263
Tempisque River Bridge 198
Tenorio, Volcán 216
Térraba 251
    Fiesta de los Diablitos 252
theaters and concert venues
    Fábrica Nacional de Licores (San
        José) 133
    José Figueras Cultural Center (San
        Ramón) 215
    Teatro Nacional (San José) 75,
        128, **129**
time zone 272
Tinoco, Federico 53
Tinoco, Joaquín 53
tipping 270
toilets 272

Tortuguero 229
Tortuguero Beach 236
Tortuguero canals 227
    boat trips 227
tourism
    effects of 69
    sustainable tourism program 69,
        219
tourist information 273
tour operators 272
transportation 260
Turrialba 150
Turrialba, Volcán 20, 150

U

Ujarrás 148
    Nuestra Señora de la Limpia
        148
Ulate, Otilio 56
Unesco Agua y Paz International
    Biosphere 82, 216
Unesco International Reserva de
    la Biosfera La Amistad 82, 256
United Fruit Company 64

V

Valle de El General 253
Villaseñor, Vicente 48
visas and passports 273
volcanoes 20, 119, 139, 177. *See
    also* by name
    eruptions 46, 213
volunteer opportunities 272

W

Wafer, Lionel 257
Walker, William 49, 179, 181
waterfalls
    Cataratas del Río Fortuna 212
    La Cangreja 178
    La Catarata Manantial de Agua
        Viva 165
    La Paz 142
    Llanos de Cortés 176
    Nauyaca Falls 243
    waterfall rapelling 99
websites 273
weights and measures 273
Wessberg, Nils Olaf 80, 195
wetlands, freshwater 21
wildlife 21, **83**, **219**. *See also* birds,
    national parks, nature reserves
    ants 244
    bats 182, 219

butterflies 143
caimans 215, 216, 227
coatimundis 248
crocodiles 163, 164, 216, 227
dolphins 243, 246
fish 94
freshwater turtles 227
iguanas 181
jaguars 247
marine life 178, 230, 246
monkeys 167, 168, 175, 227,
    247
peccaries 249
reptiles and amphibians 219,
    248, 251
sea turtles **236**, 200, 183, 204,
    228, 204
sloths 219, 227, 233
statistics 81
tapirs 247
viewing tips 83
whales 193, 243, 246
Wilson Botanical Garden 252
windsurfing **93**, 180, 214
women travelers 273

Y

yoga 202

Z

Zarcero 157
    Parque Francisco Alvarado
        157
zip-lining **98**, 185, 186
zoos and animal parks
    Aviarios Sloth Sanctuary 233
    Bat Jungle (Monteverde) 185
    Butterfly and Frog Garden 154
    El Jardín de las Mariposas
        (Monteverde) 185
    Frog Pond (Monteverde) 185
    InbioPark (Heredia) 143, 266
    La Paz Waterfall Gardens 142
    Las Pumas wildlife refuge 174
    Parque Zoológico Simón Bolívar
        (San José) 132
    Puntarenas Marine Park
        (Puntarenas) 190
    Selvatura (Monteverde) 186
    Serpentarium (Monteverde) 185
    Snake Garden 219
    Spirogyra Jardín de Mariposas
        (San José) 133
    World of Snakes (Grecia) 156
    Zoo Ave 142